THE REAL
VAN GOGH

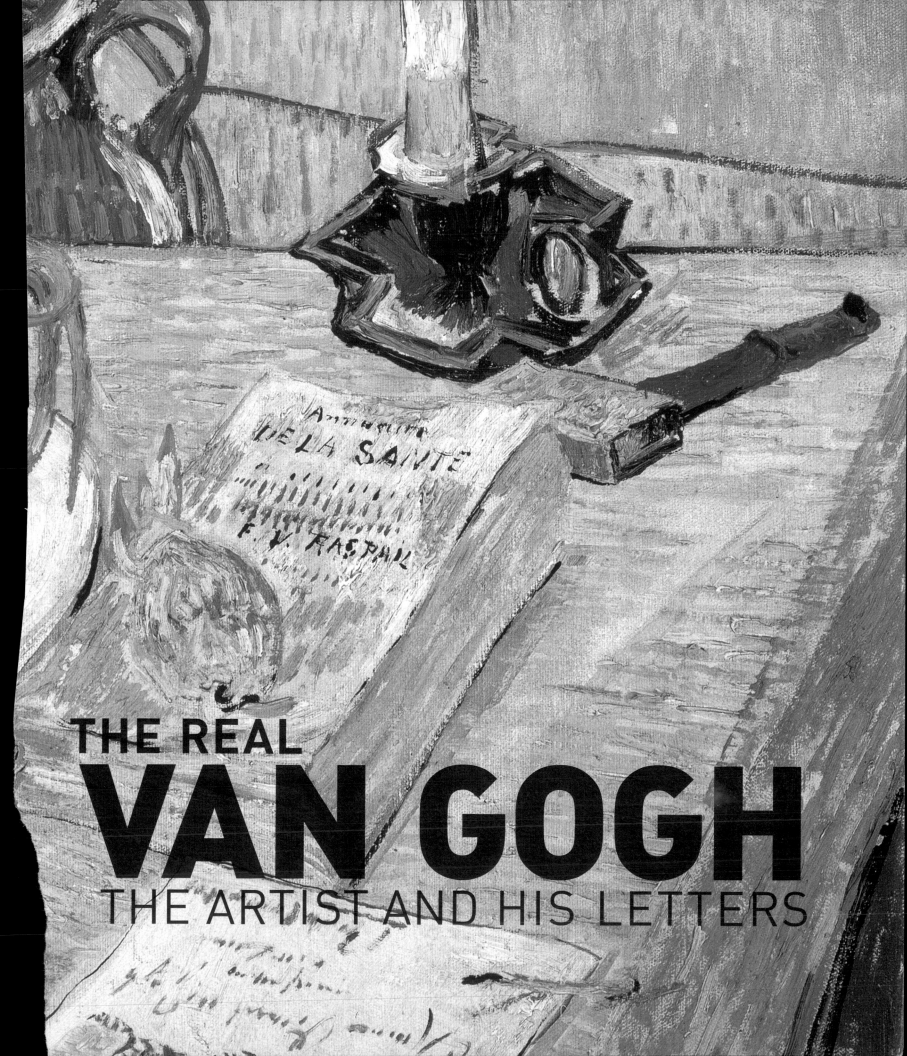

THE REAL
VAN GOGH
THE ARTIST AND HIS LETTERS

First published on the occasion of the exhibition
'The Real Van Gogh: The Artist and His Letters'

Royal Academy of Arts, London
23 January – 18 April 2010

Sponsored by

With additional support from

Travel Partner
COX & KINGS

The Royal Academy of Arts is grateful
to Her Majesty's Government for agreeing
to indemnify this exhibition under the
National Heritage Act 1980, and to MLA,
Museums, Libraries and Archives Council,
for its help in arranging the indemnity.

Exhibition Curators
Ann Dumas
with Leo Jansen, Hans Luijten
and Nienke Bakker

Exhibition Organisation
Jane Knowles
assisted by Ana B. Martinez

Curatorial Assistant
Sarah Lea

Photographic and Copyright Co-ordination
Kitty Corbet Milward

Royal Academy Publications
David Breuer
Beatrice Gullström
Carola Krueger
Sophie Oliver
Peter Sawbridge
Nick Tite

Translation from the Dutch
(Nienke Bakker, Leo Jansen,
Hans Luijten, Teio Meedendorp,
Aukje Vergeest, Roelie Zwikker):
Diane Webb
Design Kathrin Jacobsen
Picture research Sara Ayad
Colour origination DawkinsColour

Printed in Italy by Graphicom

British Library
Cataloguing-in-Publication Data
A catalogue record for this book is available
from the British Library

ISBN 978-1-905711-61-1 (paperback)
ISBN 978-1-905711-60-4 (hardback)

Distributed outside the United States and
Canada by Thames & Hudson Ltd, London

Distributed in the United States and Canada
by Harry N. Abrams, Inc., New York

Editor's Note
The publishers would like to thank the
Van Gogh Museum, Amsterdam, publishers
in association with the Huygens Institute,
The Hague, and Thames & Hudson of the
definitive new edition of Vincent van Gogh's
letters, *Vincent van Gogh – The Letters. The Complete
Illustrated and Annotated Edition*, available in six
volumes and online at www.vangoghletters.org,
for permitting their copyright texts to be used
for the purposes of quotation in this book.
Each quotation is followed by the number
(in parentheses) attached to the letter in the
book and web editions.

Each work's catalogue entry contains its
number in Faille 1970, an abbreviation of
*The Works of Vincent van Gogh: His Paintings
and Drawings* (Amsterdam, 1970), which
is a revised version of J.-B. de la Faille's
authoritative 1928 *catalogue raisonné* of the
artist's works. Illustrations of and references
to works that are not in the exhibition each
have an 'F' number, which refers the reader
to the same source.

Titles of the sketches that appear within the
artist's letters are set in italic type, after the
letter number in larger, bold type and the
names of the two correspondents in roman
type. Each sketch title is followed by a 'JH'
number in parentheses, a reference to Jan
Hulsker, *The New Complete Van Gogh: Paintings,
Drawings, Sketches* (revised and enlarged
edition, Amsterdam and Philadelphia, 1996).

All works illustrated are by Vincent van Gogh
unless otherwise stated.

Dimensions of all works are given
in centimetres, height before width.

Authorship of the catalogue entries
is indicated by the following initials:

Ann Dumas	AD
Teio Meedendorp	TM
Aukje Vergeest	AV
Roelie Zwikker	RZ

CONTENTS

PRESIDENT'S FOREWORD

Vincent van Gogh was not only a great artist, but also an impassioned letter writer. He expressed his beliefs in the most vivid and eloquent language. His letters provide a unique insight into the way he thought about and made his art. They express his ideas about life, art, literature, nature, and the people and places that he encountered in his short but astonishingly brilliant career.

The letters are at the heart of the 'The Real Van Gogh: The Artist and His Letters'. Forty of the originals, containing the sketches in which Van Gogh distilled the essence of a painting or drawing for his correspondent (usually his brother Theo), are presented alongside the works on which they are based. The selection of works has been guided by the principal themes that dominate the letters – colour, portraiture, the cycles of nature, and the artist's highly developed sense of place, expressed in the works made first in Holland and later in France, at Arles and Auvers-sur-Oise. No other artist has written so extensively or in such detail about his art. Throughout the exhibition, Van Gogh's own highly expressive words are used to illuminate his ideas about the works on display.

The exhibition takes inspiration from a new edition of this remarkable correspondence. *Vincent van Gogh – The Letters: The Complete Illustrated and Annotated Edition* is the result of fifteen years of research by Leo Jansen, Hans Luijten and Nienke Bakker, scholars at the Van Gogh Museum, Amsterdam. The publication has greatly enhanced the wealth of information contained in the letters. The Van Gogh who emerges is very different from the mad genius of popular myth. Instead, we discover a reflective, highly cultured man with systematic working methods and carefully planned artistic strategies.

'The Real Van Gogh' has been curated by Ann Dumas, in close collaboration with Leo Jansen, Hans Luijten and Nienke Bakker. They have been most generous in sharing their profound knowledge and understanding of the artist. We are immeasurably indebted to the Van Gogh Museum, without whose support it would not have been possible to realise this exhibition. The original letters are unique and precious documents that, owing to their great fragility, are hardly ever exposed. They have never been shown before in Britain. In addition, twelve major paintings from the museum's collection form the core of the exhibition. We would especially like to thank the museum's Director, Axel Rüger, and Sjraar van Heugten, Head of Collections. We would also like to thank the many other lenders, both public and private, for their commitment to the project.

Ivor Heal has been responsible for the design of the exhibition. Its organisation has been expertly handled by Jane Knowles. Sarah Lea has provided invaluable assistance throughout.

The exhibition could not have been realised without the extremely generous support of BNY Mellon. In these challenging economic times we are very grateful for their sponsorship, which has also provided free access for all state schools.

We would also like to thank Heath Lambert, Hiscox and Helena Frost for their additional support, as well as the exhibition's travel partner, Cox & Kings.

The last major exhibition of Van Gogh's works to be held in London took place over forty years ago. It is our hope that visitors to 'The Real Van Gogh' will be astonished by the power and beauty of Van Gogh's art. We hope that they will gain new insight into this great artist through his words.

Sir Nicholas Grimshaw CBE
President, Royal Academy of Arts

SPONSOR'S PREFACE

They say a picture is worth a thousand words, but in 'The Real Van Gogh: The Artist and His Letters' words redefine our understanding and appreciation of one of the most revered figures in the Post-Impressionist movement, and indeed in Western art. Through the juxtaposition of his letters and his art, the life, work and passions of Vincent van Gogh are illuminated as never before.

BNY Mellon's commitment to the arts as part of our wider philanthropic endeavours spans many projects and countries. As an organisation we are dedicated to assisting in the enrichment of the cultural life of communities around the world, and our association with this momentous exhibition is a great source of pride to our company.

Our partnership with the Royal Academy is without question a special one. With a distinguished history of scholarship, the Royal Academy is committed to opening up the arts to the broadest possible audience, and this championing of public access and education reflects the key principles that inform BNY Mellon's international programme of arts sponsorship.

We hope that you enjoy visiting 'The Real Van Gogh'. To have our understanding of an established artist recast and renewed is always a thrilling experience. In the case of an artist of such iconic stature as Van Gogh, whose life and work have been so comprehensively scrutinised, the reappraisal offered by this remarkable exhibition can genuinely be described as historic.

Helena Morrissey
Royal Academy Corporate Board Member
BNY Mellon

ACKNOWLEDGEMENTS

The curators would like to thank the following for their assistance in the making of this exhibition and its catalogue:

Anne Adriaens-Pannier, Angelika Affentranger-Kirchrath, Greet Albert Elens, Dita Amory, Irina Antonova, Alexander Apsis, Richard Armstrong, Helga Aurisch, Martin Bailey, Joseph Baillio, Maria Balshaw, Christoph Becker, Brent Benjamin, Guy Bennett, Giovanna Bertazzoni, Peter van Beveren, Szilvia Bodnár, Suzanne Bogman, Peter Boot, Rosina Buckland, Rupert Burgess, Cynthia Burlingham, Caroline Campbell, Thomas Campbell, Olivier Camu, Ernst van Claerbergen Vegelin, Timothy Clark, Michael Clarke, Erin Coe, John Collins, Michael Conforti, Francesca Consagra, James Corona, Karen Daly, Susan Davidson, Philippe de Montebello, Jean-Pierre de Rycke, DHA Design Solutions, Taco Dibbits, Jo Digger, Judith Dolkart, Benjamin Dollar, Michel Draguet, Douglas Druick, Maite van Dijk, Daniel Edelman, John Elderfield, Joenika van Es, Sjarel Ex, Charlotte Eyerman, Christopher Eykyn, Walter Feilchenfeldt, Evelyne Ferlay, Marina Ferretti, Jennifer Field, Laura Fielder, Micol Forti, David Franklin, Mathias Frehner, Flemming Friborg, Matthew Gale, Martin Gayford, Judith Gesko, Laura Giles, Lukas Gloor, Israel Goldman, Monique Hageman, Vivien Hamilton, Jodi Hauptman, Frode Haverkamp, Sandy Heller, Ella Hendricks, Lee Hendrix, Max Hollein, Nico van Hout, Jan Howard, Paul Huvenne, Geurt Imanse, Colta Ives, Kimberly Jones, Joachim Kaak, Fouad Kanaan, Adrie Kok, Stephan Koldehoff, Dorothy Kosinski, Felix Krämer, Liz Kreijn, Wim van Krimpen, Diana Kunkel, Laboratory Media, Graham Larkin, Ellen Lee, Frederik Leen, Arnold Lehman, John Leighton, Josie Lerch, Lewis Hallam Design, Louise Lippincott, Adrian Locke, Glenn Lowry, Daniella Luxembourg, Heather MacDonald, Neil MacGregor, Nicholas Maclean, Aline Magnien, Caroline Mathieu, Bernhard Mendes Bürgi, MER Services, Mitchell Merling, Olivier Meslay, Asher Miller, Jane Monroe, Mrs Minoru Mori, David Morris, Richard Nagy, István Németh, Helena Newman, Lawrence Nichols, David Norman, Alex Nyerges, Maureen O'Brien, Barbara O'Connor, Shigeru Oikawa, Mark O'Neill, Inna Orn, Fieke Pabst, Nicholas Penny, Frans Peterse, Ronald Pickvance, Wim Pijbes, Joachim Pissarro, Antonio Paolucci, Earl A. Powell III, Jussi Pylkkänen, Rebecca Rabinow, Richard Rand, Christopher Riopelle, Joseph Rishel, William Robinson, Andrew Robison, Malcolm Rogers, Betsy Rosasco, Sir Norman Rosenthal, Martin Royalton-Kisch, Timothy Rub, Kevin Salatino, Karine Sauvignon, Marijn Schaoelhoumam, Jutta Schuett, Dieter Schwarz, Yu Serizawa, Sir Nicholas Serota, David Setford, George Shackelford, John Sillevis, Stephen Snoddy, Kathleen Soriano, Paul Spencer-Longhurst, Susan Stein, Robert Steiner-Jaeggli, Verena Steiner-Jaeggli, MaryAnne Stevens, Chris Stolwijk, Hans Stomphorst, Evert van Straaten, Andreas Strobl, Luuk Struik van der Loeff, Ann Sumner, Deborah Swallow, Elizabeth Szancer Kujawski, John Tancock, Vérane Tasseau, Susan Taylor, Dodge Thompson, Louis van Tilborgh, Gary Tinterow, Aleksandra Todorovic, Jennifer Tonkovic, Kees van Twist, Olga Uhrová, Marije Vellekoop, Tom Venditti, Dominique Vieville, Bernhard von Waldkirch, Margreet Wafelbakker, Jeffrey Warda, Heinz Widauer, Nina Zimmer

intéressantes, les plus difficiles à faire
que je puis[se] imaginer.

Or il faut les voir ici contre le bleu dans le
bleu pour mieux dire

Pour faire la nature ici comme partout il faut
bien y être longtemps.

Aussi un monticard ne me donne pas
la note vraie et intime car la lumière
est mystérieuse et Monticelli et Delacroix
sentaient cela. Alors Pissarro en parlant
très bien dans le temps et je suis encore bien loin
de pouvoir faire comme il disait qu'il le faudrait

Tu me feras naturellement plaisir
en m'envoyant les couleurs si c'est
possible bientôt mais fais surtout là
dedans comme tu peux sans que
cela t'éreinte trop.

Ainsi si tu préfères me l'envoyer en
deux fois cela est bon aussi

Je crois que des deux toiles de cyprès
celle dont je fais le croquis sera la
meilleure. les arbres y sont très grands
et massifs. l'avant plan très bas des ronces
et broussailles Derrière des collines violettes
un ciel vert et rose avec un croissant de
lune. L'avant plan surtout est très empâté
des touffes de ronces ~~jau~~ à reflets jaunes
violets verts. Je t'en enverrai des
dessins avec deux autres dessins
que j'ai encore faits.

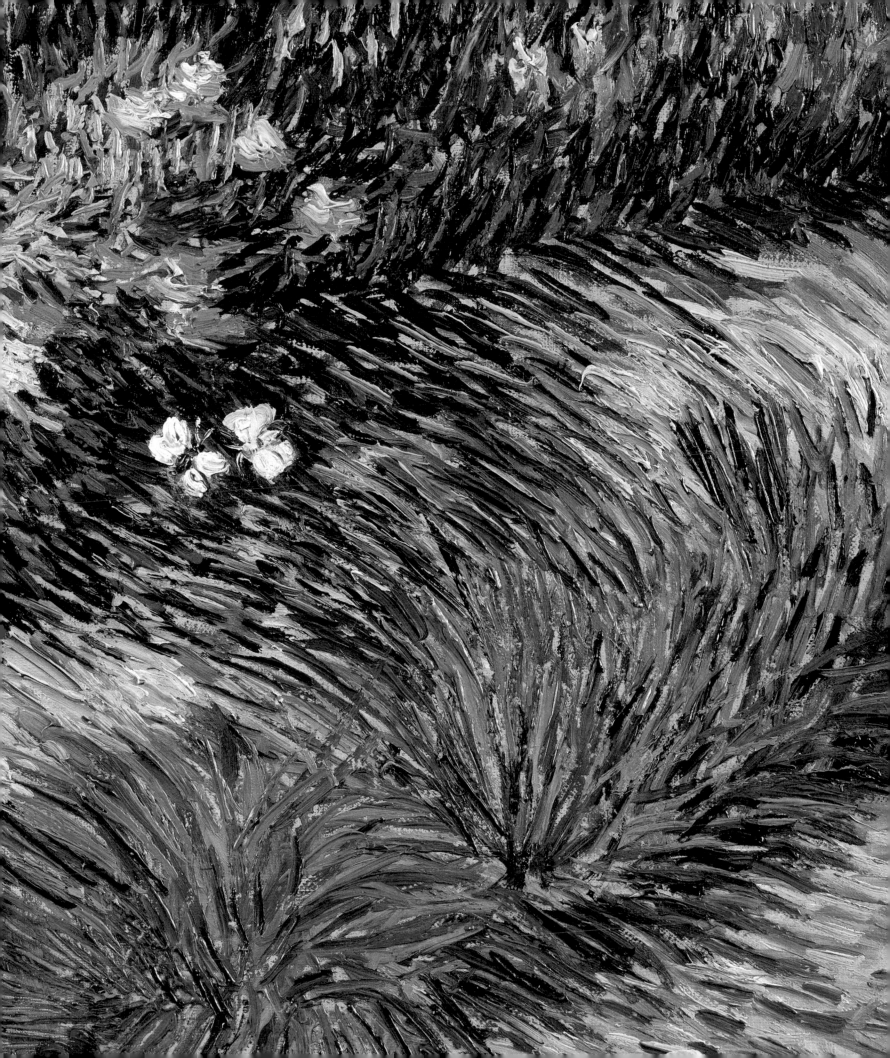

VAN GOGH'S LETTERS: WINDOWS TO A UNIVERSE

Vincent van Gogh's most fervent wish was to mean something to the people around him, to make a useful contribution to society, and if possible to offer some measure of consolation for the inevitable sorrows of human existence. He had been given life and felt compelled to prove that he deserved it. Approvingly, he quoted Ernest Renan, the controversial biographer of Jesus: 'Man is not placed on the earth merely to be happy; nor is he placed here merely to be honest, he is here to accomplish great things through society, to arrive at nobleness, and to outgrow the vulgarity in which the existence of almost all individuals drags on' (33).

To say that Van Gogh succeeded in his mission would be an understatement, but sadly he was denied the feelings of pride and satisfaction to which he was certainly entitled. Even at the end of his life, tragically cut short by suicide, his drawings and paintings were little appreciated. To be sure, he had begun to receive some recognition from a small circle of avant-garde artists and critics, but none from the broad public he had so hoped to reach. Acclaim came posthumously: since the early twentieth century Van Gogh has been viewed as a founder of modern art, and his fame and popularity among the masses is, if anything, still growing. Though he never managed to earn a living, he was, with hindsight, certainly 'worthy of his crust' (211).

His phenomenal fame, his 'star status', rests on two pillars. To begin with, there are the intrinsic qualities of his work and their meaning for art and the artists who came after him: his spontaneous, vibrant brushwork; the everyday (and thus easily recognisable) motifs, such as a pair of shoes or a postman; the beauty of his delicate draughtsmanship and the emotionally charged colours of his palette, whether dark (as in *The Potato Eaters*, fig. 1) or bright (as in *The Yellow House*, cat. 100); and the sometimes alienating effect of the ordinary things he depicted (as seen in *Wheat Field with Crows*, fig. 2).

Then there is the myth that clings to him and appeals to the imagination of many: the man who sacrificed everything, including himself, for his art; the man, living in poverty and universally misunderstood, who produced a magnificent œuvre for which he never received a penny; the mad genius who created masterpieces in a state of ecstasy and infatuation, who came out of nowhere to achieve

eternal fame; the man who cut off his ear in despair and took his own life.

The bridge between this story of the man – an amalgam of few facts and much fiction – and his unique, iconic body of works is formed by a part of Van Gogh's legacy that is less known to the broader public but can justifiably be called his second *œuvre*: his letters. Letter-writing was a natural part of Van Gogh's everyday life. He left his parents' home at the age of sixteen, and his subsequent search for his destiny was accompanied by a series of moves in the Netherlands, England, Belgium and France. In the nineteenth century, letters were the customary means of keeping in touch with friends and family, but in Van Gogh's case there was considerably more at stake. Once he had understood that it was necessary to strike out on his own, rather than comply with the conventional expectations of his milieu, writing became for him not only a means of communication but, more importantly, a way

of focusing and clarifying his thoughts, a means of carving out a place for himself and defining his intellectual identity. On the face of it, Van Gogh's letters are an account of the vicissitudes of his life – endeavours, setbacks, results – but at the same time they are an interior monologue, and as such, they are anything but quotidian: Van Gogh, a great reader and keen observer, also possessed the gift of writing well. Although he once remarked that 'writing is actually an awful way to explain things to each other' (199), he could formulate artistic and philosophical ideas in very succinct terms. His account of his thoughts and experiences is poignant and compelling. Indeed, he proved so talented at writing that his letters have been viewed as exceptional since their first publication, and are regarded by many as great literature.

Thus the letters constitute the bridge linking the man and his art. But in what sense do they contribute to a better understanding of his work?

Fig. 2 **Wheat Field with Crows**, Auvers-sur-Oise, July 1890. Oil on canvas, 51 x 103 cm. Van Gogh Museum, Amsterdam (Vincent van Gogh Foundation), s0149 V/1962 (F779)

'There – once back here I set to work again – the brush however almost falling from my hands and – knowing clearly what I wanted I've painted another three large canvases since then. They're immense stretches of wheat fields under turbulent skies, and I made a point of trying to express sadness, extreme loneliness [...] I'd almost believe that these canvases will tell you what I can't say in words, what I consider healthy and fortifying about the countryside' (from letter 898, Vincent van Gogh to Theo van Gogh and Jo van Gogh-Bonger, Auvers-sur-Oise, on or about Thursday 10 July 1890)

Fig. 3 **Letter 900** (cat. 155)
from Theo van Gogh to Vincent
van Gogh. Paris, Monday 14 July
1890. Paper, 20.2 x 26.4 cm.
Van Gogh Museum, Amsterdam
(Vincent van Gogh Foundation),
b768 V/1962

In what way do the letters – in which Van Gogh
talks about his artistic ambitions, his continuous,
homespun education, his trying out of techniques
and his satisfaction, or otherwise, with the results –
relate to the works themselves, in which all of
these ingredients come together? In searching for
answers to these questions we must be aware that
Van Gogh's correspondence, however captivating
in many respects, should not be read as a diary –
just as a self-portrait, no matter how good the
likeness, should not necessarily be regarded as a
faithful reflection of its maker. Both letter-writer
and artist seek to achieve an effect, to show a
consciously chosen side of themselves. They select
the angle of light, and choose to omit certain details
while enhancing others. The artist 'lies the truth',
in the words of the Dutch poet Gerrit Kouwenaar,
but this does not mean that Van Gogh's letters
contain little that is true to life. On the contrary,
the letters frequently afford – and not just between
the lines – sightings of the real Van Gogh.

Characterisation of the Letters

Although the known extent of Van Gogh's
correspondence is 819 letters written and 83
received, an inventory of references to other letters
sent and received shows that his correspondence in
fact totalled more than 2,000 letters. Some 90% of
the surviving corpus is preserved in the Van Gogh
Museum in Amsterdam; The Morgan Library and
Museum in New York has in its collection 21 letters
written by Van Gogh to his friend Emile Bernard
and a single letter to Paul Gauguin; and a few
others are dispersed among museums, archives
and private collections. That only 83 letters to
Van Gogh have survived is due to the fact that he
destroyed his papers at regular intervals, owing
to his frequent moves. Most of the surviving letters
written to him date from the late years; presumably
his mental state in that period prevented him from
packing his things when he moved; then again,
perhaps he had come to attach more importance
to the letters people sent him. When he died in
Auvers, all the letters he had received there came
into Theo's hands.

In this essay the letters written by Van Gogh
take centre stage. Four-fifths of them were
addressed to his brother Theo, his junior by
four years. This bias came about naturally, because
ever since a special bond had begun to develop
between Vincent and Theo, in 1872, the two had
corresponded (fig. 3). Shortly after this, Theo
went to work for an art dealer, just as Vincent had
done more than three years earlier, at the age
of sixteen, when he took up a position arranged
for him by one of his uncles. As errand boys for
the international concern Goupil & Cie, Vincent
and Theo were given a chance to prove themselves

and rise through the ranks. Both boys were enthusiastic about art and read a great deal, which was wholly in keeping with the educational ideals their parents had given them. Vincent, naturally, was the wiser of the two, and gave Theo advice – whether he wanted it or not – on which books to read, what art to look at, and how he should live his life. The letters spanned the distance between the different branches of Goupil where they were stationed (fig. 4), and although they give a good picture of Vincent's formative years, as expressions of a personal nature they are rather superficial. The brothers exchanged similar letters with all members of their family and with their friends as well. These communications usually followed the same pattern: a brief account of experiences and meetings that had taken place since the last letter, a polite enquiry after the health of the recipient, a request to write soon, the writer's best regards. The letter paper was of good quality and the handwriting neat, since each letter was a kind of visiting card and should therefore look impeccable, like a white collar and polished shoes.

Van Gogh found his own voice in the period in which he began to have serious doubts about the desirability of a future in the art business. It was also at this time that his interest in religion grew steadily until it took on pathological proportions. In around 1875 Vincent's letters stopped being an obligatory form of familial contact and became either apologies for his own behaviour or moralising and moralistic arguments and recommendations. In this period, which ended in Van Gogh's decision in 1880 to become an artist, he broke with social conventions and with the expectations his parents had for their eldest son. He set out in search of his personal destiny, determined to find something he was good at, to discover his calling in life, to do something that would have meaning for others. At first he thought he had found this in religion, in clerical office, and he sought work as a teaching assistant or lay preacher. When his plans to study theology came to nothing, he changed his life completely: living on a pittance in cramped quarters in miners' cottages, he took to reading Victor Hugo and Jules Michelet, and began to identify with artists and thinkers such as Ernest Renan and Thomas Carlyle, whose ideas were far removed from the values he had grown up with.

The substance and appearance of the letters written in this period are a direct reflection of these developments. Vincent no longer adhered to 'conventions': contact with his family tapered off and took place mainly through Theo, who received sporadic letters written hurriedly on cheap paper, with fiddly additions and corrections penned in a hasty hand. Content now took precedence over form.

Fig. 4 **Letter 39** (cat. 156) from Vincent van Gogh to Theo van Gogh. Paris, Saturday 24 July 1875. *Westminster Bridge* (F JUV. XXIII), letter sketch. Paper, 21.3 x 27.2 cm. Van Gogh Museum, Amsterdam (Vincent van Gogh Foundation), b41 V/1962

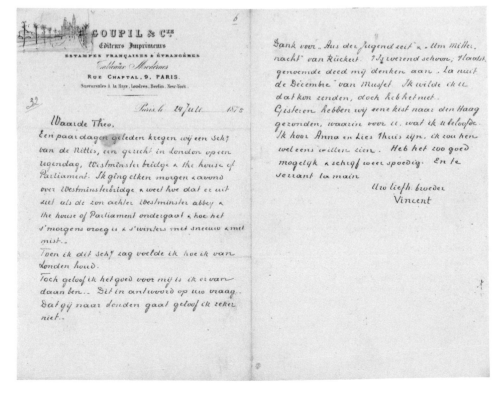

17

And it was to continue to do so. Van Gogh's handwriting had developed into a legible yet rather untraditional variant. A glance at a number of random pages shows that his handwriting could vary in appearance – sometimes squat, occasionally with a different slant, then again tending somewhat towards the smaller writing seen in the early letters – all within the same letter (see, for example, cat. 37).

In order to understand Van Gogh the artist, it is essential to read the letters written before 1880, for they reveal an important part of his moral and intellectual wellsprings, of the mentality that shaped him and of the art that informed his sensibilities and taste: the Hague School and the Barbizon School, the seventeenth-century Dutch masters and the contemporary 'salon painting' that was the mainstay of Goupil's trade.

The letters written in the 1880s focus mainly on Van Gogh's work, his daily efforts to master pencil, pen, brush and colour theory, his frustration at failing to sell anything, and his hope of collaboration with other artists with a view to breaking the old system of art dealership. In between this, we read about his ideas on society, the literature he read, his friendships, his mostly difficult love affairs, and his resistance to conventions of whatever kind. For ten years the diligent and good-natured Theo supported Vincent and made his adventure of discovery possible by sending him a monthly allowance that represented nearly 15% of his own income. He remained, until the very end, a willing sounding board for his domineering brother. Many of Vincent's letters were written to confirm the receipt of money, and more than once a lack of it prompted an epistolary plea for extra funds. Indeed, Theo's support was

indispensable to Vincent, and their whole correspondence reads like the account – punctuated by moving expressions of mutual affection – of an enduring though occasionally rocky relationship that was nonetheless deeply rooted in fraternal love.

It is impossible to name here all the topics that enrich Van Gogh's correspondence and make it worth reading; we can only urge readers to delve into the letters themselves, in both this book and the newly published editions. Suffice it to say that despite their wide-ranging subject-matter, Van Gogh's letters display an astounding cohesion. His inner world is a continuum in which ideas about life and art blend, in which old art is organically related to the art of his day, in which later notions hark back to earlier ones. In the midst of this, Van Gogh emerges as a single figure, as one big totality of countless ideas and actions.

This personage has an unmistakable voice of his own, thanks to his unerring pen; in fact, a couple of lines taken from any letter will immediately reveal his authorship. Yet these letters do not yield an unambiguous character sketch, nor do they acquaint us with their author's more intimate emotional life. Van Gogh emerges as an active, energetic man with strong views, whose life was dominated by his personal growth and the need to put his talent to use, a need that drove him to demand the utmost of himself. His efforts to augment his intellectual and cultural baggage were unflagging, his unbridled enthusiasm for art and literature downright infectious. Van Gogh's passionate, well-nigh fanatical and at times even obsessive devotion to his work contributes to his egocentricity. He sought debate, to be sure, but refused to be won over easily by others. When standing his ground in conflicts, he sometimes lost sight of reality and dismissed practical objections as unimportant. At the same time, he was able to understand that his way of life was his own choice, and that others were at liberty to live their lives as they saw fit. Yet whenever other people's ideas clashed with his own, he cast reason to the winds. It cannot have been easy to be in his company for long periods.

Ironically, the same tenacity and inflexibility that sometimes drove the people around him to rage and despair were to prove crucial to his achievements as an artist. Van Gogh's letters are a constant reflection of the struggle of a man, who showed little talent for drawing and was no longer young, to become an artist. With iron discipline he practised for years on paper and canvas, receiving neither recognition nor reward for his efforts. Somehow he found the strength within himself to do this, and to continue to have faith in his own progress, although without Theo's financial and moral support he would have had no chance whatsoever of success. Less than ten years after embarking on his artistic career, Van Gogh was counted among the avant-garde; seen in this light, the letters should provide encouragement to all those who believe in seemingly hopeless causes. Van Gogh's importance as a role model rests on his indomitable courage and perseverance, and these qualities certainly go a long way towards explaining why his letters have been read worldwide for over a century, in the course of which they have been translated into dozens of languages and appeared in scores of editions with countless reprintings.

Art and Life

Van Gogh never imagined that his correspondence would be published. That publication was possible at all is due mainly to Theo, who faithfully preserved the letters, and to his widow, Jo van Gogh-Bonger, who in 1914 published the first edition of all Vincent's letters to Theo, preceded by a detailed biographical introduction. We consequently know more about Van Gogh and the origins of his art than about any other artist. While not wishing to dwell here on his poetics, it is nonetheless worthwhile to highlight some core ideas that form the basis of his work and are illuminated in detail by the letters.

The first of these ideas actually appears as a quotation. At the end of October 1882 Van Gogh received from his friend and fellow artist Anthon van Rappard an extract of an article by the English artist Hubert von Herkomer on the position of English draughtsmen-engravers who worked for such illustrated magazines as *The Graphic* and *The Illustrated London News* – publications that Van Gogh eagerly perused, precisely because of their illustrations, which he collected (see cat. 29). The article affected him profoundly, and he mentions it in a number of subsequent letters, copying out one sentence in strikingly large handwriting in a letter to Theo: 'No result of my work would be more agreeable to me than that ordinary working men should hang such prints in their room or workplace. I believe Herkomer speaks the truth when he says *'For you – the public – it is really done'* (283). In an earlier letter he had expressed it thus: 'To you – the public – the art offers infinite pleasure and edification. For you it is really done' (278).

'Art for the people' – because Herkomer meant 'the man in the street', not the educated and well-to-do élite – was a new formulation of an ideal that had taken root, *mutatis mutandis*, in Van Gogh long before 1880. Since his idea of how he should organise his life had begun to deviate from the conventions of his milieu, he had been seeking an occupation in which he could make himself useful to his fellow human beings. His disposition and possibly also his disappointment in the attitude and mentality of the establishment in which he had been forced to work at Goupil & Cie had led him to sympathise deeply with the poor, as did the fact that his father, in performing his pastoral duties in rural villages, mainly associated with farm workers, weavers and simple peasants who led very frugal lives. When Van Gogh left the art business, his sympathy quickly changed into identification: he dressed simply (in the Borinage even shabbily), gave away his possessions and made his living conditions as spartan as possible. In this way he attempted to come closer to the people he hoped to serve, while at the same time emphasising his departure from the bourgeois, clerical culture that he thought 'Jesuitical' and hypocritical. Simple, uncultured people – who struggled to earn a living by spending the livelong day in factories or mines or working the land – were closer to nature and therefore, in his view, morally less corrupt than people with an education and a position in society, 'those who call themselves civilised people' (528). This notion also explains his fascination with the French Revolution, since it had enabled the Third Estate to throw off the yoke of centuries and had literally and figuratively dethroned the old élite.

After four or five years of searching for an occupation in which these views could help him be of service to humanity, Van Gogh found that the profession of illustrator initially presented itself as a new way of realising his goal. It was Theo who gave him this idea, which combined a practical skill with Vincent's love of art and particularly his love of prints. After all, he collected scenes of social engagement from the lives of ordinary folk, which he found, most notably, in English and French magazines. The first thing he now had to do was to learn to draw, but when he devoted himself to this task with his characteristic drive, his intention to work as an illustrator was naturally replaced by a desire to lead the life of an artist in the broader sense.

The letters written during the years of Van Gogh's artistic career bear constant witness to his unchanging ethical and social ideals, which underpin the subjects he chose, particularly the figures he first drew and later painted: peasants, fishermen, seamstresses, weavers, labourers, the elderly poor. His identification with Jean-François Millet (fig. 5), the painter of peasants who idealised in a monumental way the work and workers of rural France, is of a piece with this mentality. To get his art into the homes of simple folk, he began in late 1882 in The Hague to make lithographs, entirely in the tradition of his English exemplars. At Nuenen he depicted the peasants and farm workers of Brabant with an intentional coarseness, tending towards ugliness, in an attempt to indicate that such brutish people are closer to nature. The portraits that he hoped to sell in Antwerp show the working-class men and 'girls' whom he met in the street or in beer-halls. Later on he hoped that pictures like *Lullaby: Madame Augustine Roulin Rocking a Cradle (La Berceuse)* (cat. 81) would comfort fishermen in their solitude at sea, because that was what he wanted to do more than anything else: to comfort people.

This was, in short, his one unchanging ambition. It ran like a thread from his work with the poor in the Borinage, through the 'prints for the people' (289),

which he wanted to make in the winter of 1882–83 in The Hague, to his statement in May 1889: 'it has always been so much my desire to paint for those who don't know the artistic side of a painting' (764).

Another thread running through Van Gogh's letters is the place that art occupied in his life, although perhaps it is better to speak of his notion of the relationship between art and reality, as is demonstrated by his revealing remark: 'Books and reality and art are the same kind of thing for me' (312). In 1883 he broached this subject in a letter to Theo in which he attempted to justify living with the illiterate Sien Hoornik (see cat. 26), who knew nothing of art and literature. But – he reasoned – the fact that she stood foursquare in the midst of life meant that their relationship had a good, common basis nonetheless. Admittedly, this sounds rather naïve, and the course taken by their relationship proves that Van Gogh refused to see the reality of the situation, but it does not detract from his conviction that art must be seen as part of reality,

and that they are, in fact, one and the same thing.

In his letters, accordingly, Van Gogh deploys works of art, literary events and fictional personages as a means of taking the measure of real persons, himself included. He admires the exemplary virility in Rembrandt's portrait of the young Jan Six; he identifies with Felix Holt, the idealistic and self-assured protagonist of the eponymous novel by George Eliot; he reproaches Theo for sinking to the moral level of a narrow-minded businessman in one of Zola's novels. In the postscript to a letter he says: 'Read lots of Zola, it's healthy stuff and clears the mind' (250). Much later, in the south of France, when plagued by a series of mental breakdowns, he often quotes, completely without irony, the motto of the caricatural philosopher Pangloss in Voltaire's *Candide* – 'all is for the best in this best of all possible worlds' – to help him face the tumult of real life.

Proceeding from the same notion of the relationship between art and reality, Van Gogh took up arms against Gauguin and Bernard when they stretched the truth in the religious works they made in 1889 in Brittany by painting impossible or improbable events. Van Gogh, who enthusiastically subscribed to the idea behind Courbet's rhetorical question 'who has ever seen angels!' (515), was in essence an inveterate realist. Art need not be a photographic repetition of reality, but truthfulness and authenticity are its essential ingredients.

Not surprisingly, the words 'truthful' and 'essence' recur in the letters in this context, referring to a related aspect of Van Gogh's artistic ideas as revealed in his correspondence. 'You must really understand how I regard art. One must work long and hard to arrive at the truthful. What I want and set as my goal is damned difficult, and yet I

Fig. 5   Jean-François Millet (1814–1875), **The Sower**, 1850. Oil on canvas, 101.6 x 82.6 cm. Museum of Fine Arts, Boston, 17.1485. Gift of Quincy Adams Shaw, through Quincy Adams Shaw Jr and Mrs Marian Shaw Haughton, 1917

don't believe I'm aiming too high. I want to make
drawings that *move* some people' (249), he wrote
in July 1882 to Theo. By 'move' he meant that the
viewer feels that a work of art expresses something
real, something universal, the 'essence' of existence
(249). In Victor Hugo's *Les Misérables*, Van Gogh
encountered the figure of Fantine, a prostitute, who
made a deep impression on him: 'oh, I know as well
as anyone that in reality one won't find an exact
Fantine – but all the same this character by Hugo –
like all his characters for that matter – is *true*, being
the essence of what one sees in reality. It is the *type* –
of which one encounters only individuals' (336).
Here art is even truer than reality. This idea also
underlies the 'types of the people' (204), which Van
Gogh drew in The Hague, when he was toying with
the idea of going to Brabant. After moving there six
months later, he painted a long series of 'heads' of
farm workers to 'capture' the 'essence' of such
people in paint. These are not psychological
portraits that express the character of the individual
sitters; instead, Van Gogh was aiming to record the
universal features of the quintessential farm worker.
Precisely the same intention underpins the portraits
he painted years later of the postal employee Joseph
Roulin (cat. 70), of Roulin's wife rocking a cradle
and thus fulfilling the iconic role of comforter (cat.
81), and of Dr Paul Gachet (fig. 6), the archetypal
melancholic: 'I've done the portrait of Mr Gachet
with an expression of melancholy which might
often appear to be a grimace to those looking at the
canvas. And yet that's what should be painted,
because then one can realise, compared to the calm
ancient portraits, how much expression there is in
our present-day heads, and passion and something
like waiting and a shout. Sad but gentle but clear

and intelligent, that's how many portraits should
be done, that would still have a certain effect on
people at times. There are modern heads that one
will go on looking at for a long time, that one will
perhaps regret a hundred years afterwards' (886).

If one pays attention to Van Gogh's criteria for
judging art, it soon becomes clear that his
appreciation of a work was coloured by his regard
for the artist: 'My sympathies in the literary as well
as the artistic sphere are drawn most strongly to
those artists in whom I see the soul most at work'
(332). A work of art, therefore, was a personal
means of expression, but not in the traditional,
romantic sense of 'the spontaneous overflow
of powerful feelings', to quote Wordsworth's
definition of poetry. In his younger years Van Gogh
had read the Romantic German poets (Goethe,
Rückert, Heine), who examined and conveyed their
innermost feelings in their work; and yet in his
letters, the strictly personal was pushed almost
completely into the background. Although it is

true that he expected an artist to have a broad and profound emotional life, he thought that the writer or painter should proceed from that inner life to arrive at a general human understanding, at the same time being a thinker, an analyst: 'Whether in figures or in landscapes, I would like to express not something sentimentally melancholic but deep sorrow. In short, I want to reach the point where people say of my work, that man feels deeply and that man feels subtly. Despite my so-called coarseness – you understand – perhaps precisely because of it' (249).

In Van Gogh's letters this stance remains unchanged from first to last: however much he endeavoured throughout his artistic career to improve and perfect his technique, in the end it was the work's 'message' that was important to him. To some extent he was making a virtue of necessity, since as a self-taught late-bloomer he had never succeeded in mastering all the tricks of the trade. Even so, it was his sincere opinion of what constituted the essence of art. In the discussions he and Anthon van Rappard carried on in 1882–84 about the value of an academic training, Van Gogh constantly reiterated the primacy of content over form. Their differences of opinion became painfully obvious in 1885, when Van Rappard dismissed Van Gogh's *Potato Eaters* as a clumsily executed and caricatural work (see cat. 36). The incident was a decisive factor in the estrangement of the two artists, who in that period nevertheless had much in common in terms of their artistic proclivities.

A couple of months after the rift with Van Rappard, Vincent wrote to Theo: 'I ask you, what sort of a *man*, what sort of a visionary/observer or *thinker*, what sort of a human character is there behind some of these canvases praised for their technique – often, after all, *nothing*. But a Raffaëlli – is *someone*, a Lhermitte is *someone*, and in many paintings by virtually unknown people one feels that they were made with a *will*, with *emotion*, with *passion*, with *love*. The TECHNIQUE of a painting from peasant life or – like Raffaëlli – from the heart of urban workers – entails difficulties quite different from those of the slick painting and the rendering of action of a Jacquet or Benjamin-Constant' (515). Here, too, the discrepancy between form and content is seen as a problem, and the latter is clearly given priority. Van Gogh's conviction remained unshaken. It resounds again, for example, in a warning issued in the summer of 1888, when he was at the apex of his career: 'I must warn you that everyone will find that I work too quickly. Don't you believe a word of it. Isn't it the emotion, the sincerity of our feeling for nature, that leads us' (631). So the artist still had to feel deeply, reaching beyond his personal emotions, if he wanted to grasp and portray what was essential of man, nature and life.

Given that art and life converge to become mutually influential, a work of art is part and parcel of its maker and vice versa. This basic assumption explains why Van Gogh could sometimes identify so strongly with the men who had created the works he most admired. He had read his Carlyle and was receptive to his idea that history – and, by implication, art – had been defined by great men. In Van Gogh's eyes, the world of art had one such 'great' in Gauguin, the leader of the new generation, but he also maintained that 'the painter of the future is *a colourist such as there hasn't been before*' (604). Art of everlasting value demanded men who were larger than life.

Fig. 7 **Letter 322** (cat. 157) from Vincent van Gogh to Theo van Gogh. The Hague, on or about Friday 2 March 1883. *Five Men and a Child in the Snow* (JH323), enclosed envelope sketch. Paper, 13.8 x 10.5 cm. Van Gogh Museum, Amsterdam (Vincent van Gogh Foundation), d318 V/1970

Fig. 8 **Letter 354** (cat. 158) from Vincent van Gogh to Anthon van Rappard. The Hague, on or about Friday 15 June 1883. *Faber Pencil*, letter sketch. Paper, 20.8 x 27 cm. Van Gogh Museum, Amsterdam (Vincent van Gogh Foundation), b8369 a-b V/2006

The Letters as Commentary on Van Gogh's Own Work

Although the letters give a wide-angle view of Van Gogh's artistic agenda and thought, they are equally revealing as to the origins and meaning of individual works of art – though not all of them, for of the more than 2,000 works of art to have survived, only some 600 are mentioned in the letters. About most Van Gogh wrote no more than that they were either standing on his easel, just finished, or about to be sent. A number of works are discussed in more detail, and those passages are often extremely enlightening, not least because Van Gogh's style is clear, concrete and expressive, never woolly or abstract.

First of all, we are told a great deal about the materials Van Gogh used and the circumstances in which his works took shape. He made a drawing, for example, of his perspective frame, an aid in achieving depth and correct proportions (cat. 5); he sketched on an envelope to show Theo the effect of natural chalk (fig. 7); he mentions the kind of paper and the drawing materials used in his early,

experimental years (fig. 8). From a letter written to Anthon van Rappard in March 1883 (325), we learn that he ordered 'Korn paper' for his lithographs, that he worked with lithographic crayon and autographic ink, and that he scratched and scraped his lithographs with a 'scraper' and a 'point'. Further on in the letter he also tells his friend that he has rediscovered natural chalk: 'Now another thing – do you know *natural chalk*? Last year I was given a few large pieces by my brother, this size, no less. [Here Van Gogh drew a full-size piece of chalk.] I worked with it but didn't pay it much attention and forgot about it. Now lately I found a piece again and I was struck by how beautiful its colour was, its blackness. Yesterday I did a drawing with it, women and children at a hatch at the public kitchen where soup is sold. And I must tell you that this experiment pleased me very much indeed. [Here follow several small sketches.] I scrawl some lines here at random to show you the range of black. *Don't you think it's beautifully warm?* I immediately wrote to my brother for more of the same. Shall

I send you a piece when I get it? But if you already know of it and can get it at your place, then you send me some. For I intend to use it continually in combination with lithographic crayon. It's just as if there were soul and life in the stuff, and as if it understands what one intends and itself co-operates. I'd like to call it *Gypsy chalk*. Because the pieces are very big, there's no need to use a holder. It has the colour of a ploughed field on a summer evening! I'll get half a barrel if that's the measure it's sold by, which I doubt, however' (325). A passage like this is of great importance in understanding Van Gogh's working method and to aid the proper conservation of his works. At the same time we read how fervently he sought a means of enlivening and enhancing the expressive power of his work.

The letters from the later years in the south of France also contain detailed information about Van Gogh's studio practices: how he cut his reed pens himself from reeds found in huge quantities on the roadsides outside Arles, what size brushes he asked Theo to order (he drew them, full-size, in his letter, see fig. 9), the fact that he had rolls of primed absorbent canvas shipped to him, but worked, while with Gauguin, on coarse jute. There are also lists of paint orders that show the kinds, quantities and colours of paint he used.

Colour is a constant topic of discussion. In Van Gogh's Dutch years he considered shades of grey, brown and green the best way of putting 'sentiment' and 'mood' in his work. Writing about his masterpiece *The Potato Eaters* (fig. 1), with which he showed the world that he could produce a full-fledged figure painting based on lengthy preparatory studies – a process described in detail

in the letters – he referred as follows to the colour of the hands and faces: 'the colour they're painted now is *something like the colour of a really dusty potato, unpeeled of course*' (499). He thus chose his colours with a view to rendering the genuine, deeper truth of these peasants' lives.

Later Van Gogh came to the conclusion that colour can take on a function and meaning of its own, which is essentially independent of the image portrayed. After becoming adept in Paris at using bright colours and strong contrasts, in Arles he further increased the intensity and contrasting effect of his colours, until he had found his own, pioneering style (figs 10–11). Under the strong influence of Japanese prints, from which he adopted large, flat areas of colour and robust contours, he produced his most extremely colourful works, in which the colours no longer needed to be realistic. Their correspondence to the actual motif was not of primary importance (as it had been in *The Potato Eaters*), but rather the

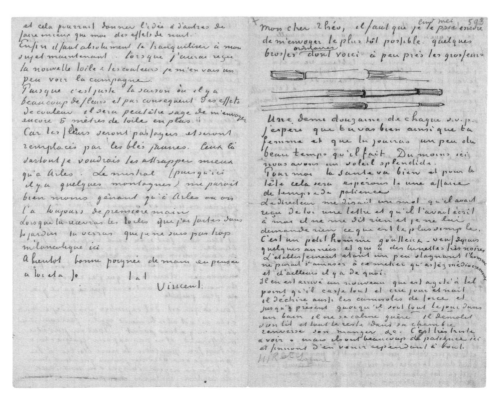

Fig. 9 **Letter 777** (cat. 159) from Vincent van Gogh to Theo van Gogh. Saint-Rémy-de-Provence, between about Friday 31 May and about Thursday 6 June 1889. Three Brushes, letter sketch. Paper, 20.9 x 26.8 cm. Van Gogh Museum, Amsterdam (Vincent van Gogh Foundation), b641 V/1962

Fig. 10 **The Harvest**, Arles, June 1888. Oil on canvas, 73 x 92 cm. Van Gogh Museum, Amsterdam (Vincent van Gogh Foundation), s0030 V/1962 (F412)

'As for landscapes, I'm beginning to find that some, done more quickly than ever, are among the best things I do. It's like that with the one of which I sent you the drawing, the harvest and the haystacks too – it's true I have to retouch everything to adjust the workmanship a little, to harmonise the brush strokes, but all the essential work was done in a single long session, and I'll spare it as much as possible when I go back to it' (from letter 635, Vincent van Gogh to Theo van Gogh, Arles, on or about Sunday 1 July 1888)

Fig. 11 **Pink Peach Trees** (**'Souvenir de Mauve'**), March 1888. Oil on canvas, 73 x 59.5 cm. Kröller-Müller Museum, Otterlo, KM 108.317 (F394)

'I'd worked on a no. 20 canvas in the open air in an orchard – ploughed lilac field, a reed fence – two pink peach trees against a glorious blue and white sky. Probably the best landscape I've done' (from letter 591, Vincent van Gogh to Theo van Gogh, Arles, on or about Sunday 1 April 1888)

sentiment or energy or tension emanating from the colour combinations themselves (fig. 12). *The Night Café* (fig. 13) depicts the rather nondescript interior of a sad-looking café with a couple of forlorn customers, but its strident colour contrasts convey a deeper meaning. The painting prompted this famous passage: 'In my painting of the night café I've tried to express the idea that the café is a place where you can ruin yourself, go mad, commit crimes. Anyway, I tried with contrasts of delicate pink and blood-red and wine-red. Soft Louis XV and Veronese green contrasting with yellow greens and hard blue greens. All of that in an ambience of a hellish furnace, in pale sulphur. To express something of the power of the dark corners of a grog-shop. And yet with the appearance of Japanese gaiety and Tartarin's good nature' (677).

Van Gogh's letters thus open up windows onto the meaning of his works – and the examples are legion. A drawing of a willow tree is not merely an impression of an element in a landscape: 'If one draws a pollard willow as though it were a living being, which it actually is, then the surroundings follow more or less naturally, if only one has focused all one's attention on that one tree and hasn't rested until there was some life in it' (175). This resonates with the Romantic tradition of the animated landscape, of nature as the revelation of creative power. Van Gogh interpreted the painting *The Garden of the Asylum* (Van Gogh Museum, Amsterdam, F659), made in melancholy circumstances in the late autumn of 1889, in a letter to Emile Bernard: 'You'll understand that this combination of red ochre, of green saddened with grey, of black lines that define the outlines, this gives rise a little to the feeling of anxiety from which some of my companions in misfortune often suffer, and which is called "seeing red"' (822; see also fig. 14, described in the same letter, and fig. 15). One of his most pitiless self-portraits is a work – made to exchange for a self-portrait of Gauguin (Fogg Art Museum, Cambridge, Mass., F476) – in which he compared himself with

a Japanese monk: 'exaggerating my personality also, I looked more for the character of a bonze, a simple worshipper of the eternal Buddha' (695), which is something we would not readily have understood without the letters. The symbolism of the sower (cat. 120) and the reaper (cat. 138) – who each stand in their own way for the natural cycle of life and who also testify to the affinity and admiration Van Gogh felt for Jean-François Millet – is documented in letters to Theo and to his artist-friends.

Nevertheless, we cannot always take Van Gogh at his word; we cannot assume that what he writes about the meaning or symbolism of a work is the last word on the subject. He painted *The Bedroom* (fig. 16), for example, to decorate the Yellow House in Arles, and he intended it to express, as he wrote to Gauguin, '*utter repose*' (706). It could thus be seen as a pendant or counterpart of the above-mentioned *Night Café*, which is seething with tension and drama. Elsewhere, however, he mentions as a pendant to *The Bedroom* the rustic *Tarascon Diligence* (cat. 59), and after painting *Wheat Field with White*

Fig. 12 **Sunflowers in a Vase**, 1888. Oil on canvas, 92.1 x 73 cm. The National Gallery, London, NG 3863 (F454)

'You talk to me in your letter about a canvas of mine, the sunflowers with a yellow background – to say that it would give you some pleasure to receive it. I don't think that you've made a bad choice – if Jeannin has the peony, Quost the hollyhock, I indeed, before others, have taken the sunflower' (from letter 739, Vincent van Gogh to Paul Gauguin, Arles, Monday 21 January 1889)

Fig. 13 **The Night Café**, 1888. Oil on canvas, 70 x 89 cm. Yale University Art Gallery, New Haven, 1961.18.34 (F463)

'The painting is one of the ugliest I've done. It's the equivalent, though different, of the potato eaters. I've tried to express the terrible human passions with the red and the green' (from letter 676, Vincent van Gogh to Theo van Gogh, Arles, Saturday 8 September 1888)

Fig. 14 **Wheat Field at Sunrise**, 1889. Oil on canvas, 71 x 90.5 cm. Private collection (F737)

'Another canvas depicts a sun rising over a field of new wheat. Receding lines of the furrows run high up on the canvas, towards a wall and a range of lilac hills. The field is violet and green-yellow. The white sun is surrounded by a large yellow aureole. In it [...] I have tried to express calm, a great peace' (from letter 822, Vincent van Gogh to Emile Bernard, Saint-Rémy-de-Provence, on or about Tuesday 26 November 1889)

Fig. 15 **The Olive Orchard**, 1889. Oil on canvas, 73 x 92.1 cm. Chester Dale Collection, National Gallery of Art, Washington, 1963.10.152 (F656)

'These are the colours: the field is violet and further away yellow ochre, the olive trees with bronze trunks have grey-green foliage, the sky is entirely pink, and 3 small figures pink also. The whole in a very discreet range. It's a canvas I'm working on from memory after the study of the same size done on the spot, because I want a far-off thing like a vague memory softened by time. There are only two notes, pink and green, which harmonise, neutralise each other, oppose each other' (from letter 829, Vincent van Gogh to Theo van Gogh, Saint-Rémy-de-Provence, on or about Thursday 19 December 1889)

Cloud (Landscape from Saint-Rémy) (cat. 134) he called it, too, a pendant to *The Bedroom*.

Comparable to these shifts in meaning and shifting interrelationships in the *œuvre* is the case of *Gauguin's Chair* (cat. 79). Van Gogh began this work in mid-November 1888, when Gauguin was staying with him at the Yellow House, and straight away it became the pendant of a work portraying Van Gogh's own chair (cat. 80). One might say that the two works are symbolic portraits of Gauguin and Van Gogh. But writing more than a year later about *Gauguin's Chair* to the critic Albert Aurier, Van Gogh gave a significant new twist to its meaning: 'A few days before we parted, when illness forced me to enter an asylum, I tried to paint "his empty place". It is a study of his armchair of dark, red-brown wood, the seat of greenish straw, and in the absent person's place a lighted candlestick and some modern novels' (853). Van Gogh had begun the 'portrait' of the chair when there was still no talk of Gauguin's departure; imparting an element of

drama to the image is characteristic of Van Gogh, who always thought in literary terms, but this narrative infuses the work with dramatic connotations it did not originally possess.

This is not to say that his interpretations and the meaning he attached to works were arbitrary, temporary or superficial. This would be unfair to Van Gogh, for it is reasonable to think that these shifts in meaning are derived more from the multivalent nature of the works in question: they could be viewed in several ways as the carriers of Van Gogh's artistic intentions, and seen as such, they are all the more firmly rooted in his *œuvre* and artistry. His letters enable us to understand this, but in trying to do so we must not take everything he writes at face value; indeed, it is necessary to read between the lines, viewing individual cases in the light of the larger whole and vice versa.

The many surviving letters of Vincent van Gogh contain countless mentions of ideas formulated and works of art produced by both himself and others. Unsuspecting readers who embark on this correspondence will almost certainly be impressed by so much drama and perseverance, and by Van Gogh's gift for expressing it all in such evocative and sympathetic terms. Inevitably, however, those readers will find their minds overrun with images, for Van Gogh's letters can seem like one long eruption of a passionate man, a sometimes obsessive seeker and artist whose boundless energy can hardly be contained. This puts us one step away from the image of Van Gogh as a mad and maladjusted genius, whose lunacy we forgive because it led to the making of so much beauty. To present things in this way, however, would be

to do Vincent van Gogh a great injustice. Despite their impression of spontaneity, his works are the product of deliberation and rational thought, and the same is true of his letters. His behaviour was inappropriate at times, and he suffered from bouts of what could be called mental derangement, but his output of letters and pictures displays a strong internal cohesion. This double *œuvre* cannot be dismissed as the product of a sick mind. On the contrary, it can only be seen as the legacy of a truly great intellect: the real Van Gogh.

Fig. 16 **The Bedroom**, Arles, October 1888. Oil on canvas, 72 x 90 cm. Van Gogh Museum, Amsterdam (Vincent van Gogh Foundation), s0047 V/1962 (F482)

'When I saw my canvases again after my illness, what seemed to me the best was the bedroom' (from letter 741, Vincent van Gogh to Theo van Gogh, Arles, Tuesday 22 January 1889)

DUTCH LANDSCAPE

In a letter to his brother Theo dated 31 July 1882 Van Gogh stated: 'The duty of the painter is to study nature in depth and to use all his intelligence, to put his feelings into his work so that it becomes comprehensible to others' (252). Nature was always the basis of Van Gogh's art. His childhood in the countryside of Brabant in the south of Holland fostered a deep and enduring love of the countryside, and the long walks he took in the forests, moors and marshes around Zundert, the village of his birth, taught him to be a keen observer of the living world in all its minute and myriad forms – to see all the world in a blade of grass. This was encouraged by his upbringing in a Protestant family that espoused the liberal teachings of the Groningen theologians for whom the beauties of nature were a manifestation of God. Although Van Gogh rejected conventional religious belief when he became an artist, his exultant view of nature as an epiphany of a deeper truth was never to leave him.

Van Gogh's primary ambition was to depict the human figure, yet from early on he displayed an instinctive talent for landscape. 'Sometimes I long so much to do landscape,' he wrote to Theo, 'just as one would for a long walk to refresh oneself, and in all of nature, in trees for instance, I see expression and a soul, as it were' (292). As he strove to teach himself the rudiments of the artist's craft Van Gogh at first concentrated on drawing. An outstanding early drawing from his first year as an artist, *A Marsh* (cat. 1), executed in the countryside near Etten, immediately reveals his innate feeling for landscape, his ability to suggest the poetry of space and atmosphere, and his ease with pen and ink, as he covers the sheet with a wealth of fluent marks that announce the varied graphic vocabulary of the great reed pen drawings he was later to make in Arles.

Van Gogh put himself through a rigorous process of self-education and as he sought to give more structure to his drawings, he studied textbooks assiduously, particularly Armand Cassagne's *Guide de*

l'alphabet du dessin (1880), which explained the laws of perspective that at first had seemed to him 'downright witchcraft or coincidence' (214). A number of early landscape drawings in which Van Gogh chooses motifs such as a road receding into the distance (cats 4, 8) are largely deliberate exercises in perspective.

Ditch beside Schenkweg is one of twelve views of The Hague that Van Gogh made in March 1882 as a commission from his Uncle Cor (Cornelis Marinus van Gogh), an art dealer in Amsterdam. Pleased with the result, Uncle Cor commissioned a further six views which Van Gogh worked on from early April to early June 1882. Van Gogh seemed to respond naturally to townscape and returned to the genre throughout his career. Turning his attention to the modern and less picturesque aspects of the city, he produced some of his most outstanding early drawings (cats 9, 10). Again he worked in pen and ink but now enriched this medium with chalk and opaque watercolour to achieve a more sophisticated and complex rendering of perspective than in the earlier series, overlaying geometric structure with richly layered marks that evoke the textural variety of the scenes.

The faint vertical and horizontal pencil lines in some of these drawings indicate that Van Gogh was using a wooden perspective frame with wires stretched across it to form a grid (see cat. 5); he would have learned about these from Cassagne's manual. He enthusiastically described and sketched the newfound device in a letter to Theo dated 6 August 1882: 'The result is that on the beach or in a meadow or a field you have a view AS IF THROUGH A WINDOW [...] I expect you can imagine how delightful it is to train this view-finder on the sea, on the green fields – or in the winter on snow-covered land or in the autumn on the fantastic network of thin and thick trunks and branches, or on a stormy sky.' He added: 'With CONSIDERABLE practice and with *lengthy* practice, it enables one to draw at lightning speed and, once the lines are fixed, to *paint* at lightning speed' (254).

The day before he had written to Theo with a sketch of himself using the frame and a palette (cat. 7), referring to his latest purchase of 'a large moist colour box for 12 pieces or tubes of watercolour with a folding lid that serves as a palette when open – there's also room for 6 brushes' (253). He had taken some lessons in watercolour at the end of 1881 from Anton Mauve, a leading artist in the Hague School and Vincent's cousin by marriage, but it was in the summer of 1882 that he began to explore this technique seriously. In part, he was responding to Theo's insistence that there was a better market for works in colour, but he also now felt sufficiently confident in drawing to take on watercolour. 'I think this is why I now work much more fluently in watercolour, because for such a long time I did my best to draw more correctly' (251).

Proud of his accomplishment, he described three watercolours made in July of that year: the bleaching grounds at the fishing village of Scheveningen, a pollarded willow by the side of an empty road and a view of the rooftops from his studio window (cats 13, 15, 17), adding watercolour sketches of each (cats 12, 14, 16) to show Theo the progress he was making. 'They're landscapes, very difficult in their delineation, with complicated perspective – but precisely because of that there's a true Dutch character and sentiment to them,' he explained (250). The beautiful view of rooftops seen from Van Gogh's studio window is particularly impressive and already we get a hint of the way he could use perspective to convey that urgent engagement with the landscape that was later to give such an emotional charge to the landscapes he painted at Saint-Rémy.

At the end of 1883 Van Gogh returned to Brabant, and lodged for two years in his parents' vicarage at Nuenen. There he concentrated largely on drawing and painting the local peasants, but did not ignore the landscape. The vicarage garden – a place that 'set me so to dreaming' (437) – was particularly resonant for

Van Gogh and inspired a number of paintings and a group of drawings that are remarkable for their poetic and melancholy mood (cat. 23); these are among the great achievements of his early work. *Behind the Hedgerows* (cat. 18), with its mesh of fine lines and soft, radiant light, recalls Rembrandt's etchings, which Van Gogh admired enormously. Other works in the series – among them *Houses with Thatched Roofs* (cat. 21), a work that captures 'the effect of light and shade – nature's mood at that moment' (441) – depict the surrounding countryside. The cottages of Brabant were a favourite motif that Van Gogh saw as particularly Dutch, and he associated them with the homely simplicity of peasant life. He pursued the theme in a number of paintings and drawings, including the large-scale canvas *Cottage in Brabant* (cat. 20).

At Nuenen, Van Gogh began to concentrate on painting in oils. In May 1885 he had completed *The Potato Eaters* (fig. 1, cat. 36), his first major work in the medium, painted in the sombre tones of the earth. But later in the year a new sense of colour began to assert itself. A visit to the newly opened Rijksmuseum in Amsterdam in the autumn rekindled Van Gogh's admiration for the colour of the great Dutch seventeenth-century painters and encouraged a 'thawing' (537) of his palette, which is manifest in the glowing colours of his majestic *Autumn Landscape* (cat. 25) and which was to burst forth in Paris under the influence of the Impressionists.

The landscape of Brabant always remained at the heart of Van Gogh's inner world, and his experience of France was coloured with nostalgia for this *lieu de mémoire*. He compared Provence to Holland repeatedly and in his last few months at Saint-Rémy, Brabant was still on his mind when he painted *Cottages at Sunset (Reminiscence of Brabant)* (Van Gogh Museum, Amsterdam, F675), 'a reminiscence of Brabant, cottages with mossy roofs and beech hedges on an autumn evening with a stormy sky, the sun setting red in reddish clouds' (864).

1 **A Marsh**
June 1881
Pen and black ink over graphite
on cream paper, 46.8 x 59.3 cm
National Gallery of Canada,
Ottawa, 15461. Purchased 1967

Selected references: Faille 1970,
no. 846; Martigny 2000, cat. 1;
Amsterdam 2005B, cat. 1

At the end of June 1881, an enthusiastic Van Gogh wrote from Etten to tell his brother that he had worked several times in the area with his artist friend Anthon van Rappard: 'We went on a fair number of excursions together, several times to the heath at Seppe, among other places, and the so-called Passievaart, a huge marsh [...] While he was painting I made a pen drawing of another spot in the marsh where many water lilies grow. (Near Roosendaalseweg.)' (168). By the Passievaart Van Gogh made this drawing and another version, with water lilies in the foreground (Virginia Museum of Fine Arts, Richmond, F845). The water of the marsh reflects the thick blanket of cloud in the sky; the trees and grass in the foreground were rendered in great detail. *A Marsh* is one of Van Gogh's best early drawings.

Even though their backgrounds were very different – Van Gogh, a clergyman's son, was self-taught and worked in isolation, whereas the aristocratic Van Rappard had received an academic training and moved in artists' circles – the two friends shared a predilection for depicting the life of the lower classes. The feeling that they were both 'painters of the people' was a powerful bond, and together they painted such subjects as the Nuenen weavers and the landscape of Brabant. Their friendship lasted four years. AV

2 Letter 172
from Vincent van Gogh
to Theo van Gogh
Etten, mid-September 1881
Storm Clouds over a Field (JH37),
Digger (JH39), *Figure of a Woman*
(JH39), letter sketches
Paper, 20.7 x 26.3 cm
Van Gogh Museum, Amsterdam
(Vincent van Gogh Foundation),
b170 a-b V/1962

3 Storm Clouds over a Field
September 1881
Pencil, black chalk and wash,
heightened with white on paper,
46.9 x 49.4 cm
Private collection, Ireland

Selected references: Faille 1970,
no. 1676; Van Haarlem 2004,
p. 37; Sotheby's 2005, lot 110

Writing to Theo in mid-September 1881, Vincent said he was delighted to report that his drawing was improving daily: 'The careful study, the constant and repeated drawing of Bargue's *Exercices au fusain* [a drawing manual] has given me more insight into figure drawing [...] So that what used to seem to me to be desperately impossible is now gradually becoming possible, thank God' (172; cat. 2). Although here he refers specifically to figure drawing, Van Gogh's progress is also apparent from his landscape drawings.

In the same letter Van Gogh made a detailed sketch of the same subject, and was probably describing the present drawing of a field beneath a stormy sky when he wrote the words: 'This is a field or stubble field which is being ploughed and sown, I have a rather large sketch of it with a storm brewing' (172). The measurements of this drawing are indeed rather large in comparison with other works from the same period. The turbulent clouds hang menacingly above the field, where several figures are still at work.

It is obvious that a piece of the drawing is missing on the right-hand side. Van Gogh worked on drawing paper of a standard format, approximately 47 x 63 cm, which means that about 14 cm of the original drawing has disappeared. It is not clear whether Van Gogh cut the drawing into a square himself. In the letter sketch he omitted much of the sky, which makes it seem as though the original composition was very elongated. AV

4 **Ditch beside Schenkweg**
March 1882
Pencil, pen and brush
and black ink, grey wash,
white opaque watercolour,
traces of a perspectival grid,
on laid paper, 18.4 x 33.7 cm
Kröller-Müller Museum,
Otterlo, KM 113.904

Selected references: Faille 1970,
no. 921; Amsterdam 1980, cat. 71;
Otterlo 1990, cat. 26; Dumas and
Van der Mast 1990, pp. 30–31;
Seattle 2004, cat. 16; Meedendorp
2007, p. 113

5 **Letter 254**
from Vincent van Gogh
to Theo van Gogh
The Hague, Saturday 5
or Sunday 6 August 1882
Post for Perspective Frame, Peg for
Perspective Frame, Perspective Frame,
letter sketches
Paper, 20.9 x 13.2 cm
Van Gogh Museum, Amsterdam
(Vincent van Gogh Foundation),
b245 V/1962

In the autumn of 1881 Van Gogh wrote from Etten to his friend Van Rappard: 'I'll carry on here for a while, I spent so many years abroad, in England as well as in France and Belgium, that it's high time I stayed here for a while. You know what's absolutely beautiful these days, the road to the station and to Leur with the old pollard willows [...] I can't tell you how beautiful those trees are now' (174). Only three drawings with pollard willows survive from the Etten period: the present *Road in Etten* (cat. 8), *Small House on a Road with Pollard Willows* (Kröller-Müller Museum, Otterlo, F900), and *Pollard Willow* (Private collection, F995).

From the moment Van Gogh decided to become an artist, he tried to produce work that was marketable. Indeed, this concern is a recurring theme in his correspondence with Theo. After his death, however, the myth arose that he gave no thought to saleability – perhaps because so few of his works were sold during his lifetime. In early March 1882, when Vincent was living in The Hague, his Uncle Cor – Cornelis Marinus van Gogh (often referred to as C. M. in the correspondence), an art-dealer in Amsterdam – gave him his first commission.

On 11 March 1882 Vincent wrote enthusiastically to Theo: 'C. M. comes, orders 12 small pen drawings from me, views of The Hague, having seen a few that were finished (Paddemoes. The Geest district – Vleersteeg were finished) for a rijksdaalder apiece, the price set by me [a rijksdaalder was worth 2.5 guilders, about a tenth of the income Van Gogh had to live on each day from his brother, so this was a modest price to ask]. With the promise that if I make them to his liking he'll order 12 more, but for which he'll fix the price higher than I do' (210). *Ditch beside Schenkweg* (cat. 4) is most probably part

of the first series, which Van Gogh finished within two weeks.

Van Gogh lived in a room with an alcove in Schenkweg (renamed Schenkstraat in 1884), at that time on the edge of the city. Part of this room was furnished as a studio. He thus found the subject of this pen-and-ink drawing close to home; visible on the far side of the ditch is part of the railway yard of the Rijnspoorweg-Maatschappij (Dutch Rhine Railway Company).

Van Gogh studied various handbooks to acquire the practical knowledge he needed to achieve proper perspective and proportions. As he explained to Theo in letter 254 (cat. 5), he also made use of technical aids, such as the perspective frame, traces of which are still visible in some of his drawings and paintings. He illustrated the frame in use in letter 253 (cat. 7), and letter 400 (cat. 6) contains a fine example of his use of perspective. AV

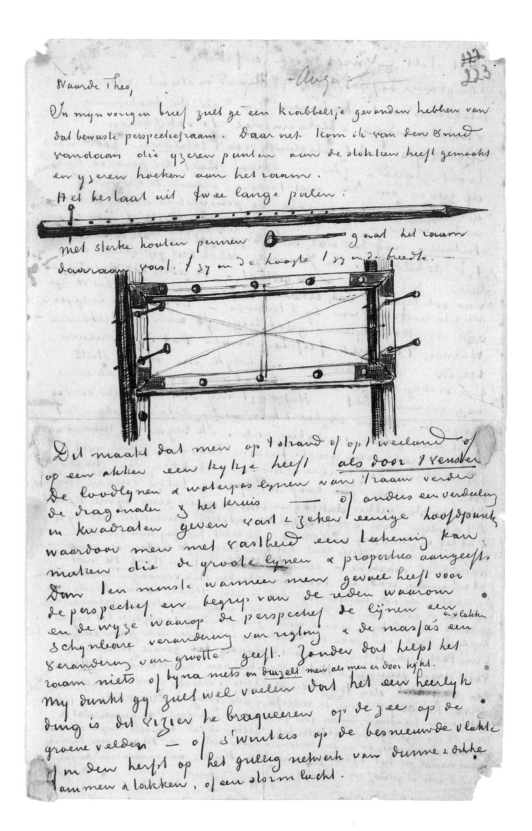

6 **Letter 400**
from Vincent van Gogh
to Theo van Gogh
Nieuw-Amsterdam,
Sunday 28 October 1883
Man Pulling a Harrow (JH 420),
letter sketch
Paper, 20.9 x 26.7 cm
Van Gogh Museum, Amsterdam
(Vincent van Gogh Foundation),
b359 a-b V/1962

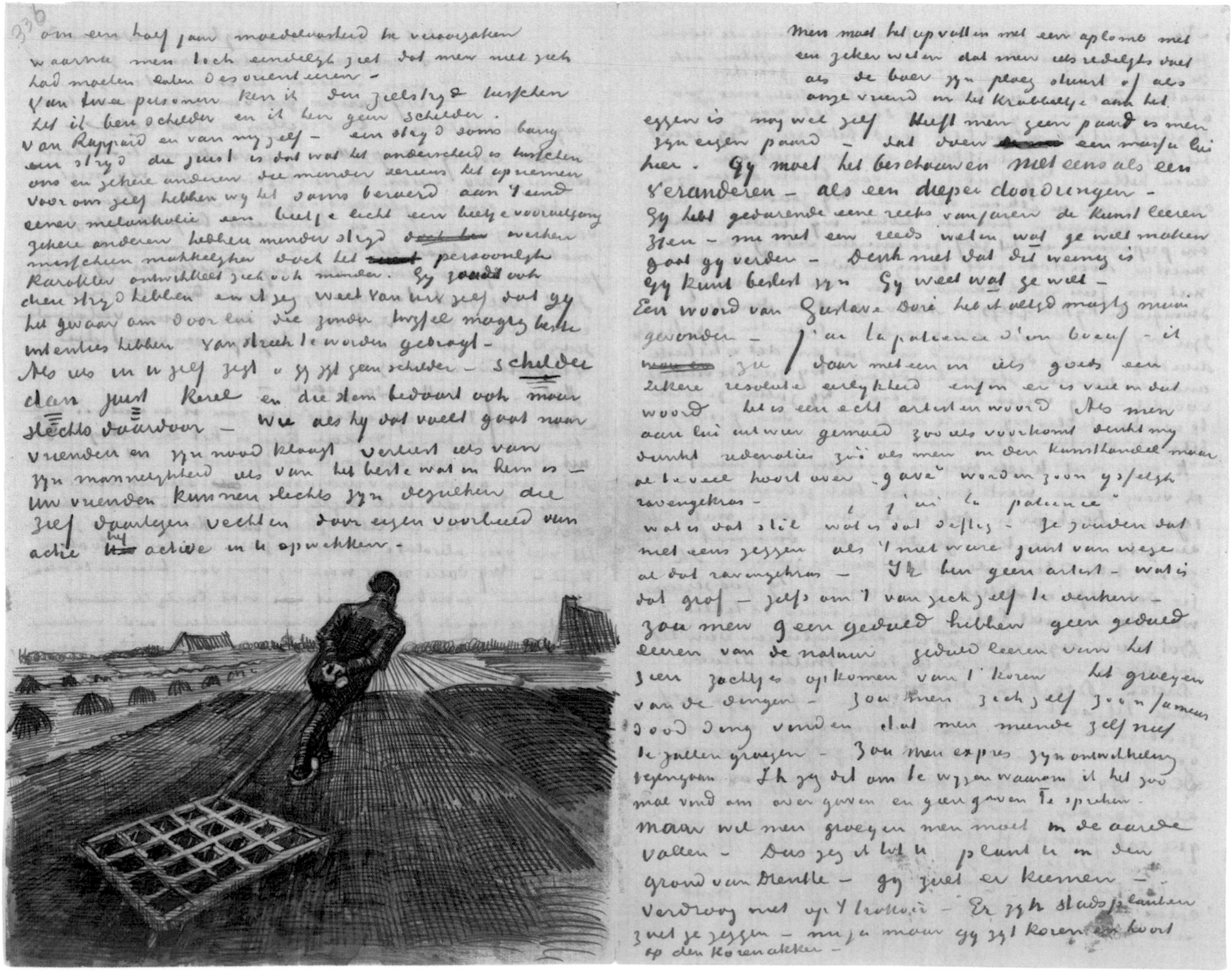
om een half jaar moedeloosheid te veroorzaken waarna men toch eindelijk ziet dat men niet zich had moeten laten desorienteeren – Van twee personen ken ik den zelfstrijd tusschen het ik ben schilder en ik ben geen schilder. Van Rappard en van mijzelf – een strijd soms bang een strijd die juist is dat wat het onderscheid is tusschen ons en zekere anderen die minder ernstig het opnemen voor ons zelf hebben wij het soms benauwd aan 't eind eener melankolie een beetje licht een beetje vooruitgang zekere anderen hebben minder strijd werken misschien makkelijker doch het persoonlijk karakter ontwikkelt zich ook minder. Gij zoudt ook dien strijd hebben en ik zeg weet van uzelf dat gij het gevaar om door lui die zoo'n tusschel mogelijk beste intenties hebben van streek te worden gebracht – Als iets in u zelf zegt u gij zijt geen schilder – schilder dan juist kerel en die stem bedaart ook maar slechts daardoor – wie als hij dat voelt gaat naar vrienden en zijn nood klaagt verliest iets van zijn mannelijkheid iets van het beste wat in hem is – uw vrienden kunnen slechts zijn dezulken die zelf daartegen vechten door eigen voorbeeld van actie hij active in u opwekken –

Men moet het opvatten met een aplomb met een zeker weten dat men iets redelijks doet als de boer zijn ploeg stuurt of als onze vriend in het krabbeltje aan het eggen is nog wel zelf. Heeft men geen paard is men zijn eigen paard – dat doen een massa lui hier. Gij moet het beschouwen niet eens als een veranderen – als een dieper doordringen – Gij hebt gedurende eene reeks van jaren de kunst leeren zien – nu met een reeds weten wat ge wilt maken gaat gij verder – Denk niet dat dit weinig is gij kunt beslist zijn Gij weet wat ge wilt – Een woord van Gustave Doré heb ik altijd mogelijk mooi gevonden – j'ai la patience d'un boeuf – ik zie daar met een in iets goeds een zekere resolute eerlijkheid enfin er is veel in dat woord het is een echt artistenwoord. Als men aan lui uit wien gemaald zoo als voorkomt denkt mij dunkt redenaties zooals men in den kunsthandel maar al te veel hoort over „gave" worden zoo'n ijselijk ravengekras – „j'ai la patience" wat is dat stil wat is dat deftig – Ze zouden dat niet eens zeggen als 't niet ware juist van wege al dat ravengekras – Ik ben geen artist – wat is dat grof – zelfs om 't van zich zelf te denken – zou men geen geduld hebben geen geduld leeren van de natuur geduld leeren van het zien zachtjes opkomen van 't koren het groeien van de dingen – zou men zich zelf zoo'n faameus dood ding vinden dat men meende zelfs niet te zullen groeien – zou men expres zijn ontwikkeling tegengaan. Ik zeg dit om te wijzen waarom ik het zoo mal vind om over gaven en geen gaven te spreken. Maar wil men groeien men moet in de aarde vallen – Dus zeg ik tot u plant u in den grond van Drenthe – gij zult er kiemen – verdroog niet op 't trottoir – Er zijn stadsplanten zult ge zeggen – nu ja maar gij zijt koren en hoort op den korenakker –

7 **Letter 253**
from Vincent van Gogh
to Theo van Gogh
The Hague, Saturday
5 August 1882
*Van Gogh's Palette, Beach at
Scheveningen with Perspective Frame,
letter sketches*
Paper, 21 x 26.6 cm
Van Gogh Museum, Amsterdam
(Vincent van Gogh Foundation),
b244 V/1962

8 Road in Etten

October 1881
Chalk, pencil, pastel, watercolour
on laid paper; pen and brown ink
underdrawing, 39.4 x 57.8 cm
Lent by the Metropolitan Museum
of Art, New York, Robert Lehman
Collection, 1975 (1975.1.774)

Selected references: Faille 1970,
no. 1678; 's-Hertogenbosch 1987,
pp. 196–99; Otterlo 1990, p. 49

9 **Sien's Mother's House Seen from the Back Yard**
c. May 1882
Pencil, pen and black ink, heightened with white on laid paper, 29 x 45 cm
Signed lower left: *Vincent*
Nahmad Collection, Switzerland

Selected references: Faille 1970, no. 941; Sotheby's 1990, lot 255; Faille 1992, p. 242; Heenk 1995, pp. 57–58; Christie's 2006, lot 52

10 **Nursery on Schenkweg**
April–May 1882
Black chalk, graphite, pen, brush, and ink, heightened with white body colour on laid paper, 29.6 x 58.5 cm
Signed lower left: *Vincent*
Lent by the Metropolitan Museum of Art, New York. Bequest of Walter C. Baker, 1971 (1972.118.281)

Selected references: Faille 1970, no. 930; Dumas and Van der Mast 1990, pp. 35–36, 172–73; Heenk 1995, pp. 56–58; Budapest 2006, cat. 8

After drawing a series of views of The Hague for his Uncle Cor, Van Gogh was immediately commissioned to do more, and wrote to Theo on c. 2 April 1882 to tell him the news: 'C.M. paid me, and a new order, but difficult enough, 6 detailed, specific, townscapes. I'll see that I make them in any case, because if I understand correctly I'll get for these 6 as much as for the first 12. And then perhaps sketches of Amsterdam' (214).

From early April to early June he worked on these drawings, which are more accurately worked out and more characteristic views of The Hague than the first series, as his uncle had requested.

These two sheets belong to the second series, about which Van Gogh wrote on 23 May 1882: 'I'm working again on the drawings for C.M. But will he like them? Perhaps not. I can't see such drawings as anything other than studies of perspective – and so I'm doing them mainly to practise.

Even if His Hon. doesn't take them I won't regret the effort I'm putting into them, because I'd like to keep them myself and get some practice in the matter on which such an enormous amount depends – perspective and proportion' (230).

While drawing Van Gogh gladly made use of the perspective frame and the perspectival grid, aids in capturing the correct perspective and proportions on the drawing paper. He also experimented with various drawing materials, as can be seen in *Nursery on Schenkweg*, in which pen and pencil alternate with black chalk. AV

11 **Snowy Yard (View from the Artist's Studio in The Hague)**
March 1883
Gouache and watercolour, ink and chalk on paper, 40 x 60 cm
Collection Jan Krugier and Marie-Anne Krugier-Poniatowski

Selected references: Faille 1970, no. 1022; Heenk 1995, p. 75; Vienna 2005, cat. 47; Vienna 2008, cat. 3

12 **Letter 251**
from Vincent van Gogh to Theo van Gogh
The Hague, Wednesday 26 July 1882
Fishing Boats on the Beach (JH159), *Rooftops* (JH157): '*Meadows and Carpenter's Yard at Rijswijk*', letter sketches
Paper, 21 x 13.3 cm
Van Gogh Museum, Amsterdam (Vincent van Gogh Foundation), b242 a-d V/1962

In late July 1882 Vincent sent Theo several watercolours, to show him that by concentrating on drawing he had also become more proficient in the technique of watercolour: 'And for myself I did them to test whether now, after doing nothing but drawing for a time (around six months), I found watercolours easier, and secondly to see where I still need to do more work on the foundation or basic drawing on which everything depends. They're landscapes, very difficult in their delineation, with complicated perspective – but precisely because of that there's a true Dutch character and sentiment to them. They look like the last ones I sent, and are no less conscientiously delineated, only now there's also: colour – the gentle green of the meadow contrasting with the red tiled roof, the light in the sky set off

by the matt tones of the foreground, a yard with earth and damp wood' (250).

This description probably refers to the sheet *Rooftops* (cat. 13) that Van Gogh had just finished, which displayed the red tiled roof and the view of the Rijswijk meadows stretching into the distance. In his next letter (251; cat. 12) he sent his brother a sketch of these rooftops.

In the previous letter, written on a summer Sunday, 23 July 1882, Van Gogh describes his view enthusiastically: 'So you must imagine me sitting at my attic window as early as 4 o'clock, studying the meadows and the carpenter's yard with my perspective frame – as the fires are lit in the court to make coffee, and the first worker ambles into the yard. Over the red tiled roofs comes a flock of white pigeons flying between the black smoking

Zomerdag op 't strand

Rijswijksche Weilanden · Timmermanswerf

219

13 Rooftops

21 July 1882
Watercolour and gouache
on paper, 39 x 56.5 cm
Joe L. Allbritton

Selected references: Faille 1970,
no. 943; Faille 1992, no. 943;
Heenk 1995, p. 63; Hulsker 1996,
no. 156; Journal 2002, p. 113;
Sotheby's 2006, pp. 70–73, lot 18

→

chimneys. But behind this an infinity
of delicate, gentle green, miles and miles
of flat meadow, and a grey sky as still, as
peaceful as Corot or Van Goyen. That view
over the ridges of the roofs and the gutters
in which the grass grows, very early in the
morning and the first signs of life and
awakening – the bird on the wing, the
chimney smoking, the figure far below
ambling along – this is the subject of my
watercolour, I hope you'll like it' (250).

Snowy Yard (View from the Artist's Studio
in The Hague) (cat. 11) was made a year later,
in March 1883. This watercolour, too, was
probably intended to show the mastery
he had gained in this technique: Van Gogh
drew the subject several times before
attempting the watercolour. AV

14 Letter 251
from Vincent van Gogh
to Theo van Gogh
The Hague, Wednesday
26 July 1882
Bleaching Ground (JH163):
'*Bleaching Ground Scheveningen*',
letter sketch
Paper, 21 x 13.3 cm
Van Gogh Museum, Amsterdam
(Vincent van Gogh Foundation),
b242 a-d V/1962

**15 Bleaching Ground
at Scheveningen**
Late July 1882
Watercolour, heightened
with white on paper (recto),
31.8 x 54 cm
The J. Paul Getty Museum,
Los Angeles, 98.GC.2

Selected references: Faille 1970,
no. 946r; Dumas and Van der
Mast 1990, p. 68; Meedendorp
2007, pp. 138–43

'I've also done a bleaching ground at Scheveningen, on the spot in one go, entirely in wash almost without preparation, on a very coarse piece of torchon. Here are a couple of small sketches of it' (251; cat. 14). In his letter of 26 July 1882, Van Gogh did, in fact, make a small sketch of the bleaching ground, to give Theo an impression of the watercolour he had made on the spot.

In the summer of 1882 Van Gogh drew the rural surroundings of The Hague, including the nearby fishing village of Scheveningen. He used a variety of drawing materials – pencil, pen and ink, black chalk, watercolour and gouache – to try out various effects. At bleaching grounds, washing was laid out on the ground to dry and bleach in the sun. Here Van Gogh depicted the public bleaching grounds in the Kerklaan at Scheveningen, with the Church of St Anthony Abbot in the background. AV

On Monday 31 July 1882 Vincent wrote to Theo about cat. 17: 'I've attacked that old giant of a pollard willow, and I believe it has turned out the best of the watercolours. A sombre landscape – that dead tree beside a stagnant pond covered in duckweed, in the distance a Rijnspoor depot where railway lines cross, smoke-blackened buildings – also green meadows, a cinder road and a sky in which the clouds are racing, grey with an occasional gleaming white edge, and a depth of blue where the clouds tear apart for a moment' (252; cat. 16).

At the end of the same letter he added a coloured sketch and the words: 'Where the black is darkest in this little sketch is where the greatest strengths are in the watercolour – dark green, brown, dark grey'.

Vincent found the question of colour and the use of black very intriguing; he and Theo had already discussed the subject at length in their letters. AV

18 Behind the Hedgerows

March 1884
Pencil, pen and ink on paper,
40 x 53 cm
Signed lower left: *Vincent*
Rijksmuseum, Amsterdam,
SK-A-2225

Selected references: Faille 1970,
no. 1129; Otterlo 1990, p. 129;
Van Heugten 1997, pp. 82–98;
Amsterdam 2005B, cat. 20

In the first half of March 1884, Van Gogh
made seven pen-and-ink drawings,
of which six have survived. *Behind the
Hedgerows* belongs to this series, in which
the artist gives proof of great proficiency
with the pen and achieves fully resolved
compositional schemes. This sheet depicts
the garden behind the parsonage in
Nuenen – the lane is still called 'Achter de
Heggen' (the Dutch title of this drawing).
Van Gogh used much hatching and a
strong graphic hand to characterise the
sky, the road and the pollarded trees.

He was evidently satisfied with these
pen-and-ink drawings, for in March he
sent them to Van Rappard for assessment
with the words: 'I'm sending you [...] a few
others, namely sepia sketch, in the marsh,
pen drawing, Pollard birches – Avenue of
poplars – Behind the hedgerows – The
kingfisher and Winter garden. I'm sending
them to you on a little roll; be so good as
to put them in the portfolio with the others,
particularly when you send them back, so
that they stay flat if possible' (437). AV

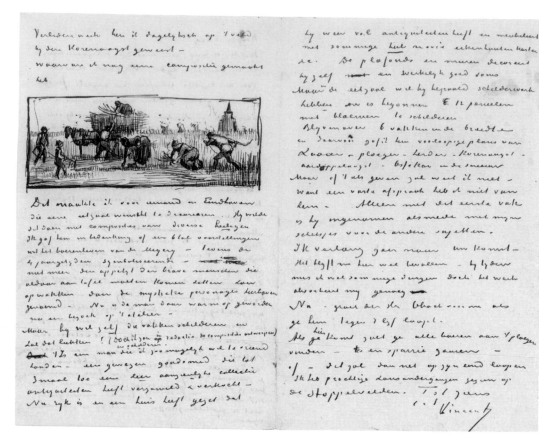

19 Letter 453
from Vincent van Gogh
to Theo van Gogh
Nuenen, on or about
Monday 4 August 1884
Wheat Harvest (JH508),
letter sketch
Paper, 20.7 x 26.3 cm
Van Gogh Museum, Amsterdam
(Vincent van Gogh Foundation),
b408 V/1962

20 Cottage in Brabant
End of July–August 1885
Oil on canvas, 63 x 113 cm
Signed lower left: *Vincent*
An American family

Selected references: Bowness
1969; Faille 1970, no. 1669;
Van Tilborgh and Vellekoop 1999,
pp. 10–11, note 21; Compton
Verney 2006, pp. 29–31

**21 Houses with
Thatched Roofs**
March 1884
Pen and ink, graphite,
watercolour on wove paper,
30.5 x 44.8 cm
Tate, 4715. Bequeathed
by C. Frank Stoop, 1933

Selected references: Faille 1970,
no. 1242; 's-Hertogenbosch 1987,
pp. 205–06; Amsterdam 2005B,
cat. 24; Compton Verney 2006,
pp. 21, 30–31

Van Gogh tried to capture the character of the Brabant countryside in the pen-and-ink drawing *Houses with Thatched Roofs* (cat. 21), which he sent to Van Rappard at the end of March. In the accompanying letter he apologised to his friend for having made the drawing so hastily: 'As far as the execution is concerned, of course I would wish right heartily that the direction of the pen strokes had followed the forms more expressively, and the forces that establish the tone of the masses also expressed their shape better. I think you'll grant me that the way things fit together – the shape of them – hasn't been systematically or deliberately neglected – but I had to make a rough stab at it in order somehow to render the effect of light and shade – nature's mood at that moment – the overall aspect – in a relatively short time' (441).

During the summer months of that year (1884) he worked outside, trying to capture peasants working in the fields, a favourite theme: 'Last week I was in the fields every day during the wheat harvest – of which I've made a composition' (453; cat. 19). Van Gogh had started working on a set of designs for decorations for the dining room of the retired goldsmith Antoon Hermans in Eindhoven, and *Wheat Harvest* (now lost) was the first of his compositions.

Cottage in Brabant (cat. 20) shows Van Gogh beginning to master the plasticity he had previously thought himself incapable of rendering. Brabant's farmhouses and thatched cottages were among his favourite motifs. Van Gogh was referring to this canvas, among others, when he wrote to Theo on 12 July 1885: 'I'm working a good 2 hours from here. I want to get a few more fine cottages in the middle of the heath. I now have four as big as the last two I sent, and a few small ones [...] I wanted to tell you now, though, that for the time being, because

there are now 6 or so large canvases, I plan to make only small ones' (513)

Cottage in Brabant has an extraordinary early history in Britain. The painting appears to have been acquired in the early twentieth century by a doctor in Stafford, from whom it passed to a farmer, John Holme, in the late 1920s to repay a debt for grain and straw. At some point the connection to Van Gogh had been lost. Holme's son Charles inherited the painting in 1952 and it was sold for £4 in an auction of agricultural equipment at Billington Farm, on the fringes of Stafford. It then resurfaced in a Hampstead antique shop in 1968 where, still unrecognised as a Van Gogh, it was bought that year by Dr Luigi Grosso, an Italian BBC journalist, for £45. Grosso spotted the signature and the painting was then authenticated by the art historian Alan Bowness (see Martin Bailey, in Compton Verney 2006, pp. 29–30). AV

22 **Letter 444**
from Vincent van Gogh
to Theo van Gogh
Nuenen, early April 1884
Parsonage Garden with
Trees in Blossom (JH476),
letter sketch
Paper, 20.7 x 27 cm
Van Gogh Museum, Amsterdam
(Vincent van Gogh Foundation),
b400 V/1962

23 **The Vicarage Garden**
at Nuenen
May 1884
Oil on paper, 25 x 57 cm
Collection Groninger Museum,
Groningen, 1962.0200

Selected references: Faille 1970,
no. 185; Vienna 1996, cat. 55;
Brescia 2005, cat. 18; Budapest
2006, cat. 24

In May 1884 Van Gogh wrote to Anthon van Rappard: 'Well, it pleases me that you like my little winter garden. This garden set me so to dreaming, and I've since made another of the same subject' (437).

In an earlier letter (probably 433, 2 March 1884) Van Rappard had received a sketch after this painting on paper, and had apparently expressed a favourable opinion of it. Van Gogh depicted the garden of the vicarage where he lived with his parents on a number of occasions, and remarked on 'the astonishingly authentic and half old-fashioned, half rustic

character of this garden' (444; cat. 22). In the same letter he sketched 'an effect of trees in blossom in the late afternoon'.

Although Van Gogh's technique still recalls that of his great example Millet and of the painters of the Hague School, he is clearly beginning to develop a personal style of painting.

The work also testifies to his progress in the art of perspective: the trees on either side, which are just beginning to blossom, afford a fine view of the farmland behind the vicarage garden, with the old church tower of Nuenen visible in the distance. AV

From 6 to 8 October 1885, Van Gogh was in Amsterdam – 'went Tuesday, back Thursday' (534) – to see the new Rijksmuseum, which had opened a few months earlier. He was wildly enthusiastic about the masterpieces he had seen, and gave Theo a lively account of painting techniques, modelling and the mixing of colours. Colour was a particular point of interest, since he and Theo were engaged in a discussion about the use of black in his paintings, which was something Theo had advised against. In Paris Theo saw the impressionist palette of contemporary French artists, and was trying to persuade Vincent to adopt a 'lighter' manner, which he thought would result in work that was more saleable.

In imitation of his great example Delacroix, however, Van Gogh came to the conclusion that he would do well to start 'from the colours on his palette instead of starting from the colours in nature' (537). While nature remained an important starting point, he did not want to copy it 'mechanically and slavishly' (537).

That same month he made various studies of autumn landscapes, one of which was *Autumn Landscape* (cat. 25): 'Presently my palette is thawing, and the bleakness of the earliest beginnings has gone' (537). Compared with earlier landscapes, this work is certainly much brighter in colour. Using primarily a warm shade of brown-orange, Van Gogh portrayed the trees in all their autumn glory. They stand against a bright, clear sky, which he filled in only after painting the trees.

The following month he made another colourful autumn landscape (Museum Boijmans Van Beuningen, Rotterdam, F45), of which he sent Theo a sketch (cat. 24): 'The horizon is a dark line against a light line of sky in white and blue. In this dark line little flecks of red, bluish and green or brown, forming the silhouette of the roofs and orchards, the field greenish. The sky higher up, grey, against it the black trunks and yellow leaves. Foreground completely covered with fallen yellow leaves, in which 2 little black figures and one blue. On the right a birch trunk, white and black, and a green trunk with red-brown leaves' (542). AV

'WRESTLING WITH THE FIGURES'

When Van Gogh first embarked on his career as an artist – a decision that he took in the Borinage in Belgium in 1880 – it was not all plain sailing. In the first place, he tried to acquire the basic skills by studying handbooks. Because he hoped to earn his living as an illustrator, he was mainly interested in the rendering of figures and began by copying examples, lent to him by H. G. Tersteeg, that were part of the standard fare of every art student: Charles Bargue's *Cours de dessin* (1868–70) and *Exercices au fusain* (1871), loose-leaf series of black-and-white lithographs in large format of antique statues and nudes in various poses. Van Gogh copied these a number of times, and studied books on anatomy and perspective. He also copied the ten prints belonging to Jean-François Millet's series *Les Travaux des Champs* (*The Labours of the Fields*) (1853). Even in his work from this early period, his idealisation of simple folk who live close to nature is clearly visible.

After a short time he decided to move to Brussels to take a more serious approach to his new career. Although he enrolled at the Academy – we do not know if he actually attended any lessons – and occasionally received advice from other artists, he worked for the most part alone, following a course he mapped out for himself. He continued diligently to copy Bargue's sheets, and informed Theo on 1 November 1880 that he was copying a skeleton with the help of a handbook of anatomical examples, Albert de Zahn's *Esquisses anatomiques à l'usage des artistes* (1865). 'And what I'm now going to do is complete the drawing of the muscles, i.e. that of the torso and legs, which will form the whole of the human body with what's already made. Then there's still the body seen from the back and from the side. So you see that I'm pushing ahead with a vengeance, those things aren't so very easy, and require time and moreover quite a bit of patience [...] There are laws of proportion, of light and shadow, of perspective, that one *must know* in order to be able to draw anything at all. If one lacks that knowledge, it will always remain a fruitless struggle and one will never give birth to anything [...] Drawing is a hard and difficult struggle' (160). And it continued to be so, particularly figure drawing: 'much as I love landscape, I love figures even more. Still, it's the hardest part' (250), he wrote in July 1882.

In Etten, where he lived with his parents from April to December 1881, Van Gogh mainly drew figures working the land, using his fellow villagers as models. He firmly believed that figure studies were the basis of everything: 'I feel more and more as time goes on that figure drawing in particular is good, that it also works indirectly to the good of landscape drawing. If one draws a pollard willow as though it were a living being, which it actually is, then the surroundings follow more or less naturally, if only one has focused all one's attention on that one tree and hasn't rested until there was some life in it' (175). During his stay in The Hague (1881–83), Van Gogh had a plentiful supply of models, thanks to Sien Hoornik and her family and the occupants of the House for Old Men and Women. Not surprisingly, he made much progress. Compositions with a number of figures were particularly challenging: 'I assure you that there's a lot involved in compositions with figures, and I'm very busy. It's like weaving: you have to give it all your attention to keep the threads apart; you must control and keep an eye on several things at once' (271).

Not only was it difficult to group the figures, but their poses and proportions also continued to create problems for Van Gogh. His figures at work often remained too static and their bodies lacked volume. At Nuenen, after reading in Jean Gigoux's *Causeries sur les artistes de mon temps* (1885) about Delacroix's creed that one must work by proceeding from volumes and not from lines, he applied that manner of drawing and was, as he himself said, better able to endow his figures with life and form. 'In these new drawings I'm starting the figures with the torso, and it seems to me that they're fuller and broader as a result. If 50 aren't enough, I'll draw 100 of them, and if that's still not enough, even more, until I've got what I want solidly, that's to say that everything is round, and there is as it were neither beginning nor end anywhere on the form, but it constitutes a single, harmonious, living whole' (506). The large drawings of working figures made with this in mind in the summer of 1885 are among his most convincing figure studies (cats 41–47). Even though he had passionately defended his *Potato Eaters* a couple of months earlier, when Anthon van Rappard had been so extremely critical of the work (see fig. 1, cat. 36), Van Gogh knew that his friend's criticism was not entirely unfounded. He must have realised that large compositions with groups of figures were not his strong suit, since afterwards he no longer ventured to make such pictures. Figures continued to populate his landscapes, but from now on he depicted them at a greater distance and in less detail.

All these efforts served to further his mission of depicting the heroic quality of simple peasant life. In the spring of 1885 he wrote:

'When I say that I'm a peasant painter, that is really so, and will become clearer to you in future; I feel at home there. And it's not for nothing that I've spent so many evenings sitting pondering by the fire with the miners and the peat-cutters and the weavers and peasants here – unless I had no time to think – because of the work. I've become so absorbed in peasant life by continually seeing it at all hours of the day that I really hardly ever think of anything else' (493).

Even so, in November 1885 Van Gogh moved to Antwerp and shifted his attention to portraiture, not only because he thought this would make his work more marketable, but also because portrait painting came much more easily to him. In a letter written to Emile Bernard in July 1888 he exclaimed, 'I want to do figures, figures and more figures, it's stronger than me' (665), by which he was referring to portraiture, which he had come to consider his principal aim: 'it's the only thing in painting that moves me deeply and that gives me a sense of the infinite' (652), he wrote to Theo. His attention was still focused on the human figure, but while in his Dutch years he was intent on depicting work and people in action, in the last two years of his life he tried to capture his models' character and type.

In Saint-Rémy, where recollections of the North sometimes filled him with nostalgia, he began again to sketch farm workers and toyed with the idea of making a new version of *The Potato Eaters*, even though in the intervening period he had devoted little attention to such compositions. This did not lead him to produce any important works, however, and in Auvers the idea faded away altogether.

26 Sien Sewing

April–May 1882
Pencil, pen and brush in black
ink (partly faded to brown),
grey washes, white opaque
watercolour on laid paper
(two sheets), 53 x 37.5 cm
Signed lower left: *Vincent*
Museum Boijmans Van
Beuningen, Rotterdam,
MB1949/T6

Selected references: Faille 1970,
no. 1025; Soth 1994; Van Heugten
1996, pp. 34–37, 217–18;
Alexandria 1998, cat. 54;
The Hague 2005, pp. 170–78;
Meedendorp 2007, pp. 120–28

In December 1881 Van Gogh moved to The Hague, where he was to live for nearly two years. In January or February 1882 he met Sien Hoornik, whom he paid to pose for him. Sien was a former prostitute, pregnant and ill at that time; Van Gogh wanted to help her, as he explained to Theo: 'A pregnant woman who roamed the streets in winter – who had to earn her bread, you can imagine how. I took that woman as a model and worked with her the whole winter. I couldn't give her a model's full daily wage, but all the same, I paid her rent and have until now been able, thank God, to preserve her and her child from hunger and cold by sharing my own bread with her. When I met this woman, she caught my eye because she looked ill' (224). Sien soon moved in with Van Gogh, which gave him easy access to a model; he was no doubt overjoyed, because models were expensive and difficult to find.

Van Gogh portrayed Sien a number of times in various poses during the year and a half that they lived together. This drawing is often wrongly connected with a letter from late March or early April 1883, in which Van Gogh reports that 'I've already written that I've drawn with the natural chalk – yesterday I began a second drawing with it, a woman sewing' (333). In fact, Van Gogh used no chalk at all for this drawing. AV

27 Woman Peeling Potatoes

c. December 1882
Crayon and pencil on paper,
61.3 x 39.4 cm
Collection Gemeentemuseum
Den Haag, The Hague.
On long-term loan from
a private collection

Selected references: Faille 1970,
no. 1053a; The Hague 2005,
pp. 106–07; Meedendorp 2007,
pp. 61–65

Van Gogh had captured the motif of a woman peeling potatoes as early as 1881, and even though in 1882 (during his time in The Hague) he was more inclined to depict city scenes and people out and about, this domestic theme crops up again. The figure is probably Sien Hoornik, with whom Van Gogh was living at the time, who is seated here on a bench, peeling potatoes.

Van Gogh liked to portray folk types going about their daily work; it was also a way for him to gain necessary practice. He preferred to draw figures in large formats, as he explained to Theo in a letter dated Sunday 3 December 1882: 'You write about the question of making drawings in a smaller format [...] Do you know what I think – all formats have their pros and cons. In general, for my own study, I definitely need to have the figure in fairly large proportions, so that head, hands, feet aren't too small and one can draw them robustly' (290). AV

28 Sower

December 1882
Pencil, pen, brush and ink, wash,
white opaque watercolour,
on watercolour paper, 61 x 40 cm
Stichting Collectie P. en
N. De Boer, Amsterdam

Selected references: Faille 1970,
no. 852; Amsterdam 1988, p. 172;
Otterlo 1990, cat. 65; Hulsker
1996, no. 275; Vienna 1996,
cat. 30; Paris 1998, cat. 43

After experimenting with lithography in November 1882, Van Gogh resolved to draw large figures actively engaged in performing a task as possible subjects for new lithographs. By the beginning of December he had finished several of these figure drawings, including two sowers. Van Gogh was presumably referring to the present sheet in a letter that he wrote to Theo between 4 and 9 December: 'Then a second sower with a light brown bombazine jacket and trousers, so this figure comes out light against the black field bounded at the end by a row of pollard willows. This is a very different type, with a fringe of beard, broad shoulders, a little stocky, a little like an ox in the sense that his whole appearance has been shaped by working on the land. If you like, more the type of an Eskimo, thick lips, broad nose' (291). Further on he wrote: 'expressing action is very difficult, and in the eyes of many the effect is "more pleasing" than anything else'.

The sower's pose suggests a powerful forward movement, and Van Gogh placed his model in more or less the same position as his famous example, Millet's *Sower* (fig. 5), which he copied many times. Van Gogh, however, depicted the right foot of his model pointing quite far outwards, so that the longer one looks at this sower, the more he seems to be executing a ballet step. TM

Van Gogh was fascinated by prints of all kinds, but particularly by the illustrations in such English magazines as *The Graphic* and *The Illustrated London News*, which appealed to him because they depicted social hardship and the lives of the poor. These themes were attuned to his interests at the time and were echoed in the novels of Charles Dickens and George Eliot that he so esteemed. He also admired the expressive qualities of the black-and-white graphic medium.

Van Gogh first encountered these wood engravings when he was working for the art dealer Goupil & Cie in London in the 1870s, but he began collecting them on an impressive scale when he moved to The Hague in 1882. In January 1883 he acquired 21 volumes of *The Graphic* dating from 1870 to 1880 for 21 guilders, a price he considered cheap but which was still quite a substantial sum for him to find. 'I now have *The Graphics* in my possession. I sat looking at them deep into the night' (303), he wrote to his friend the painter Anthon van Rappard, a fellow enthusiast and collector of magazine illustrations. After much hesitation, Van Gogh decided to remove the prints from their bindings and to paste them onto pieces of grey, green or brown paper so that he could sort them methodically, according to subject or artist.

As he studied his collection, a print would sometimes provide him with an idea for a pose or a composition. Some of the sketches he made in Drenthe in late 1883, for example, reflect the compositional design of these graphic images. Writing to Theo on 3 October 1883 from 'the very back of beyond in Drenthe, where I arrived after an endless trip through the heath on a barge', Van Gogh added a group of sketches, explaining: 'The figures that now and then appear on the plain usually have great character, sometimes they're really charming. I drew, among others, a woman in the barge with crepe around her cap brooches because she was in mourning, and later a mother with a small child – this one had a purple scarf around her head' (392; cat. 30). His presentation of these letter sketches, grouped together on a single page in a montage-like arrangement, recalls certain wood-engraving illustrations in *The Graphic*, such as *Market Gardening: A Winter's Journey to Covent Garden* (cat. 29), a print that Van Gogh owned and that is still mounted on the paper to which he attached it. AD

MARKET GARDENING—A WINTER'S JOURNEY TO COVENT GARDEN

31 Letter 421

from Vincent van Gogh
to Antoine Furnée
Nuenen, between about Sunday
6 and Friday 18 January 1884
Gardener with a Wheelbarrow (JH440),
Interior with a Woman Sewing (JH441),
Weaver (JH442), letter sketches
Paper, 20.9 x 26.6 cm
Van Gogh Museum, Amsterdam
(Vincent van Gogh Foundation),
b382 V/1962

32 Weaver

March 1884
Oil on canvas, 62.5 x 84.4 cm
Museum of Fine Arts, Boston,
58.356. Tompkins Collection –
Arthur Gordon Tompkins Fund

Selected references: Faille 1970,
no. 29; Zemel 1985;
's-Hertogenbosch 1987, pp. 47–
58; Amsterdam 1990, cat. 2,
pp. 38–39; Brescia 2005, p. 320

In December 1883, when Van Gogh arrived at his parents' house in rural Nuenen, the first theme he depicted was weaving. As a result of the industrial revolution, Brabant's once-proud 'home weavers' had been reduced to an impoverished group on its way to extinction. Van Gogh idealised their craft and straitened circumstances, and he thought the looms 'such almighty beautiful affairs' (445), with their heavy oak beams, colourful threads and that 'black apparition' (437), the weaver, who formed the very heart of the composition. He enclosed sketches of weaving themes in various letters (cat. 31, for example).

Van Gogh documented the Nuenen weavers in various ways and in a variety of techniques: there are approximately thirty watercolours, pen-and-ink drawings and paintings. One of the first was this painting. In a letter written on 30 April, Vincent told Theo that he was working on two weavers at the same time: 'I'm doing a fairly large painting of a weaver – the loom straight on from the front [...] And at the same time also the one I started in the winter, a loom on which a piece of red cloth is being woven – there the loom is seen from the side' (445). Evidently Van Gogh had already started on this work and took it up again in March/April. The loom is a nineteenth-century model. AV

33 **Letter 489**
from Vincent van Gogh
to Theo van Gogh
Nuenen, on or about
Saturday 4 April 1885
Head of a Woman (JH723),
Head of a Woman (JH723),
letter sketches
Paper, 21 x 13.5 cm
Van Gogh Museum, Amsterdam
(Vincent van Gogh Foundation),
b435 V/1962

34 **Head of a Woman**
March 1885
Oil on canvas, 43 x 30 cm
Van Gogh Museum, Amsterdam
(Vincent van Gogh Foundation),
s6 V/1962

Selected references: Faille 1970,
no. 160; Van Tilborgh and
Vellekoop 1999, pp. 84–104;
Journal 2001, p. 65; Ten Berge,
Meedendorp, Vergeest and
Verhoogt 2003, pp. 78–97

From October 1884 to November 1885
Van Gogh – now in Nuenen – made
numerous studies of heads, more than
fifty of them in oil. One of his sources of
inspiration was a series appearing in the
English magazine *The Graphic* entitled
'Heads of the People'. These were wood
engravings of characteristic heads of
working folk.

He diligently set about documenting
the faces of the Brabant peasants. These
'heads' are not portraits but types, who
represented the simple country life that
Van Gogh, following the example of
Millet, so much admired. 'Don't forget
that I'm definitely convinced that a
painter of peasant life can do no better
than follow the example of Barbizon –
dwelling and living right in the midst
of what one is painting' (489; cat. 33),
he wrote to Theo in early April 1885.

In making these studies, Van Gogh
hoped to improve his technique in a number
of areas, such as colour, form and the effect
of light and shade. In February 1885 he
wrote to Theo: 'I'm hard at work on painting
those heads. I paint during the day and
draw in the evening [...] I think that it will
help me with the figure in general' (483).

Van Gogh was probably referring to the
present study when he wrote to Theo: 'As
to colour, it's a contrast of bright red and
pale green against the colour of the little
face; there's already a head like it among
those you took with you' (489). In the same
letter he made a sketch after this study, in
which the young woman wears a green jacket
and a red cap of the kind worn indoors. AV

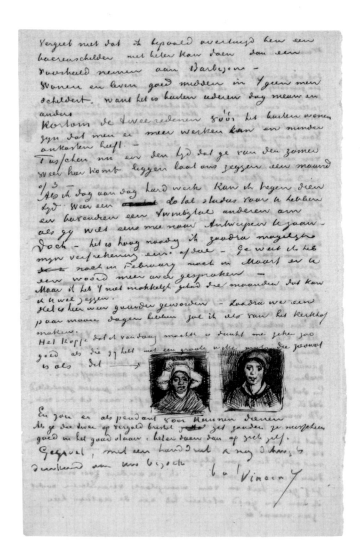

76

35 Letter 492
from Vincent van Gogh
to Theo van Gogh
Nuenen, Thursday 9 April 1885
The Potato Eaters (JH735),
letter sketch
Paper, 20.7 x 26.4 cm
Van Gogh Museum, Amsterdam
(Vincent van Gogh Foundation),
b437 V/1962

36 The Potato Eaters
April 1885
Lithograph, 31.3 x 37 cm
Signed lower left: *Vincent*
Collection Gemeentemuseum
Den Haag, The Hague,
PRE-1929-0128

Selected references: Faille 1970,
no. 1661; 's-Hertogenbosch 1987,
no. 42; Van Heugten and Pabst
1995, pp. 74–78, 97–98;
Meedendorp 2007, pp. 280–84

Van Gogh's first (and last) large figure painting – *The Potato Eaters* (fig. 1) – was preceded by several months of study. That entire winter he devoted himself intensively to painted and drawn studies of heads and interiors, all intended to lead to a large composition. On 9 April he reported to Theo: 'I'm working on those peasants around a dish of potatoes again. I've just come home from there – and have worked on it further by lamplight – although this time I started it in daylight. See, this is what the composition has now become. I've painted it on a fairly large canvas, and as the sketch is now, I believe there's life in it' (492; cat. 35). By 13 April he had finished a painted study (Kröller-Müller Museum, Otterlo, F78), and proceeded to work on the final version.

In the meantime he produced the present lithograph after the painted study. To the amazement of the printer, Van Gogh drew the composition from memory, directly onto the stone, without first making a sketch, so the printed impressions show the composition (and signature) in reverse.

Van Gogh sent prints to several people, including Van Rappard, whose reaction was devastating: 'You'll agree with me that such work isn't intended seriously [...] what connection is there between the coffee pot, the table and the hand lying on top of the handle? [...] And with such a manner of working you dare to invoke the names of Millet and Breton? Come on! Art is too important, it seems to me, to be treated so cavalierly' (503). Van Gogh, deeply wounded, returned the letter with these words: 'My dear friend Rappard, I just received your letter – to my surprise. You hereby get it back' (504).

Although he planned to make a series of lithographs on peasant life, Van Gogh made only *The Potato Eaters*. His graphic work is a modest group: although he admired reproductive prints he made only nine lithographs and one etching (cat. 85) himself. These works can best be seen as warming-up exercises and experiments to capture what he saw in his mind's eye. AV

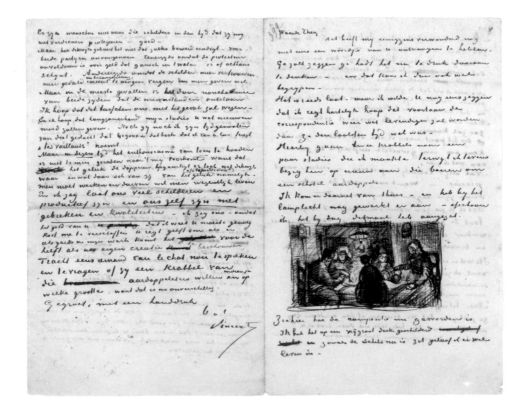

In the summer of 1885, after producing his first large figure painting, *The Potato Eaters* (fig. 1), Van Gogh threw himself with renewed energy into making countless studies of peasants at work – mainly on paper, but also on canvas. He deliberately avoided portraying them according to academic rules. In a letter written to Theo in mid-July, he fervently defended his own vision, which had been criticised by the painter Charles Serret and others: 'tell him that I don't *want* them academically correct [...] Tell him that in my view Millet and Lhermitte are consequently the true painters, because they don't paint things as they *are*, examined drily and analytically, but as *they* [...] feel them. Tell him that my great desire is to learn to make such inaccuracies, such variations, reworkings, alterations of the reality, that it might become, very well – lies if you will – but – truer than the literal truth' (515).

In May–June 1885, shortly before harvest time – when models were almost impossible to find – Van Gogh made many drawings of peasant figures. In the following months he worked up several of those drawings into paintings (see also cat. 40) and included similar figures in letter sketches at this time (see cat. 37). A study of a peasant woman lifting potatoes (Van Gogh Museum, Amsterdam, F1257r) was the model for this painting. The woman's rather stiff bearing betrays the fact that she is posing; Van Gogh failed to emphasise the action. The thickly impasted coarse brown brush strokes seem literally to refer to the dark clay or earth in which the woman's clogs appear to have sunk. AV

39 **Postcard**
from Vincent van Gogh
to Anton Kerssemakers
Nuenen, Thursday 9 April 1885
Man and a Woman Planting Potatoes
(JH728), letter sketch
Card, 9.1 x 13. 8 cm
National Gallery of Art,
Washington, 1995.47.44.
Collection of Mr and Mrs
Paul Mellon

40 **Peasant Woman
Digging Potatoes**
Summer 1885
Oil on canvas on panel,
30.5 x 38 cm
Koninklijk Museum voor Schone
Kunsten, Antwerp, 2889

Selected references: Faille 1970,
no. 98; Paris 1960, cat. 16; Ten
Berge, Meedendorp, Vergeest
and Verhoogt 2003, pp. 117–21;
Budapest 2006, cat. 37;
Vienna 2008, cat. 30

Van Gogh continually put his painting skills to the test: 'I keep on making what I can't do yet in order to learn to be able to do it' (528), he wrote to his friend and fellow painter Anthon van Rappard in mid-August 1885. In the summer and autumn of that year, Van Gogh painted many peasants at work – diggers, weeders, planters, reapers – to get a grip on colour and form. After the criticism that both Van Rappard and Theo had levelled at his first large figure painting, *The Potato Eaters* (fig. 1), made in May of that year, he again threw himself into making studies.

The motif of peasant men and women lifting potatoes appears in Van Gogh's early work: in 1880 he made a copy in pencil and chalk after Millet's famous *Peasants Digging* (1856; Museum of Fine Arts, Boston). In the summer of 1885, the theme of the digging labourer recurs in various paintings (see also cats 42, 46). In the above-mentioned letter to Van Rappard, he sent a 'little scratch of a study I did yesterday' (528; cat. 37), of two digging women with farms or cottages in the background, which is closely related to the present painting; the postcard (cat. 39) shows figures in similar poses. At the bottom of the letter Van Gogh added remarks about his own work and about a sketch that Van Rappard had sent: 'You can see from my croquis that, for my part, I take a lot of trouble specifically to get action – being occupied – doing something – into my figures. I think it's good that one figure in your composition, at any rate, is already stooping' (528). Having figures stoop was an effective means of suggesting movement. AV

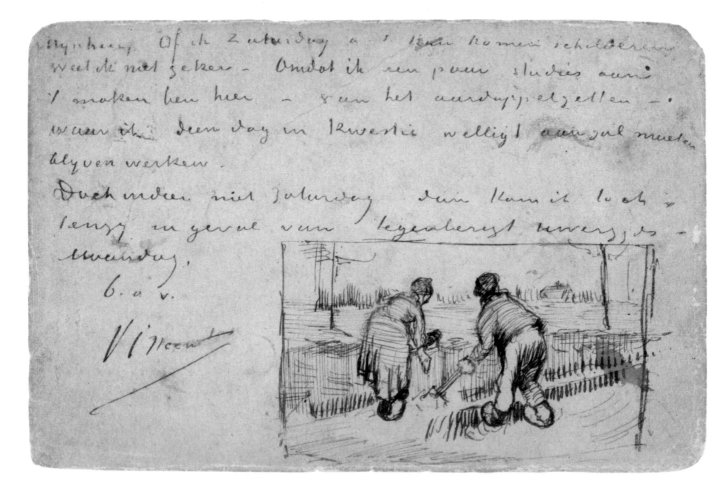

41 Reaper

July–August 1885
Black chalk, grey-white opaque
watercolour on wove paper,
56 x 37.8 cm
Signed lower left: [Vin]cent
Kröller-Müller Museum,
Otterlo, KM 121.581

Selected references: Faille 1970,
no. 1313; New York 1973, cat. 49;
London 1974, cat. 49;
Van Heugten 1997, pp. 222–39;
Meedendorp 2007, pp. 312–15,
316, 323

Peasants working the land were a source of inspiration for Van Gogh, both in his early years and during the time he spent in France. In the summer of 1885, after completing *The Potato Eaters* (fig. 1), he embarked with renewed energy on a series of studies of working figures. Cats 41–47 are a selection of drawings from this period, in which Van Gogh documented the harvest and other labours of the land. During the busy harvest season it was difficult to find models, so he made various studies – such as the *Reaper* – in his studio and later added the wheat surrounding the figure. On 28 June he wrote to Theo: 'And we're heading towards harvest – and then I must make the wheat harvest and the potato lifting a campaign time. It's twice as difficult to get a model then and yet it's essential, because the older I get, the more convinced I become that one can't be too conscientious, that one must always and eternally exert oneself in what *Daudet* (in "L'histoire de mon livre", an article by him that I read recently about "Les rois en exil") calls *the hunt for the model*' (510).

The monumentality of the figures in these studies is new for Van Gogh; he used larger sheets than usual, which enabled him to pay more attention to detail and also to adopt them later as examples for painted compositions with much smaller figures. On 12 July 1885 he therefore asked Theo to return the drawings to him on his next trip to the Netherlands: 'These figure studies – I'd like you to bring them back with you when you come, though. For there are going to be many more that I need for painting. They're to serve for figures that are definitely not larger than a span, say, or even less – so that what's in them becomes even more concentrated' (513).

It seems clear that Van Gogh planned to make another large painting, probably with figures reaping the harvest, given the activities portrayed here: binding sheaves of wheat, reaping the wheat, and lifting potatoes and beets. Despite his thorough preparation, he never got around to producing the large work he probably had in mind, although he did make several small paintings of harvest scenes. Years later, in Arles and Saint-Rémy, he was again to take up the theme of the peasants' labours at harvest time, but in those works the figures are less important. AV

44 Peasant Woman Planting Potatoes

August 1885
Black chalk on charcoal
on ribbed handmade paper,
heightened with an eraser,
partial wash, 41.7 x 45.3 cm
Signed lower left: *Vincent*
Inscribed lower left: *Planteuse
de pommes de terre*
Städel Museum, Frankfurt am
Main. Property of the Städelscher
Museumsverein e.V., 16738

Selected references: Faille 1970,
no. 1272; 's-Hertogenbosch 1987,
p. 185; Vienna 1996, cat. 75;
Van Heugten 1997, pp. 222–39;
Meedendorp 2007, pp. 312–15

45 Peasant Woman Planting Beets

June–July 1885
Black chalk on wove paper,
53.5 x 44 cm
Inscribed lower left: *planteuse
de betteraves (juin)*
Museum Boijmans Van
Beuningen, Rotterdam, MB744

Selected references: Faille 1970,
no. 1270; Van Heugten 1997,
pp. 222–39; Amsterdam 2005B,
p. 26; Budapest 2006, cat. 38;
Meedendorp 2007, pp. 312–15

Planteuse de betteraves (Brut)

89

46 **Peasant Woman, Kneeling,
Seen from the Back**
July 1885
Black chalk on paper, 43 x 52 cm
The National Museum of Art,
Architecture and Design, Oslo,
NG.K&HB00165

Selected references: Faille 1970,
no. 1280; Van Heugten 1997,
pp. 222–39; Meedendorp 2007,
pp. 312–15

47 **Peasant Woman**
Binding Sheaves
August 1885
Black chalk, wash, traces
of fixative, on wove paper,
44.4 x 56.4 cm
Kröller-Müller Museum,
Otterlo, KM 124.603

Selected references: Faille 1970,
no. 1264; Van Heugten 1997,
pp. 222–39; Meedendorp 2007,
pp. 312–15, 323

COLOUR AND JAPONISME

In the first years of his artistic career Van Gogh was preoccupied mainly with problems of technique: the proportions and grouping of figures, for example, and the rendering of perspective. He focused on drawing, his primary concerns being the handling of line and the effect of the materials used. Colour was of secondary importance, but that changed at Nuenen, where he decided to devote himself completely to painting and became thoroughly immersed in colour theory. The anecdotes of the artists Théophile Silvestre and Jean Gigoux and Van Gogh's discoveries about Delacroix's palette in the art-theoretical handbooks by Charles Blanc were a revelation to him. He was particularly struck by 'how in his paintings the MOOD *of colours and tone was at one with the meaning*. The contrast of colours, breaking, reciprocal effect from black to white, from yellow to violet, from orange to blue, from red to green' (526).

Delacroix based his unconventional use of colour on the theories of the physicist Michel-Eugène Chevreul, who had described the optical effect of complementary colours and the result of mixing them in *De la loi du contraste simultané des couleurs* (1839). This treatise exerted a great influence not only on Delacroix's notions but also on those of the Impressionists, and in particular on two painters of the younger generation, Georges Seurat and Paul Signac, whose innovative stipple technique would not have been possible without this scientific basis. Of course, Van Gogh did not yet know any of this in 1885, when he began to apply to his own work the knowledge he had obtained from his attentive reading of Blanc's *Grammaire des arts du dessin, architecture,*

sculpture, peinture (1867) and *Les Artistes de mon temps* (1876). These new ideas did not immediately lead him to use brighter colours, however; he stuck to his subdued palette, and a lack of examples prevented him from putting his book-learning into practice.

Although a radical change in Van Gogh's palette did not take place until midway through his first year in Paris, his last landscapes from Nuenen were already much more colourful. For one thing, his visit in October 1885 to the Rijksmuseum in Amsterdam and his reacquaintance there with the Dutch masters had inspired him to use brighter colours, while Theo had been urging him for some time to introduce more colour into his work to increase its saleability. In Antwerp Van Gogh studied the palette of Rubens, from whom he learned how to achieve stronger flesh tones. 'Rubens is certainly making a strong impression on me,' he told Theo, 'I'm utterly carried away, for instance, by his way of drawing the features in a face with strokes of pure red or, in the hands, modelling the fingers with similar strokes' (547).

Although he was eagerly searching for new ways to use colour, Van Gogh's first acquaintance with the work of the Impressionists in Paris no doubt came as a shock, and at first he was more attracted to the use of colour he saw in Delacroix's work and that of the relatively unknown Provençal painter Adolphe Monticelli. Following in their footsteps, he painted numerous flower still-lifes as studies in complementary colours, since colour had meanwhile become an independent means of expression: 'in COLOUR seeking LIFE, the true drawing is modelling with colour' (569).

Van Gogh's acquaintance with young avant-garde artists, particularly Emile Bernard and Henri de Toulouse-Lautrec, in the autumn of 1886, as well as his growing admiration for Japanese prints, led him to develop rapidly into a fervent colourist. From this moment on, colour was of paramount importance to him, and he began to try out various modern styles to find out what form his colour should take. After the loose brushwork of Impressionism and the dots and dashes of pointillism, the well-defined areas of colour and clear lines of Japanese prints provided Van Gogh with the ideal starting point for his own bold style. The most daring and colourful paintings he made in Arles – *Sunflowers in a Vase* (fig. 12), *The Tarascon Diligence* (cat. 59), *The Bedroom* (fig. 16), *Lullaby: Madame Augustine Roulin Rocking a Cradle (La Berceuse)* (cat. 81) – would have been inconceivable without those Japanese examples. 'All my work is based to some extent on Japanese art' (640), he declared in July 1888. But he also remained true to the lessons of Delacroix, invariably seeking the contrast of complementary colours to achieve the best possible effect. The colours of Provence were wonderfully in keeping with 'the simplification of colour in the Japanese manner', as Van Gogh argued in a letter to Bernard. 'What I'd like to know is the effect of a more intense blue in the sky. Fromentin and Gérôme see the earth in the south as colourless, and a whole lot of people saw it that way. My God, yes, if you take dry sand in your hand and if you look at it closely. Water, too, air, too, considered this way, are colourless. NO BLUE WITHOUT YELLOW and WITHOUT ORANGE, and if you do blue, then do yellow and orange as well, surely'

(622). Colour could express emotions and did not have to be true to life: in *The Night Café* (fig. 13) red and green portrayed 'the terrible human passions' (676), whereas the colours in *The Bedroom* expressed 'utter repose' (706).

After such furious experimentation with colour in Arles, in Saint-Rémy Van Gogh sought peace and harmony in his colour schemes. Japanese examples faded into the background, and he returned to Delacroix and Millet, whose black-and-white prints he 'translated' into colour. He compared this with a musician's interpretation: 'And then I improvise colour on it [...] but seeking memories of their paintings – but the memory, the vague consonance of colours that are in the same sentiment, if not right – that's my own interpretation' (805).

In this period he more frequently explained in writing what his colours were meant to evoke, as he made clear in his last letter to Bernard, in which he explains his painting of the garden of the asylum: 'You'll understand that this combination of red ochre, of green saddened with grey, of black lines that define the outlines, this gives rise a little to the feeling of anxiety from which some of my companions in misfortune often suffer, and which is called "seeing red". And what's more, the motif of the great tree struck by lightning, the sickly green and pink smile of the last flower of autumn, confirms this idea' (822). Although he no longer sought out extremes in colour, in the last year of his life he made various paintings, such as *Wheat Field with Crows* (fig. 2), in which the hues are greatly intensified. A colourist at heart, Van Gogh always remained true to his nature.

48 Terrace in the Luxembourg Gardens

Summer 1886
Oil on canvas, 27.1 x 46.1 cm
Sterling and Francine Clark
Art Institute, Williamstown,
Massachusetts, 1955.889

Selected references: Faille 1970,
no. 223; Clark 1996, p. 112;
Vellekoop and Van Heugten 2001,
cat. 229; Amsterdam 2005A,
pp. 18–25

Van Gogh was a great lover of nature. Time and again he chose gardens, orchards, parks and other public patches of green as the subject of drawings and paintings. His letters reveal that nature made him melancholy, but it also gave him comfort and inspiration.

When he went to live in Paris in the spring of 1886, Van Gogh first saw the work of the Impressionists, under whose influence he increasingly abandoned the dark tones of his earlier work in favour of livelier colours. Commenting on this in a letter to his friend the English painter Horace Livens, he wrote: 'So as we said at the time in COLOUR seeking LIFE, the true drawing is modelling with colour' (569). In addition to many flower still-lifes, in which he did a great deal of experimenting with colour (see cat. 49), he depicted parks, such as *Terrace in the Luxembourg Gardens*, which he most probably painted on location. This work was previously thought to be a view of the Tuileries, but it is apparent from the white column in the right background, which stands near the pond in the lower-lying part of the grounds, that this is a view of the garden of the Palais du Luxembourg.

Although Van Gogh said in his letter to Livens that he did not consider himself an Impressionist, this painting's broad manner of painting, fresh palette and subject-matter – a scene from everyday life – is very much in keeping with the kind of work the Impressionists produced. Van Gogh framed the composition within a painted black border, which he likewise applied to two other paintings from the summer of 1886: *View from Theo's Apartment* (National Gallery of Ireland, Dublin, F265) and *Still-life with Gladioli and Chinese Asters* (Private collection, F247). The *Head of a Woman with Her Hair Loose* (Van Gogh Museum, Amsterdam, F206) of December 1885 also has a border, but only on the left-hand side (I am grateful to Louis van Tilborgh for sharing his findings with me). RZ

49 **Vase of Cornflowers,
Daisies, Poppies
and Carnations**
June–July 1886
Oil on canvas, 80 x 67 cm
Signed upper left: *Vincent*
Collection Triton Foundation,
The Netherlands

Selected references: Faille 1970,
no. 324; Seoul 2007, p. 244;
Hendriks and Van Tilborgh
forthcoming

After his spell in Cormon's studio, Van Gogh wanted to become more skilled at painting figures, but lacked the models necessary to put this plan into action. Instead, he took the 'opportunity to study the question of colour' (574). He did this by the conventional method of painting still-lifes. 'Last year I painted almost nothing but flowers' (574), he informed his sister Willemien in October 1886. To this end, helpful acquaintances sent him flowers, 'a beautiful bunch every week', as emerges from a letter that Theo wrote to their mother. It was around this time that Van Gogh told Horace Livens, an artist from England, about his exercises in colour, writing to him in English as follows: 'I have made a series of colour studies in painting simply flowers, red poppies, blue corn flowers and myosotys. White and rose roses, yellow chrysantemums [sic] – seeking oppositions of blue with orange, red and green, yellow and violet, seeking THE BROKEN AND NEUTRAL TONES to harmonise brutal extremes. Trying to render intense COLOUR and not a grey harmony' (569).

Vase of Cornflowers, Daisies, Poppies and Carnations must have been produced in June or the first half of July, considering the presence of poppies and cornflowers. The use of thickly impasted paint applied with varied, spontaneous brush strokes makes it one of the first of Van Gogh's paintings to display the direct influence of Adolphe Monticelli, who had inspired him at the time. Van Gogh used blue for the background, however, thus deviating from Monticelli, who chose dark colours for this purpose. The fact that the canvas is signed suggests that it was either ready for sale or intended as a present. RZ

50 Grass and Butterflies

May–July 1887
Oil on canvas, 51 x 61 cm
Private collection

Selected references: Faille 1970,
no. 460; Hendriks and
Van Tilborgh 2006, p. 32;
Van Maanen 2006, pp. 9–10

It was long thought that Van Gogh painted the colourful *Grass and Butterflies* in Arles in April 1889, but recent research has led to a new dating. Its style, characterised by the fairly systematic use of long brush strokes, is related to Neo-Impressionism, and displays similarities mainly to paintings made in the period May–July 1887, when Van Gogh was working near Asnières. The ground of the canvas and the pigments used also indicate the work's origin in Paris.

The painting can be connected with a letter written at the end of March 1888 to H. G. Tersteeg (1845–1927), manager of The Hague branch of Goupil & Cie. Van Gogh, hoping to spark Tersteeg's enthusiasm for modern art, had suggested that Theo send several studies to him. Vincent describes one of the works he considered suitable as 'the butterflies' (589). No other painting of butterflies is known from the Paris period, so in all likelihood he was referring to *Grass and Butterflies*. Later, in Saint-Rémy, he was to return to the motif, painting close-ups of butterflies and flowers in nature. RZ

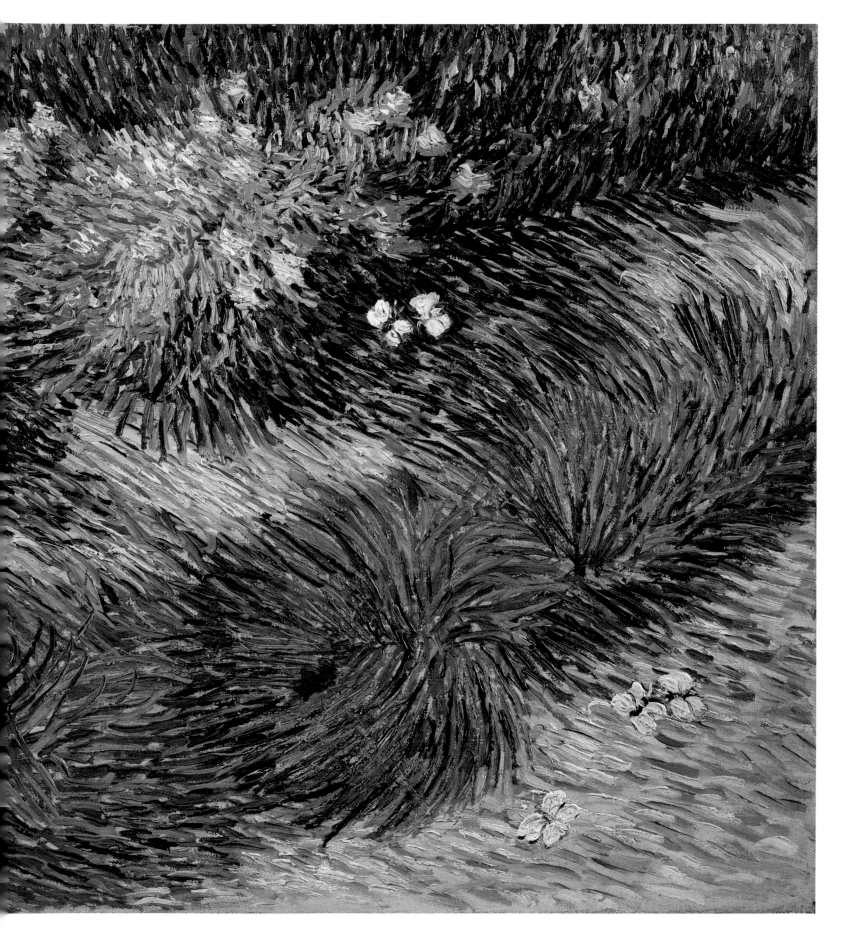

51 Two Cut Sunflowers
August–September 1887
Oil on canvas, 50 x 60.7 cm
Signed and dated lower right:
Vincent 87
Kunstmuseum Bern,
Schenkung Prof. Dr Hans
R. Hahnloser, Bern, G2140

Selected references: Faille 1970,
no. 376; Amsterdam 1990, p. 69;
Welsh-Ovcharov 1998, fig. 32;
Hendriks and Van Tilborgh 2006,
fig. 124a, p. 135; Van Tilborgh
2008, no. 18, pp. 19–32

Van Gogh painted a total of eleven sunflower still-lifes, four of which were made towards the end of his stay in Paris. *Two Cut Sunflowers* is the first of the four paintings featuring cut sunflowers that originated in Paris in the late summer of 1887 (he subsequently painted F377, F375 and F452). The present work displays a graphic, rather draughtsmanlike style. The dark colour of the flower on the left contrasts with the background of red, orange, yellow and blue-green brush strokes, whereas the light-coloured flower on the right stands out much less.

It was a novel idea to depict sunflowers that had gone to seed. 'I indeed, before others, have taken the sunflower' (739), Van Gogh later wrote to Gauguin from Arles. When he was living in Paris, he was familiar with a 'decoration' of sunflowers in the inexpensive eating-place Bouillon Duval on the Boulevard Montmartre, and this may have been what gave him the idea to paint sunflowers himself. Perhaps he was even toying with the idea of exhibiting flower still-lifes there, because since July 1887 he had no longer been able to show his work at the Café du Tambourin, as his former girlfriend Agostina Segatori had lost her job as manageress there.

Although in the end Van Gogh never had an exhibition at Bouillon Duval, he mentioned it once more in a letter to Theo, written after he had taken up the motif of sunflowers again: 'Next door to your shop, in the restaurant, as you know, there's such a beautiful decoration of flowers there; I still remember the big sunflower in the window' (666). RZ

52 Basket of Oranges

March 1888
Oil on canvas, 45 x 54 cm
Signed lower left: *Vincent*
Private collection, courtesy
of Heather James Fine Art

Selected references: Faille 1970,
no. 395; New York 1984, cat. 7;
Ten Berge, Meedendorp, Vergeest
and Verhoogt 2003, p. 396

After working for two years in Paris, where he was confronted with, and inevitably influenced by, modern art and the Paris art world, Van Gogh left for the south of France, 'the land of the *blue* tones and gay colours' (569). Shortly after his arrival in Arles, he wrote to Theo about this still-life: 'Now I've just finished a study like the one of mine Lucien Pissarro has, but this time it's of oranges. That makes eight studies I have up to now. But that doesn't count, as I haven't yet been able to work in comfort and in the warm' (583).

In this painting Van Gogh combined the complementary colours of orange and blue. Besides these bright contrasting colours, the work is characterised by daring brush strokes, particularly in the basket.

In early April, Van Gogh conceived a plan to renew his ties with Dutch acquaintances by dedicating a study to the painter George Hendrik Breitner, with whom he had drawn in The Hague in 1882 – and who, tradition has it, for he was not without a sense of humour, reproached Van Gogh for making 'art for Eskimos'. Having given earlier still-lifes to the artist Lucien Pissarro and the art-dealer Alexander Reid (see cat. 67), he intended to give the present work to Breitner: 'I have one exactly like the study I exchanged with L. Pissarro and Reid's one, oranges, foreground white, background blue' (592). *Basket of Oranges* never came into Breitner's possession, however; it bears no inscription such as the one found on the work made for Pissarro. Theo's widow, Jo van Gogh-Bonger, finally sold it in 1905 to the collector L. C. van Enthoven. RZ

53 Boats at Sea,
Saintes-Maries-de-la-Mer
June 1888
Oil on canvas, 44 x 53 cm
Signed lower right: *Vincent*
Pushkin State Museum
of Fine Arts, Moscow

Selected references: Faille 1970,
no. 417; Amsterdam 2005B,
cat. 55; Vellekoop and Zwikker
2007, pp. 7–9

Between late May and early June 1888 Van Gogh made an excursion to Les Saintes-Maries-de-la-Mer, a fishing village on the Mediterranean Sea. 'I've finally seen the Mediterranean, which you'll probably cross before me', he wrote to his friend Emile Bernard. 'Spent a week in Saintes-Maries, and to get there crossed the Camargue in a diligence, with vineyards, heaths, fields as flat as Holland […] On the completely flat, sandy beach, little green, red, blue boats, so pretty in shape and colour that one thought of flowers; one man boards them, these boats hardly go on the high sea – they dash off when there's no wind and come back to land if there's a bit too much' (622).

Van Gogh made a total of nine drawings and three paintings of Les Saintes-Maries-de-la-Mer. In the above-mentioned letter to Bernard, he enclosed a small sketch of *Boats at Sea* with colour notations (fig. 17). Later, when the canvas now in Moscow (cat. 53) was drying in his studio in Arles, he made no fewer than three drawn copies of it, which differ somewhat from one another. The drawing intended for John Peter Russell is now in the Guggenheim Museum (cat. 54); the work he sent to Theo is in Brussels (cat. 55). In both cases Van Gogh rendered the sky by means of dots. Because he knew that Emile Bernard did not like Pointillism, he omitted the dots in the drawing intended for him (Kupferstichkabinett, Staatliche Museen zu Berlin, F1430), using brisk lines instead to depict the sky. Vincent told Theo that 'the painted studies lack clarity of touch. One more reason why I felt the need to draw them' (657). RZ

Fig. 17 **Letter 622** from Vincent van Gogh to Emile Bernard. Arles, on or about Thursday 7 June 1888. *Fishing Boats at Sea* (JH1464), enclosed sketch. Paper, 23.2 x 35.8 cm. The Morgan Library and Museum, New York. Thaw Collection

54 Boats at Saintes-Maries
31 July – 6 August 1888
Reed pen and ink over graphite
on wove paper, 24.3 x 31.9 cm
Solomon R. Guggenheim
Museum, New York.
Thannhauser Collection,
Gift of Justin K. Thannhauser,
1978, 78.2514.21

Selected references: Faille 1970,
no. 1430a; New York 1984,
cat. 73; Amsterdam 2005в,
cat. 58, pp. 273–75; Van Heugten
2005, cat. 108; Vellekoop and
Zwikker 2007, fig. 11, pp. 13–15

55 Fishing Boats at Sea

c. 6–8 August 1888
Reed pen, quill, and pen
and ink over graphite on paper,
24 x 31.5 cm
Signed lower right: *Vincent*
Royal Museums of Fine Arts
of Belgium, Brussels, 6743

Selected references: Faille 1970,
no. 1430b; New York 1984, p. 138;
Amsterdam 2005B, cat. 59,
pp. 276–77; Vellekoop and
Zwikker 2007, fig. 12, pp. 13–15

56 Letter 644
from Vincent van Gogh
to Theo van Gogh
Arles, between Tuesday 17
and Friday 20 July 1888
Garden with Flowers (JH1511),
letter sketch
Paper, 21.1 x 26.8 cm
Van Gogh Museum, Amsterdam
(Vincent van Gogh Foundation),
b553 V/1962

**57 Flowering Garden
with Path**
July 1888
Oil on canvas, 73 x 91 cm
Collection Gemeentemuseum
Den Haag, The Hague.
On long-term loan from the
Instituut Collectie Nederland
(The Netherlands Institute
for Cultural Heritage)

Selected references: Faille 1970,
no. 429; New York 1984, cat. 80;
Amsterdam 1990, cat. 50; Stolwijk
and Veenenbos 2002, p. 172;
Amsterdam 2005B, fig. 164;
Vellekoop and Zwikker 2007,
cat. 345

In a letter written on 8 August 1888, Vincent told Theo how impressed he was by the magnificent colours of Provence: 'Under the blue sky, the orange, yellow, red patches of flowers take on an amazing brilliance, and in the limpid air there's something happier and more suggestive of love than in the north. It vibrates – like the bouquet by [Adolphe] Monticelli that you have' (657).

The origin of *Flowering Garden with Path* might be connected with the 'very interesting tour round the farms' that Van Gogh had recently made 'with someone who knows the area' (657). What he had seen at the time had left a deep impression on him: 'Ah, these farmhouse gardens with the lovely big red Provence roses, the vines, the fig trees; it's quite poetic, and the eternal strong sun, in spite of which the foliage stays very green' (657). In addition to the *Flowering Garden with Path* shown here, characterised by its profusion of lively and colourful brush strokes, Van Gogh painted a garden view in vertical format (fig. 18).

In the second half of July, Vincent wrote to Theo about the above-mentioned works and made a sketch of the motif, to which he added colour notations: 'I have a new drawing of a garden full of flowers; I also have two painted studies of it' (644; cat. 56). RZ

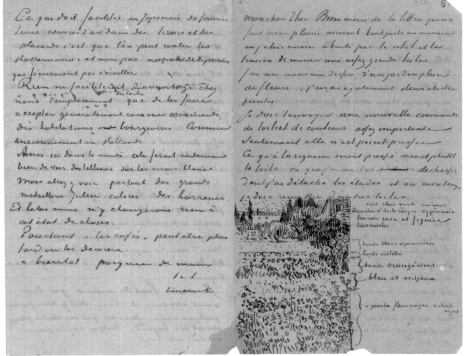

Fig. 18 **Flowering Garden**, 1888.
Oil on canvas, 92 x 73 cm. Private collection (F430)

58 Letter 703
from Vincent van Gogh
to Theo van Gogh
Arles, Saturday 13 October 1888
The Tarascon Stagecoach (JH1606),
letter sketch
Paper, 20.7 x 13.5 cm
Van Gogh Museum, Amsterdam
(Vincent van Gogh Foundation),
b596 a-c V/1962

59 The Tarascon Diligence
October 1888
Oil on canvas, 71.4 x 92.5 cm
The Henry and Rose Pearlman
Foundation; on long-term
loan to the Princeton
University Art Museum

Selected references: Faille 1970,
no. 478a; Seznec 1950; New York
1984, cat. 112

When he decided to depict *The Tarascon Diligence* Van Gogh had in mind a passage from the satirical novel *Tartarin de Tarascon* by the Provençal writer Alphonse Daudet. More specifically, he drew inspiration from the chapter 'Les Diligences déportées', in which the 'old stagecoach' complains about its hard life. On 13 October 1888, Vincent wrote to Theo: 'Have you re-read the Tartarins yet? Ah, don't forget to! Do you remember in Tartarin the complaint of the old Tarascon diligence – that wonderful page? Well, I've just painted that red and green carriage in the yard of the inn. You'll see. This hasty croquis gives you its composition' (703; cat. 58).

He went on to talk about the colour and style of the painting: 'Simple foreground of grey sand. Background very simple too, pink and yellow walls with windows with green louvred shutters, corner of blue sky. The two carriages very colourful: green, red, wheels yellow, black, blue, orange. A no. 30 canvas once again. The carriages are painted in the style of [Adolphe] Monticelli, with impastos. You once had a very beautiful Claude Monet, of four colourful boats on a beach [Art Institute of Chicago]. Well, here it's carriages, but the composition is of the same kind' (703).

In contrast to the painting, in the letter sketch he drew in the left foreground several chickens and placed a figure in the cart on the right. Later on in the letter Van Gogh apologised for the 'very poor croquis': working on *The Tarascon Diligence* had tired him so much that he no longer felt able to draw. RZ

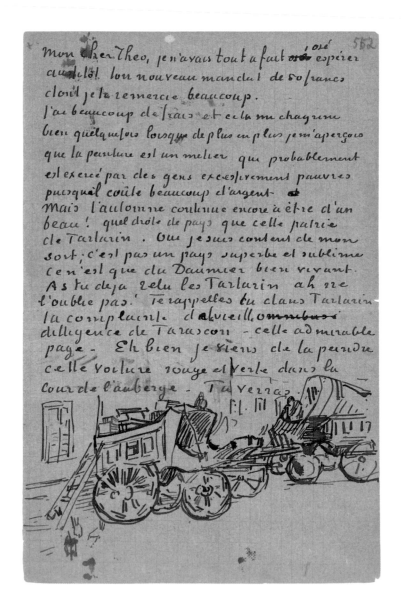

Letter 615

from Vincent van Gogh
to Theo van Gogh
Arles, Monday 28 May 1888
Album of Drawings,
letter sketch
Paper, 20.3 x 26.4 cm
Van Gogh Museum, Amsterdam
(Vincent van Gogh Foundation),
b532 a-c V/1962

Like many artists in the late nineteenth century, Van Gogh had a passion for Japanese prints. He first discovered them in Antwerp at the end of 1885: 'My studio's quite tolerable, mainly because I've pinned a set of Japanese prints on the walls that I find very diverting. You know, those little female figures in gardens or on the shore, horsemen, flowers, gnarled thorn branches' (545). When Van Gogh moved to Paris in February 1886, he and Theo became enthusiastic collectors of Japanese prints, scouring the shops selling oriental wares and buying prints in bulk from the dealer Samuel Bing, often for only a few centimes each. Writing later from Arles, Van Gogh encouraged his brother to visit Bing's attic where he would find 'a heap of 10 thousand Japanese prints, landscapes, figures, old Japanese prints too. One Sunday he'll let you choose for yourself, so take plenty of old sheets too' (640).

Eventually, the brothers were to own about 350 Japanese sheets, among them many ukiyo-e prints, 'visions of the floating world'. In his portrait of the Montmartre colour merchant Julien Tanguy (1824–1894) (fig. 19), Van Gogh poses his sitter against a colourful backdrop of Japanese prints from his own collection. We can easily identify two prints by the great Japanese printmaker Utagawa Hiroshige (1797–1858) that

belonged to Van Gogh: *Yoshitsune's Cherry Tree* (1855; cat. 63) and *Mount Fuji from Sagami Gawa River* (1858; cat. 61) (the impressions shown here are identical to those owned by Van Gogh, which are now in the Van Gogh Museum, Amsterdam). Also identifiable, at the lower right, is the flamboyant figure of a courtesan by Kesai Eisen (1790–1848), which appeared on the front cover of a Japanese-themed issue of the magazine *Paris illustré* (May 1886). Van Gogh was so taken with this print that he made a painted copy of it, as he did with cat. 62: *The Courtesan: after Eisen* (1887, Van Gogh Museum, Amsterdam, F373) and *Flowering Plum Tree: after Hiroshige* (fig. 20).

The impact of Japanese prints on Van Gogh's art cannot be overestimated and, in the end, was far greater than that of the Impressionists. 'All my work is based to some extent on Japanese art' (640), he informed Theo. In his second year in Paris and especially in Provence Japanese prints provided him with the stimulus he needed to reject the dark palette of his early years and to embrace colour directly. Van Gogh found the 'flat tones' (686) of Japanese prints very compelling, as he did their brilliant, unmodulated colour, bold contours and daring non-Western perspectives. As he wrote to Emile Bernard: 'the Japanese disregards reflection, placing his solid tints one beside the other –

Tu me diras que Détaille par exemple en a une trentaine peutche d'années de Paris et qu'il se tient droit comme un i

Bon fais comme cela si tu as des capacités pareilles. je ne m'y opposepas et notre famille a une vie tenace

Tout ce que je désirerais due je résume à ceci si ces messieurs te font prendre des marrons au feu pour eux à de pareilles distances fais toi payer cher ou refuses et mets toi dans les impressionnistes faisant moins d'affaires au point de vue des sommes remuées mais en vivant davantage dans la nature.

Pour moi je me refais décidemment et l'estomac depuis le mois écoulé a gagné énormement. Je souffre encore d'émotions mal motivées mais involontaires ou d'hébêtement de certains jours mais cela va en se tranquilisant.

Je compte faire une excursion à Ste Marie pour voir enfin la Méditerranée

Sans doute les deux soeurs seront bien contentes de venir à Paris et cela ne leur fera aucun mal c'est bien sur.

Je voudrais que tout le monde vienne ici dans le midi également

Je me fais toujours des reproches que ma peinture ne vaut pasce qu'elle coûte

Il faut pourtant travailler - seulement sache que si jamais les circonstances rendraient désirable que je m'occupe plutôt dans le commerce pourvu que cela te décharge je le ferais sans regrets

Mourier te donnera encore deux dessins à la plume.

Sais tu ce qu'il faudrait en faire de ces dessins — des albums de 6 ou 10 ou 12 comme les albums de dessins originaux japonais

J'ai grand envie de faire un tel album pour Gauguin et un pour Bernard. Car cela deviendra mieux que ça les dessins

Couverture orange ou jaune citron

61 Utagawa Hiroshige (1797–1858)
**Mount Fuji from
Sagami Gawa River**
1858
Woodblock print, 60.1 x 44.9 cm
On loan from the British
Museum, London,
1948,0508,0.25

62 Utagawa Hiroshige (1797–1858)
Plum Orchard at Kameido
1857
Woodblock print, 60.1 x 44.9 cm
On loan from the British
Museum, London,
1948,0410,0.65

63 Utagawa Hiroshige (1797–1858)
Yoshitsune's Cherry Tree
1855
Woodblock print, 60.1 x 44.9 cm
On loan from the British
Museum, London,
1915,0823,0.766

→ characteristic lines naively marking off movements or shapes' (622).

Van Gogh's obsession with Japanese prints went far beyond aesthetic appreciation. They were the basis of a Utopian vision of Japan as a paradise of colour and beauty that he projected onto Provence. 'I want to begin by telling you that this part of the world seems to me as beautiful as Japan for the clearness of the atmosphere and the gay colour effects. The stretches of water make patches of a beautiful emerald and a rich blue in the landscapes, as we see it in the Japanese prints' (587), he wrote to Emile Bernard a month after he arrived in Arles. Moreover, he idealised the simplicity and dedication of Japanese artists' lives and their way of working. In a letter to Theo (615; cat. 60) he sketched a concertina-fold album to demonstrate how he would like to present his own drawings in the way the Japanese artists did (he had seen such albums; the one that belonged to the brothers is in the collection of the Van Gogh Museum, Amsterdam). His notions about the Japanese way of life were confirmed by his reading of Pierre Loti's popular novel *Madame Chrysanthème* (cat. 163) in the summer of 1888.

Japanese prints acted as a catalyst for Van Gogh: he succeeded brilliantly in fusing their abstract and decorative qualities with his own vision, which was grounded in realism and observation. AD

Fig. 19 **Portrait of Père Tanguy**, autumn 1887.
Oil on canvas, 92 x 73 cm. Musée Rodin, Paris, P.7302 (F363)

Fig. 20 **Flowering Plum Tree: after Hiroshige**, Paris 1887.
Oil on canvas, 55 x 46 cm. Van Gogh Museum, Amsterdam
(Vincent van Gogh Foundation), s0015 V/1962 (F371)

64 The Ramparts of Paris

Summer 1887
Watercolour, gouache, chalk
and pencil on laid paper,
39.5 x 53.5 cm
The Whitworth Art Gallery,
University of Manchester,
D.1927.4

Selected references: Faille 1970,
no. 1403; Heenk 1995, pp. 150–
51; Martigny 2000, cat. 27;
Vellekoop and Van Heugten 2001,
pp. 286–303, no. 315c;
Amsterdam 2005B, pp. 46–47;
Hendriks and Van Tilborgh 2006,
p. 30, note 25

The ramparts of Paris were constructed between 1841 and 1845. More than eighteen miles long, these fortifications – including barracks and 52 entrance gates – encircled the city and were surrounded by a wide, deep canal. By Van Gogh's day, the overgrown fortifications no longer served any military purpose. On Sundays and holidays they functioned as a recreational area for the working classes, but at night they were a place of crime and prostitution.

It was recently discovered that in the autumn of 1886 Van Gogh made his first painting of this subject, namely a view of the one of the pedestrian walkways below the ramparts (Solomon R. Guggenheim Museum, New York, F239) (I am grateful to Teio Meedendorp and Louis van Tilborgh for sharing their discovery with me). In the summer of 1887 Van Gogh produced three pencil drawings (Van Gogh Museum, Amsterdam, SD1719r and SD1719v) and four colourful watercolours of the ramparts (F1400 and F1401 belong to the Van Gogh Museum, Amsterdam; F1402 is in a private collection; F1403 is the current work from Manchester). He presumably made the pencil studies in his search for a suitable composition for the watercolour drawings. The ramparts and the building in the present work also occur, but seen from a different angle, in one of the pencil studies (SD1719v). The couple strolling in the foreground were sketched in with brush and ink over the underdrawing but never finished (I am grateful to Marije Vellekoop and Sjraar van Heugten, respectively Curator of Prints and Drawings and Head of Collections at the Van Gogh Museum, for sharing their findings with me).

Like other drawings made in the summer of 1887, the composition and palette of *The Ramparts of Paris* betray the influence of Japanese prints. When Vincent began to correspond with Theo again after his move to Arles, he often mentioned this source of inspiration. At the beginning of 1888, for example, he said: 'I have an enormous amount of drawing to do, because I'd like to do drawings in the style of Japanese prints' (594). The series of watercolours from Paris can be seen in this context. RZ

65 La Mousmé, half-figure

31 July – 6 August 1888
Reed pen, pen and ink over
graphite on wove paper,
31.5 x 24 cm
Signed lower left: *Vincent*
Private collection, courtesy
of Thomas Gibson Fine Art

Selected references: Faille 1970,
no. 1503; Millard 1974, p. 160;
New York 1984, cat. 81; Heenk
1995, pp. 170–71; Amsterdam
2005B, cat. 80, pp. 273, 275

During the first months of his stay in
Arles, Van Gogh's work was inspired by
Japanese prints, and he associated the
landscape of Provence with that of Japan.
Inspired by *Madame Chrysanthème* – a novel
with a Japanese setting by Pierre Loti – he
described his newest paintings in a letter
to Theo of 29 July: 'Now, if you know what
a '*mousmé*' is (you'll know when you've
read Loti's Madame Chrysanthème), I've
just painted one. It took me my whole week
[...] A mousmé is a Japanese girl – Provençale
in this case – aged between 12 and 14. That
makes 2 figures, the Zouave, and her, that I
have' (650). On the same day he described
the work in a letter to Emile Bernard: 'Have
just finished portrait of young girl of 12,
brown eyes, black hair and eyebrows, flesh
yellow grey, the background *white*, strongly
tinged with veronese, jacket blood-red
with violet stripes, skirt blue with large
orange spots, an oleander flower in her
sweet little hand' (649).

Van Gogh made a drawn copy of
the painting (National Gallery of Art,
Washington, F431) to send to his friend
John Peter Russell. In the drawing,
he concentrated on the girl's head and
upper body. On 3 August he sent Russell
La Mousmé and eleven other drawings
made after paintings. RZ

66 Two Crabs

January 1889
Oil on canvas, 47 x 61 cm
Private collection

Selected references: Faille 1970,
no. 606; Stolwijk and Veenenbos
2002, pp. 180, 46, 92; Compton
Verney 2006, pp. 20, 56;
Pickvance 2006, pp. 500, 501;
Seoul 2007, p. 120

In this still-life we see two crabs, one of which lies on its back. Van Gogh painted this work with quick, spontaneous brush strokes. The warm, bright red and shades of yellow used for the crustaceans provide a lively contrast to the green background. Similar use of complementary colours is found in a smaller painting, *A Crab on Its Back* (Van Gogh Museum, Amsterdam, F605); its colours are slightly less bright, but the greater amount of detail suggests that it is the later of the two works.

It is usually assumed that Van Gogh painted both works at the beginning of January 1889, when he announced upon returning from hospital: 'I'm going to get back to work tomorrow, I'll begin by doing one or two still-lifes to get back into the way of painting' (732). Although the autumn and winter of 1887–88 and the late summer of 1888 have been suggested as alternative datings, here it is assumed that Van Gogh painted these works in Arles upon his release from hospital.

A source of inspiration for Van Gogh's crab was perhaps the reproduction of Hokusai's woodcut *Crabs* in the journal *Le Japon artistique* (fig. 21), which Theo had sent to Vincent in mid-September 1888.

The painstaking depiction of the crab's anatomy suggests that Van Gogh had a dead crab in front of him. Fresh crabs would not have been available every day in Arles. Van Gogh remarked in June 1888 that even in Saintes-Maries on the coast, fish were not to be had every day: 'there isn't fish to eat every day, as the fishermen go off to sell in Marseille' (619). RZ

Fig. 21 Katsushika Hokusai (1760–1849), **Crabs**. Woodcut from
Le Japon artistique: Documents d'art et d'industrie, 1, May 1888. Van Gogh
Museum, Amsterdam (Vincent van Gogh Foundation)

THE MODERN PORTRAIT

Van Gogh attached the greatest importance to portraits, as his letters continually reveal. As he wrote to his sister Willemien on 5 June 1890: 'What I'm most passionate about, much much more than all the rest in my profession – is the portrait, the modern portrait' (879). For him portraits were the essence of modern art. He saw them as a means of capturing his own times in a way that would have meaning for the future, explaining in the same letter: 'I *would* like to do portraits which would look like apparitions to people a century later.'

Following his decision to become an artist in 1880, Van Gogh's primary aim was to master the human figure. It was in The Hague (1882–83) that he first seriously tackled the portrait, using his companion Sien Hoornik and her family as models (cat. 26) as well as the residents of an old people's home whom he persuaded to sit for him. These forceful early drawings, often drawn in velvety black lithographic crayon combined with ink and graphite, are not so much portraits as representations of social types, in particular the poor and the socially oppressed – subjects inspired by Van Gogh's admiration for the illustrations in such English magazines as *The Graphic* and *The Illustrated London News*, and his empathy with the criticism of social inequality to be found in the novels of Charles Dickens and George Eliot.

During the two years that he spent in his parents' vicarage at Nuenen (1883–85), Van Gogh found his models in the rural community. An impressive group of paintings and drawings of weavers at their looms (cats 31, 32) was followed by a series of heads of peasants (cats 33, 34) that he called 'Heads of the People', echoing the title of a series of illustrations published in *The Graphic* (cat. 29) beginning in 1875. These sometimes almost grotesque heads culminated in Van Gogh's first major painting, *The Potato Eaters* (fig. 1), and they are remarkable for the sheer force of their execution. The muddy colours, Van Gogh felt, evoked the very soil on which the peasants worked and he laid on his paint in thick, broad strokes.

Already we see his use of exaggeration for the sake of greater emotional truth, a characteristic of all Van Gogh's portraits.

In Paris (1886–88), as Van Gogh sought to redefine himself as an avant-garde artist, he developed a new and more expressive approach to the portrait. His discovery of the Impressionists and the younger generation of experimental artists that included Signac, Bernard, Gauguin and Seurat led him to work in brilliant colour contrasts applied with a lively and varied touch, as in his portrait of the Scottish art dealer Alexander Reid (cat. 67), who was resident in Paris. Van Gogh painted an impressive number of self-portraits in Paris, partly because he could not afford models. He increasingly used colour arbitrarily for expressive effect and emotional impact, deploring the imitative realism of the photograph. 'I myself still find photographs frightful', he wrote to his sister Wil on 19 September 1889, 'and don't like to have any, especially not of people whom I know and love. These portraits, first, are faded more quickly than we ourselves, while the painted portrait remains for many generations. Besides, a painted portrait is a thing of feeling made with love or respect for the being represented' (804). Shortly before he left Paris for Arles, Van Gogh painted one of his greatest self-portraits (cat. 68) in which he pays homage to Rembrandt's famous self-portrait with a palette of 1660 in the Musée du Louvre. Boldly he proclaims his professional identity: the vivid pigments on his palette that are used so dramatically in the face, hair and beard assert Van Gogh's sense of himself as a modern artist excited by the power of colour.

'The best thing one could do, from all points of view, would be to paint portraits of women and children' (604), Vincent wrote to Theo from Arles in May 1888. At first, however, Van Gogh was immediately absorbed by the landscape. It was only at the end of May and in early June that he turned his attention to portraits. His subject was a young Zouave, a French infantryman from a regiment accustomed to service in French North Africa, with 'the neck of a bull, the eye of a tiger' (629) whom he depicted in watercolour, oil and reed pen (cats 73–75). In July Van Gogh painted his portrait of the postal worker Joseph Roulin (cats 69–70) and at the beginning of December 1888, he announced to Theo that he had made portraits of 'an entire family' (723), repeating and underlining this phrase. The result was a series of portraits of his friend the postal worker Joseph Roulin, his wife Augustine, his sons Armand and Camille, and his baby daughter Marcelle (cats 69, 76–77). Perhaps Van Gogh's wish to record a whole family owed something to Zola's Les Rougon Macquart, an ambitious cycle of novels charting the life of a family in the Second Empire, which he read with enthusiasm (Dorn 2000, p. 171). He made several variations of the Roulin portraits, no less than seven of Madame Roulin and many versions of the head of Joseph Roulin. Once again, Van Gogh pursued his notion of portrait types. Although each sitter certainly retains his or her individuality, Van Gogh fits his subjects into his scheme of types, and this is more important to him than the accurate rendering of appearance or achieving a penetrating psychological likeness. Joseph Roulin is a 'Socratic type' and 'a fierce republican' (655) while Madame Roulin, the berceuse who rocks the cradle, is the archetype of maternity. In November he had painted Marie Ginoux (cats 71–72), proprietress of the Café de la Gare in Arles, whom he presented as a stylish and coquettish woman, one of the celebrated attractive women of Arles (Arlésiennes). The books on the table in front of her suggest a penchant for contemporary French literature, which almost certainly reflects Van Gogh's own enthusiasm rather than his sitter's.

Two of the most striking 'portraits' that Van Gogh painted in Arles are the symbolic portrayals of himself and of Gauguin in the form of their empty chairs (cats 79–80). Curiously, Vincent seems to have avoided making portraits of the people to whom he was closest: there are no known portraits of Theo, for example, and only a sketchy one of

Gauguin made in Arles (Van Gogh Museum, Amsterdam, F546). These chairs, however, evoke a palpable presence of the absent sitters. Not only are the two compositions a contrast in light and dark, day and night, but also in the two artists' characters: Van Gogh's rustic chair with his pipe and tobacco symbolised, in his view, his rough and simple nature, in comparison with the elegant chair, candle and books that evoked for him the presence of the more sophisticated Gauguin.

Although his landscapes are the best-known works from the last phases of his life in Saint-Rémy and Auvers (1888–90), Van Gogh continued to care passionately about portraiture. He was hampered by the 'impossibility of having models' (798), a problem that was exacerbated by his fear of the other patients in the asylum of Saint-Paul-de-Mausole at Saint-Rémy and his self-imposed isolation. Nevertheless, he painted some portraits of people he met and a number of outstanding self-portraits.

In his last few months at Auvers in northern France Van Gogh achieved great intensity in his portraits through the medium of colour. This is evident in his last great portrait, that of Dr Gachet (fig. 6), the homeopathic doctor and amateur artist who took care of Van Gogh and whom the artist also captured, characteristically smoking his pipe, in an etching printed in the doctor's studio (cats 84–85). With Portrait of a Peasant Girl in a Straw Hat (cats 82–83) he returned to a favourite theme of his early career, but now the sombre Dutch palette is recast in a dazzling display of complementary oranges and blues. Colour was the means by which Van Gogh created a sense of the universal and timeless in his portraits. 'And in a painting I'd like to say something consoling, like a piece of music. I'd like to paint men or women', he explained to Theo, 'with that je ne sais quoi of the eternal, of which the halo used to be the symbol, and which we try to achieve through the radiance itself, through the vibrancy of our colorations' (673).

67 **Portrait of Alexander Reid**

Spring 1887

Oil on cardboard, 42 x 33 cm
Signed lower right: *Vincent*
Lent by Culture Sport Glasgow on
behalf of Glasgow City Council.
Bought with the assistance of a
special Government Grant, The
Art Fund, the National Fund for
Acquisitions, an anonymous
donor and public subscription,
1974, 3315

Selected references: Faille 1970,
no. 343; Glasgow 1990, cat. 29;
Fowle 1991; Amsterdam 2000,
pp. 90–91; Louisville 2002, cat.
28; Compton Verney 2006, cat. 2

Alexander Reid (1854–1928) was an influential Scottish art dealer who came in June or July 1886 to work with Theo at the gallery of Boussod, Valadon & Cie (formerly Goupil & Cie) in Paris. He became friendly with the Van Gogh brothers, and probably even stayed with them for a while in the summer of 1886 and spring of 1887 at their apartment in the Rue Lepic.

Like Theo, Reid collected contemporary art, including that of the Impressionists Monet and Degas and the practically unknown Provençal painter Adolphe Monticelli. These shared interests caused their friendship to cool later on, to the extent that Vincent often spoke of Reid in negative terms: 'That Reid was ambitious, and being hard up for money like all of us, he was beside himself when it came to earning money' (604). In Saint-Rémy, however, Van Gogh took a milder view of him: 'How I think of Reid as I read Shakespeare, and how I've thought of him several times when I was iller than at present. Finding that I'd been infinitely too harsh and perhaps discouraging towards him in claiming that it was better to love painters than paintings' (784).

At first this work was viewed as a self-portrait by Van Gogh. It was included as such in Baart de la Faille's 1928 *catalogue raisonné* – until Alexander McNeil Reid recognised his father in the painting. Contemporaries of Van Gogh and Reid apparently said that the two men could have been mistaken for twins. AV

68 Self-portrait as an Artist
January 1888
Oil on canvas, 65.5 x 50.5 cm
Signed and dated on the stretcher
lower right: *Vincent / 88*
Van Gogh Museum, Amsterdam
(Vincent van Gogh Foundation),
s22 V/1962

Selected references: Faille 1970,
no. 522; Van Lindert and Van
Uitert 1990, pp. 104–05; Tokyo
1993, pp. 97–106; Amsterdam
2003, pp. 213, 215

Van Gogh described this self-portrait in a long letter to his sister Willemien: 'First I start by saying that to my mind the same person supplies material for very diverse portraits. Here's an impression of mine, which is the result of a portrait that I painted in the mirror, and which Theo has: a pink-grey face with green eyes, ashcoloured hair, wrinkles in forehead and around the mouth, stiffly wooden, a very red beard, quite unkempt and sad, but the lips are full, a blue smock of coarse linen [...] You'll say that this is something like, say, the face of – death [...] but anyway isn't a figure like this [...] in any event *something different* from a photograph? And you see – this is what Impressionism has – to my mind – over the rest, it isn't banal, and one seeks a deeper likeness than that of the photographer' (626).

The last self-portrait Van Gogh made in Paris, this work is the monumental result of self-examination, painted in bright, unmixed, complementary colours. The red and green in the face and the orange of the beard against the blue of the smock (displaying strokes of orange) stand out in particular, showing that in the space of only two years Van Gogh had mastered the Impressionists' palette and colour theory. The grim expression on his face clashes with the cheerful colours. It was not without reason that he emphasised in his letter that a painting is not a photograph: this canvas illuminates his character to some extent, whereas a photograph, in Van Gogh's view, is merely a one-dimensional picture of a person's outward appearance. AV

69 **The Postman**
    Joseph Roulin
    1888
    Brown ink over black chalk
    on paper, 51.44 x 42.23 cm
    Los Angeles County Museum
    of Art, George Gard de Sylva
    Collection, M.49.17.1

    Selected references: Faille 1970,
    no. 1459; Otterlo 1990, p. 233;
    Belluno 2003, p. 64; Ten Berge,
    Meedendorp, Vergeest and
    Verhoogt 2003, pp. 265–71;
    Amsterdam 2005B, p. 224;
    Vienna 2008, cat. 99

70 **The Postman**
    Joseph Roulin
    August 1888
    Oil on canvas, 81.3 x 65.4 cm
    The Museum of Fine Arts,
    Boston, 35.1982. Gift of
    Robert Treat Paine, 2nd

    Selected references: Faille 1970,
    no. 432; Journal 2001, p. 72; Ten
    Berge, Meedendorp, Vergeest
    and Verhoogt 2003, pp. 265–71;
    Brescia 2005, cat. 95;
    Amsterdam 2005B, p. 224

'I'm now working on the portrait of a postman with his dark blue uniform with yellow. A head something like that of Socrates, almost no nose, a high forehead, bald pate, small grey eyes, high-coloured full cheeks, a big beard, pepper and salt, big ears. The man is a fervent republican and socialist, reasons very well and knows many things. His wife gave birth today and so he's in really fine feather and glowing with satisfaction. In fact I much prefer to paint something like this than flowers', Van Gogh wrote from Arles to his sister Willemien on 31 July 1888 (653).

Although Van Gogh calls him a postman, Joseph Roulin was actually an 'Entreposeur des Postes', a postal employee at Arles railway station. Van Gogh had frequent dealings with him – whenever he sent work to Theo, for instance – and the two men became friends. When Van Gogh suffered a mental breakdown in late December

1888, Roulin was his help and stay, looking after the house while he was in hospital and keeping Theo informed about the state of his brother's health. Upon his release from hospital Vincent wrote to Theo: 'Roulin has been excellent to us, and I dare believe that he'll remain a staunch friend' (732).

Even after Van Gogh's admission to the asylum in Saint-Rémy, he and Roulin remained in touch for a long time, but they never saw each other again. Van Gogh drew and painted Roulin and members of his family on various occasions in the months preceding his breakdown. Two examples are shown here. In the larger version (cat. 70) he portrayed Roulin three-quarter length, wearing his impressive blue uniform with gold buttons and embroidery. During the same session Van Gogh also painted a bust-length portrait (Detroit Institute of Arts, F433). AV

The legendary beauty of the women of Arles appealed greatly to Van Gogh's imagination, and their handsomeness was only enhanced by their 'colourful costume, worn well' (686). In November, after the arrival of Gauguin, Vincent wrote to Theo: 'Then I have an Arlésienne at last, a figure (no. 30 canvas) knocked off in one hour, background pale lemon – the face grey – the clothing dark dark dark, just unmixed Prussian blue. She's leaning on a green table and is sitting in a wooden armchair – coloured orange' (717). Gauguin, too, portrayed Madame Ginoux, possibly at the same time. Van Gogh was clearly proud to have reached a level of proficiency that enabled him to capture a likeness on canvas in only one hour.

Marie and Joseph Ginoux ran the Café de la Gare in Arles, and Van Gogh was a regular customer. They became friends, and he kept in touch with them even after his admission to the asylum at Saint-Rémy.

He painted Marie Ginoux seven times in all, including two versions of this portrait. The version he describes is probably the work in the Musée d'Orsay, which is indeed painted more thinly and more hastily than the canvas from New York. In this second version he changed only the objects on the table, depicting several books instead of gloves and a parasol. The influence of Gauguin and Japanese prints is apparent here, in the 'synthetist' use of line and colour, the bright palette, the large monochrome areas and the strong contours.

The subject of *L'Arlésienne* continued to preoccupy Van Gogh and, later, in June 1890, he wrote to his sister Willemien about his recent paintings, among them a portrait based on a drawing by Gauguin, and tried to describe the colours and the tone, complaining that he couldn't 'manage to do a good croquis of it' (879; cat. 71). AV

73 **The Zouave**
June 1888
Oil on canvas, 65 x 54 cm
Van Gogh Museum, Amsterdam
(Vincent van Gogh Foundation),
s67 /1962

Selected references: Faille 1970,
no. 423; Van Uitert and Hoyle
1987, pp. 240–41; Van Lindert
and Van Uitert 1990, pp. 68–69;
Tokyo 1993, cat. 8; Amsterdam
2005 B, pp. 222–28

In Arles Van Gogh made a series of character portraits, one of which was this Zouave. The Zouaves, the French Algerian light infantry, were quartered in Arles, and in June 1888 Van Gogh became friendly with one of them. On 21 June he wrote an enthusiastic letter to Theo to say that he finally had a model: 'he's a lad with a small face, the neck of a bull, the eye of a tiger' (629). From 20 to 23 June – four consecutive days of rain – Van Gogh painted and drew him a number of times. In this 'bust-length' version, he placed the Zouave against a wall, wearing a traditional uniform: 'the blue of blue enamel saucepans, with dull orange-red trimmings and two lemon-yellow stars on his chest, a common blue and very hard to do. I've stuck his very tanned, feline head, wearing a bright red cap, in front of a door painted green and the orange bricks of a wall. So it's a coarse combination of disparate tones that isn't easy to handle [...] and yet I'd always like to work on portraits that are vulgar, even garish like that one. It teaches me, and that's what I ask of my work above all' (629).

At first Van Gogh expressed his dissatisfaction with this 'terribly hard' portrait to both Bernard and Theo, but he later changed his opinion and even suggested to Bernard that he take it in exchange for one of his paintings. In the end he was proud of this powerful portrait that radiates masculine vigour. AV

74 The Zouave, half-figure
31 July – 6 August 1888
Reed pen, pen and ink over
graphite on wove paper,
31.9 x 24.3 cm
Signed lower left: *Vincent*
Solomon R. Guggenheim
Museum, New York,
Thannhauser Collection,
Gift of Justin K. Thannhauser,
1978, 78.251423

Selected references: Faille 1970,
no. 1482a; Minnesota 1962,
cat. 119; New York 1984, cat. 77;
New York 1990, cat. 82;
Amsterdam 2005 B, cat. 79

75 The Zouave
c. 20 June 1888
Reed pen and brown ink,
wax crayon and watercolour
over graphite on wove paper,
31.5 x 23.6 cm
Inscribed and signed upper right:
*à mon cher copain | Emile Bernard |
Vincent*
Lent by the Metropolitan
Museum of Art, New York.
Gift of Emanie Philips, 1962
(62.151)

Selected references: Faille 1970,
no. 1482; Amsterdam 2005 B,
cat. 77, pp. 222–23; New York
2007, fig. 37, p. 198; Vienna
2008, cat. 96

In June 1888 Van Gogh wrote to Bernard: 'I would make you some croquis were it not that having drawn and painted for three or four days with a model – a Zouave – I'm exhausted – on the contrary, writing is restful and diverting. What I've done is very ugly: a drawing of the Zouave, seated [cat. 74], a painted sketch of the Zouave against an all-white wall and lastly his portrait against a green door and some orange bricks of a wall [cat. 73]. It's harsh and, well, *ugly* and badly done. However, since that's the real difficulty attacked, it may smooth the way in the future. The figures that I do are almost always detestable in my own eyes, and all the more so in others' eyes – nevertheless, it's the study of the figure that strengthens us the most' (632).

The next day he informed his friend: 'If you wished, I would earmark for an exchange with you the head of a Zouave that I've painted' (633). Bernard never received this painting, although he did receive the watercolour (cat. 75) with the dedication 'à mon cher copain Emile Bernard, Vincent'.

Bernard was enthusiastic about it, as emerges from a letter to his parents, in which he reports that Vincent had sent him by post 'six truly remarkable pen drawings. There's a head of a Zouave that amazes me. Vincent's becoming very good. At the same time that he's an excellent artist, he's a thinker, because every one of his works contains an idea that flashes on the eye of the man who looks for it' (641, see note 1). AV

à mon cher copain
Emile Bernard
Vincent

76 Portrait of Madame Augustine Roulin and Baby Marcelle
December 1888
Oil on canvas, 92.4 x 73.5 cm
Philadelphia Museum of Art.
Bequest of Lisa Norris Elkins,
1950, 1950-92-22

Selected references: Faille 1970,
no. 490; Sutton 1990, pp. 92–94;
Journal 2001, p. 71; Winterthur
2002, cat. 12

During his stay in Arles, Van Gogh became very friendly with the Roulins. He painted the father, a postal employee, a number of times (cats 69–70), and the other members of the family as well. At the beginning of December 1888 he wrote to Theo: 'But I've done the portraits of *an entire family*, the family of the postman whose head I did before – the man, his wife, the baby, the young boy and the 16-year-old son, all characters and very French, although they have a Russian look. No. 15 canvases. You can sense how in my element that makes me feel' (723).

He painted Madame Roulin no fewer than eight times, including the five well-known '*berceuses*'. But while the *berceuses* are more the portrayal of a type (a woman rocking a baby), this painting of Madame Roulin with her baby Marcelle is a true portrait. Augustine Roulin's third child was born on 31 July 1888, and in December Van Gogh painted the portrait of the mother and her four-month-old daughter. Marcelle could not sit or stand on her own, so her mother had to hold her up. The baby, with her plump little hands, looked straight at the painter, but it is unlikely that she kept still while 'posing'. In fact, it is obvious that Van Gogh had to lay in his painting quickly, hence the hasty handling of paint in the figures and the background. The large areas of colour are striking: bright yellow for the background and green for Augustine's clothing, which contrasts with the red-brown of the back of her chair and the white of Marcelle's clothes. AV

77 Portrait of Camille Roulin

November–December 1888
Oil on canvas, 43.2 x 34.9 cm
Philadelphia Museum of Art.
Gift of Mr and Mrs Rodolphe
Meyer de Schauensee, 1973,
1973-129-1

Selected references: Faille 1970,
no. 537; Feilchenfeldt 1988,
p. 103; Sutton 1990, cat. 34,
pp. 95–97; Journal 2001, p. 75

'There's no better or shorter way to improve my work than to do figures. Also, I always feel confidence when doing portraits, knowing that that work is much more serious – that's perhaps not the word – but rather is the thing that enables me to cultivate what's best and most serious in me' (654), as Van Gogh wrote on or about Friday 3 August 1888. His constant lack of money meant that he could seldom afford models, and therefore relied on the readiness of acquaintances to pose for him.

In Arles these willing models included the members of the Roulin family. After the postal employee Joseph Roulin had posed on various occasions (cats 69–70) and the two had struck up a friendship, Van Gogh painted the rest of the family in late 1888 and early 1889 (cats 76–77). He produced this portrait of the 'young boy' – eleven-year-old Camille, the youngest son of the family – in late November or early December: 'And if I manage to do *this entire family* even better, I'll have done at least one thing to my taste and personal' (723).

Two versions of this portrait are known: one was intended for Theo, the other for the Roulin family. The work that Theo received is now in the Van Gogh Museum, Amsterdam (F538). AV

78 **Letter 646**
from Paul Gauguin
to Vincent van Gogh
Pont-Aven, on or about
Sunday 22 July 1888
The Young Wrestlers,
letter sketch
Paper, 21 x 27 cm
Van Gogh Museum, Amsterdam
(Vincent van Gogh Foundation),
b844 V/1962

79 **Gauguin's Chair**
November 1888
Oil on canvas, 90.5 x 72.5 cm
Van Gogh Museum, Amsterdam
(Vincent van Gogh Foundation),
s48 V/1962

Selected references: Faille 1970,
no. 499; Van Uitert and Hoyle
1987, cat. 71, pp. 236–37;
Amsterdam 1990, cat. 77,
pp. 184–87; Amsterdam 2000,
pp. 202–03; Amsterdam 2003,
cat. 85, pp. 225, 307

Van Gogh eagerly awaited Gauguin's arrival in Arles. However, Gauguin constantly delayed his departure from Pont-Aven in Brittany and did not leave until October 1888. In a letter (646; cat. 78) he explained: 'If it weren't for this damned money, my bags would soon be packed. I don't know why, but for the past ten days or so I have lots of painted follies in my head which I plan to execute in the south', including a sketch of his painting *The Young Wrestlers* (1888; Private collection).

Van Gogh considered portraiture 'the painting of the future' (716), the highest genre but also the most difficult to work in, owing to the costliness of models. It is strange, therefore, that while he was living and working with him in Arles, Van Gogh painted only one likeness of Gauguin, a sketchy portrait in profile (Van Gogh Museum, Amsterdam, F546). Perhaps he was too much in awe of this artist, who had, moreover, just advised him to stop basing his work on reality and to proceed instead from the imagination: 'Gauguin,

in spite of himself and in spite of me, has proved to me a little that it was time for me to vary things a bit – I'm beginning to compose from memory' (721), Vincent wrote to Theo in the second half of November 1888.

Van Gogh sometimes thought of ingenious solutions to the problem of his shortage of models. Empty chairs could personify their owners, and this chair is a portrait, at it were, of his friend Gauguin. Van Gogh also painted a pendant, a self-portrait, of his own empty chair (cat. 80).

Over a year later Van Gogh wrote the following about Gauguin's chair: 'A few days before we parted, when illness forced me to enter an asylum, I tried to paint "his empty place"' (853). Chronologically speaking, Van Gogh gives a slightly distorted version of events, because he painted the chair in November, when there was still no talk of discord; it was not 'several days' but several weeks later that relations between Van Gogh and Gauguin became strained to breaking point. AV

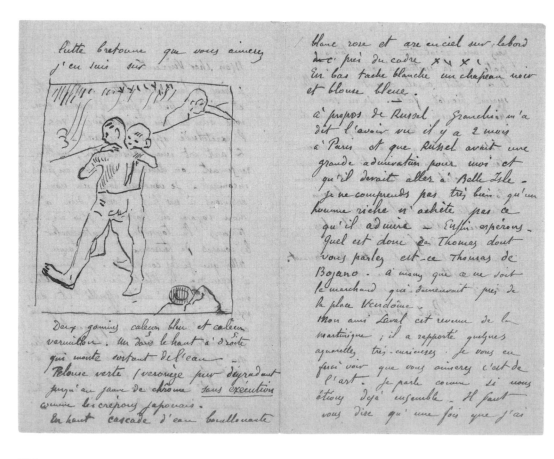

80 **Van Gogh's Chair**
November 1888 – January 1889
Oil on canvas, 91.8 x 73 cm
Signed on the crate upper left:
Vincent
The National Gallery, London,
NG 3862. Bought 1924

Selected references: Faille 1970,
no. 498; London 1992, cat. 32,
p. 126; Stolwijk and Veenenbos
2002, pp. 136, 176; Bristol 2005,
p. 12; Compton Verney 2006,
pp. 25, 27, 128

In a letter written in the second half of November 1888, Vincent told Theo that 'the last two studies are rather funny. No. 30 canvases, a wooden and straw *chair* all yellow on red tiles against a wall (*daytime*). Then Gauguin's armchair, red and green, night effect, on the seat two novels and a candle' (721). The first chair he described is a 'self-portrait': a simple chair with a wickerwork seat, on which his pipe and tobacco pouch stand. His presence is almost palpable. *Gauguin's Chair* (cat. 79) displays costlier workmanship, including armrests and more decoration. The atmosphere of simplicity that Van Gogh conjures up in his 'self-portrait' is heightened by the box of onions in the left-hand corner, the floor tiles and the cool daylight in which the scene is bathed. Gauguin's chair, by contrast, is a 'night effect', illuminated by a gas-lamp and candlelight, in mysterious blue and red. Gauguin – whom Van Gogh considered the very embodiment of a modern artist – is personified by two contemporary novels, recognisable by the colour of their covers: yellow and pink.

Van Gogh completed the painting of his own chair in January, after Gauguin's departure: 'I've just been working on the pendant again today, my own empty chair, a deal chair with a pipe and a tobacco pouch' (736). These canvases are sometimes taken as symbolic of the way the two artists worked: Gauguin from his imagination, Van Gogh from reality. AV

81 Lullaby: Madame Augustine Roulin Rocking a Cradle (La Berceuse)
February 1889
Oil on canvas, 92.7 x 72.7 cm
Museum of Fine Arts, Boston, 48.548. Bequest of John T. Spaulding

Selected references: Faille 1970, no. 508; New York 1984, no. 146, pp. 246–48; Journal 2001, pp. 62–83; Ten Berge, Meedendorp, Vergeest and Verhoogt 2003, pp. 272–76; Brescia 2005, pp. 389–90

Between the end of December 1888 and the end of March 1889 Van Gogh painted no fewer than five versions of *La Berceuse*. Augustine Roulin, the wife of Van Gogh's friend Joseph Roulin, a postal employee, sat for these pictures. This is the first version, which Van Gogh described in a letter to Gauguin of 21 January 1889: 'Today I made a fresh start on the canvas I had painted of Mrs Roulin, the one which had remained in a vague state as regards the hands because of my accident. As an arrangement of colours: the reds moving through to pure oranges, intensifying even more in the flesh tones up to the chromes, passing into the pinks and marrying with the olive and Veronese greens. As an Impressionist arrangement of colours, I've never devised anything better' (739).

Painting the berceuses was a comforting activity for Van Gogh in this period of illness and uncertainty. In these pictures his aim was not so much to produce a good likeness as to portray a type: a mother rocking a baby (Augustine Roulin holds a cord with which to rock the cradle). This motif recurs frequently in Van Gogh's correspondence. In the same letter to Gauguin he writes: 'And I believe that if one placed this canvas just as it is in a boat, even one of Icelandic fishermen, there would be some who would feel the lullaby in it'. This is a reference to Pierre Loti's novel *Pêcheur d'Islande* (1886), which Van Gogh often mentions in this period. The book, which Gauguin had also read, is the sad tale of Breton fishermen who sail each summer to fish for cod in the Icelandic seas. AV

82 **Letter 896**
from Vincent van Gogh
to Theo van Gogh
and Jo van Gogh-Bonger
Auvers-sur-Oise,
Wednesday 2 July 1890
*Girl against a Background
of Wheat* (JH2054), *Couple Walking
between Rows of Poplars* (JH2042),
Wheat Fields (JH2039),
letter sketches
Paper, 27 x 41.8 cm
Van Gogh Museum, Amsterdam
(Vincent van Gogh Foundation),
b694 V/1962

83 **Portrait of a Peasant Girl
in a Straw Hat**
June 1890
Oil on canvas, 92 x 73 cm
The Steven and Alexandra Cohen
Collection

Selected references: Faille 1970,
no. 774; Las Vegas 1999,
pp. 101–05; Martigny 2000, p. 116

'Here are three croquis – one of a figure of a peasant woman, big yellow hat with a knot of sky-blue ribbons, very red face. Coarse blue blouse with orange spots, background of ears of wheat' (896; cat. 82). This passage from Vincent's letter to Theo of 2 July 1890 describes the portrait (cat. 83) he was working on, a sketch of which he included in the letter.

The backdrop is almost abstract. Among the ears of wheat are several poppies, which are now pale orange, as are the girl's cheeks, though both must originally have been bright red.

Several weeks before starting work on this canvas, Van Gogh stressed yet again, in a letter to his sister Willemien dated 5 June 1890, how important portrait painting was to him: 'What I'm most passionate about, much much more than all the rest in my profession – is the portrait, the modern portrait. I seek it by way of colour, and am certainly not alone in seeking it in this way. I WOULD LIKE, you see I'm far from saying that I can do all this, but anyway I'm aiming at it, I *would like* to do portraits which would look like apparitions to people a century later. So I don't try to do us by photographic resemblance but by our passionate expressions, using as a means of expression and intensification of the character our science and modern taste for colour' (879). AV

84 **Letter 877**
from Vincent van Gogh
to Theo van Gogh
Auvers-sur-Oise,
Tuesday 3 June 1890
Portrait of Dr Gachet (JH2008),
letter sketch
Paper, 27 x 42 cm
Van Gogh Museum, Amsterdam
(Vincent van Gogh Foundation),
b687 V/1962

85 **Portrait of Dr Gachet
with Pipe**
June 1890
Etching, 18 x 15 cm
Van Gogh Museum, Amsterdam
(Vincent van Gogh Foundation),
p472 V/1962

Selected references: Faille 1970,
no. 1664; Gachet and Mothe 1994,
pp. 55–57, 142; Van Heugten
and Pabst 1995; Meedendorp
2007, pp. 370–73

In June 1890, after painting two portraits of Dr Gachet (see fig. 6) and sending a sketch to Theo (877; cat. 84), Van Gogh unexpectedly made a third, this one an etching (cat. 85), a technique that was completely new to him.

Paul Gachet was Van Gogh's physician in Auvers, and the two men had become friends. Gachet, an amateur artist who also collected art, owned a printing press. He could easily reproduce the etchings Vincent made, as he reported enthusiastically to Theo: 'I really hope to do a few etchings of subjects from the south, let's say 6, since I can print them free of charge at Mr Gachet's; he's very willing to run them off for nothing if I do them' (889).

Van Gogh had conceived a plan to make etchings of some of his works, which would enable him to reach a wider public: 'Of course we'll leave him free to run off copies for himself. Mr Gachet will come one day to see my canvases in Paris, and then we'd choose the ones to be engraved' (889).

On 28 June Gauguin reported the receipt of an artist's proof, which was most likely this portrait, Van Gogh's only known etching: 'My dear Vincent, On my return from a little trip I found both your letter and your proof etching [...] I don't know Doctor Gachet but I've often heard *père* Pissarro speak of him. And it must be pleasant for you to have someone close to you who sympathises with your work, your ideas' (892).

It is not clear why Van Gogh stopped etching after making just this one. He and Gachet printed a number of impressions of this portrait, which Gachet called *L'Homme à la pipe*. After Van Gogh's death, Gachet and, later, his son produced further impressions: more than 70 are in circulation. The original plate is now in the Musée d'Orsay in Paris. AV

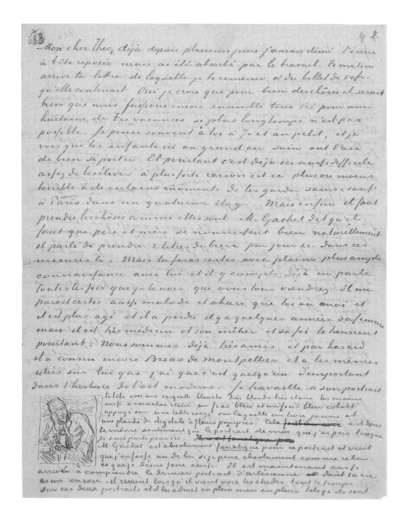

153

THE REVELATION
OF THE SOUTH

In the spring of 1886 Vincent van Gogh went to Paris to find out what was happening in the world of art, to come into contact with other artists, and, if possible, to sell his work. For the first time in his life, he met like-minded individuals: Henri de Toulouse-Lautrec, Emile Bernard, Paul Gauguin, Paul Signac. In their midst he developed in a way that was truly spectacular, evolving from a backward-looking, tonal painter who concentrated on atmosphere and sentiment into a forward-looking colourist determined to contribute to the art of the future. He discovered the beauty of Japanese prints and managed to make some of their elements a natural part of his own idiom. He also discovered Adolphe Monticelli, whose expressive and almost sculptural impasto provided him with a liberating example.

But two years in Paris were more than enough for Van Gogh: he grew tired of his Bohemian existence, the unhealthy city, and envious artists who did not understand that there was power in unity. In February 1888 he decided to leave for Marseilles – the city of Monticelli, who had died two years earlier in sorrowful circumstances – but what was intended to be a brief stay *en route* in Arles led to his staying in that small garrison town on the Rhône. After the comparatively letterless Paris years, Van Gogh's time in Arles (from February 1888 to May 1889) represents a dramatic high point in his correspondence, not only because the letters he wrote there shed light on the debilitating circumstances of the ear incident and his psychological crises, but primarily because they elucidate his artistic output and self-evaluation. They explain how the modern attainments of the Paris years enabled Van Gogh to plumb his most creative and original depths in Provence, even though he later came to the conclusion that he had failed in his ambition to make a contribution to the art of the future.

Van Gogh travelled from Paris to Arles by train. 'How I watched out to see "if it was like Japan yet"! Childish, isn't it?' (706), he later wrote to Gauguin. Apart from hoping that the climate would do him good – which in fact it did – he expected to encounter in the South the Mediterranean equivalent of the Japan he had envisioned from the hundreds of brightly coloured Japanese prints he had seen, and in this he was not disappointed. Van Gogh also intended to carry out some reconnaissance work, exploring the market for modern art in Marseilles and Theo's possibilities as an art dealer there, but nothing ever came of these plans.

Vincent's correspondence with Theo, as well as the letters he exchanged with Gauguin and Bernard, meant a great deal to him. They enabled him – despite the isolation of Arles – to keep abreast of artistic trends in Paris and Brittany (where Gauguin and Bernard stayed on several occasions) and to compare his own efforts with theirs.

Van Gogh spent most of his fifteen-month sojourn in Arles attempting, directly or indirectly, to realise his dream of founding an artists' colony, the 'Studio of the South', in the Yellow House, in which he hoped that his ideal of solidarity and collaboration among artists would come to fruition. When it appeared that Gauguin, whom he greatly admired, might join him there, Van Gogh threw himself heart and soul into preparations. The letters give a detailed account of his preoccupation with Gauguin's uncertain arrival, and how Van Gogh, when he was sure Gauguin was actually coming, spent day and night – to the point of physical and mental exhaustion – getting the house ready for him. This resulted in dozens of peerless works which show Van Gogh at the summit of his artistic creativity.

Van Gogh's self-confidence grew. He knew that he had struck out on a path all his own, having spent years practising and following the examples of others in his search for a technique and style that would enable him to express the deep truths of reality. The tone of his letters is self-assured; he dares to say, for example, that his still-lifes of sunflowers had made him the sunflower painter *par excellence* (fig. 12). In his letters to Bernard, he does not hesitate to speak out boldly and to lecture him about important artists of the past and about the path he should take. He no longer felt himself to be in a subordinate position to Theo, because he knew that his work was worth the money invested in it, even if no one wanted to buy it.

Van Gogh's collaboration with Gauguin turned into a fiasco. As regards technique, the two artists definitely profited from each other, passing on ideas that were mutually stimulating. But the differences in their egocentric personalities and artistic temperaments caused considerable tension after only a couple of weeks. Gauguin, who certainly understood that Van Gogh was developing into an exceptional artist, looked down on his taste in art and literature, which was marked by his preference for a fairly uncomplicated form of realism. While Gauguin sought to express himself in other spheres –

dream, fantasy, recollection – reality remained the be-all and end-all for Van Gogh. He found it difficult to follow Gauguin, who tended towards symbolism and took fantasy and imagination as his point of departure. In style and technique, an artist could take great liberties, but, as Van Gogh wrote to Bernard, with whom he carried on similar discussions by post, he could not work with 'abstractions': 'I can't work without a model. I'm not saying that I don't flatly turn my back on reality to turn a study into a painting – by arranging the colour, by enlarging, by simplifying – but I have such a fear of separating myself from what's possible and what's right as far as form is concerned [...] I have so much curiosity for what's possible and what really exists that I have so little desire or courage to search for the ideal, in so far as it could result from my abstract studies [...] I exaggerate, I sometimes make changes to the subject, but still I don't invent the whole of the painting; on the contrary, I find it ready-made – but to be untangled – in the real world' (698).

The breakdown of his collaboration with Gauguin and the consequent collapse of the 'Studio of the South', culminating in the ear incident on 23 December 1888, undermined Van Gogh's self-confidence. When he returned to the Yellow House after a period of hospitalisation in Arles, Van Gogh's neighbours objected to his presence, and at last he felt compelled to have himself admitted to the psychiatric clinic in Saint-Rémy for a long period of treatment. The olympic heights he had attained in Arles seemed to him like the flight of Icarus.

86 Arles in the Snow
February 1888
Oil on canvas, 50 x 60 cm
Signed on the fence: *Vincent*
Private collection, London

Selected references: Faille 1970, no. 391; New York 1984, cat. 6; Otterlo 1990, p. 223; Toledo 2003, cat. 8

Van Gogh left Paris because he felt drawn to the warm climate and bright colours of Provence. When he arrived in Arles on 20 February 1888, however, he was surprised by the bitter cold: 'Now I'll tell you that for a start, there's been a snowfall of at least 60 centimetres all over, and it's still snowing' (577), he wrote to Theo from his new home. The winter landscape reminded him of Japanese prints of this subject: 'And the landscape under the snow with the white peaks against a sky as bright as the snow was just like the winter landscapes the Japanese did' (577).

Having completed a small study of a winter landscape a couple of days after his arrival (Solomon R. Guggenheim Museum, New York, Thannhauser Foundation, F290), Van Gogh painted another winter landscape: *Arles in the Snow*. This work must have been produced after the first snow had almost completely melted and a couple of centimetres of fresh snow had fallen on 25 February, as recorded in the meteorological reports of Provence in this period. On about 5 March he wrote to his brother: 'There's a hard frost here, and out in the country there's still snow – I have a study of a whitened landscape with the town in the background' (582). This reference to the town in the background makes it clear that Van Gogh was alluding to *Arles in the Snow*. He signed the work on the wooden fence in the foreground. RZ

87 Tiled Roof with Chimneys and a Church Tower, Arles
March–April 1888
Pencil, reed pen, pen and brown
ink on wove paper, 25.5 x 34.5 cm
Private collection

Selected references: Faille 1970,
no. 1480a; New York 1984, cat. 14;
Arles 1989, cat. 2, pp. 14–15;
Heenk 1995, p. 178; Amsterdam
2005B, p. 149

'I now have a terrace for a studio' (599),
Van Gogh wrote to Bernard on 19 April
1888. He ended this letter by saying:
'Write to me soon, still same address,
Restaurant Carrel, Arles'. Van Gogh drew
this view from the terrace of his hotel at
30 Rue Amédée-Pichot, in the northern
part of the town, where he stayed from
late February to early May.

In drawing and painting his surroundings,
Van Gogh was generally more interested
in capturing ordinary, everyday sights than
in portraying picturesque, historical
monuments. A couple of days after his
arrival in Arles, he summarised his first
impressions as follows: 'The women really
are beautiful here, it's no joke – on the
other hand, the Arles museum is dreadful
and a joke, and fit to be in Tarascon –
there's also a museum of antiquities,
they're genuine' (578).

*Tiled Roof with Chimneys and a Church
Tower, Arles* belongs to an early group of
drawings in which Van Gogh explored, as
it were, his new surroundings. A roof and
three chimneys figure prominently in the
foreground, while the city's monuments
are visible in the distance. Van Gogh was
looking from the terrace towards the
southwest, where he could see – from left
to right – one of the towers of the arena,
the spire of the Church of the Cordeliers,
the distant cupola of the Homme de
Bronze and the tower of Saint-Julien.
At the far right is the Church of the
Dominicans. RZ

161

88 **The Road to Tarascon**
April 1888
Pencil, pen, reed pen and brown
ink on wove paper, 25.8 x 35 cm
Kunsthaus Zürich, Grafische
Sammlung, 1940/1

Selected references: Faille 1970,
no. 1502; Roskill 1971, p. 167;
Martigny 2000, cat. 47;
Amsterdam 2005B, cat. 45;
Vellekoop and Zwikker 2007, p. 5

Van Gogh made this rapidly drawn depiction
in April 1888. As in several other drawings
from that year, it shows the Avenue de
Montmajour, which ran from the Place
Lamartine in Arles, where the Yellow
House stood, to Tarascon.

The walking figure – sometimes
interpreted in the Van Gogh literature
as a symbolic self-portrait – was added
later in the studio, after Van Gogh had
erased and scratched out an earlier attempt.
The drawing was probably among the
works sent to Theo on 7 May 1888.

This work can be connected with a
painting made in July of that year, *The Painter
on the Road to Tarascon* (F448), which was
unfortunately lost in the Second World
War. The figure in that painting, unlike
the one in the drawing, is clearly an artist
walking. Van Gogh called the painting
'a quick sketch I made of myself laden
with boxes, sticks, a canvas, on the sunny
Tarascon road' (660). RZ

89 **Letter 609**
from Vincent van Gogh
to Theo van Gogh
Arles, Saturday 12 May 1888
Farmhouse in a Wheat Field
(JH1418), *View of Arles with Irises
in the Foreground* (JH1418),
letter sketches
Paper, 20.3 x 26.4 cm
Van Gogh Museum, Amsterdam
(Vincent van Gogh Foundation),
b527 V/1962

View of Arles with Irises in the Foreground (cat. 91) was the first painting Van Gogh made after completing a series of blossoming orchards on about 20 April. He mentioned it in a letter to Theo written on 12 May 1888, illustrating his written description of the canvas by adding a sketch with colour notations: 'A meadow full of very yellow buttercups, a ditch with iris plants with green leaves, with purple flowers, the town in the background, some grey willow trees – a strip of blue sky. If they don't mow the meadow I'd like to do this study again, because the subject matter was really beautiful and I had trouble finding the composition. A little town surrounded by countryside entirely covered in yellow and purple flowers. That would really be a Japanese dream, you know' (609; cat. 89).

Van Gogh must have experienced the same difficulties with the composition when making, with the help of a perspective frame, the virtuoso reed-pen drawing that preceded the painting (cat. 90). It is apparent that the drawing pre-dates the painting from the grass, the mowing of which is less advanced in the drawing.

Van Gogh again mentioned the painted 'view of Arles' ten days later in a letter to Bernard: 'of the town you see only a few red roofs and a tower, the rest's hidden by the foliage of fig-trees, &c. All that far off in the background and a narrow strip of blue sky above. The town is surrounded by vast meadows decked with innumerable buttercups – a yellow sea. These meadows are intersected in the foreground by a ditch full of purple irises. They cut the grass while I was painting, so it's only a study and not a finished painting, which I intended to make of it. But what a subject – eh – that sea of yellow flowers with a line of purple irises, and in the background the neat little town of pretty women' (612). RZ

J'ai trouvé un restaurant meux
ou je mange pour 1 franc.
La santé va mieux ces jours ci
maintenant j'ai deux nouvelles
études comme ceci

bleu

Tu en as un
dessin déja d'une
ferme au bord de la
grande route dans
les blés

Bleu   Violet

Une prairie pleine de boutons d'or
très jaune un fossé avec des
plantes d'Iris au feuilles vertes à fleurs
violettes dans le fond la ville
quelques saules gris — une bande de
ciel bleu.

Si on ne coupe pas la prairie je voudrais
refaire cette étude car la donnée était bien
belle et j'ai eu du mal a trouver la composition
une petite ville entourée d'une campagne
entierement fleurie de jaune & de violet
tu sais ce serait joliment un reve japonais.
Ayant demandé le prix de transport de l'envoi
qui est parti par petite vitesse cela sera 7 francs
jusqu'a en gare à Paris Vu qu'il ne me reste
pas grand chose je n'ai pas affranchi ici — mais
si on demandait davantage il faudrait
réclamer. la caisse est marquée V V & W 1042
Hier & aujourdhui nous avons de nouveau
le mistral. J'espère que mon
envoi arrivera avant que Tersteeg
ne vienne a Paris.
Poignée de main ecris moi bientot
à t
Vincent

165

90 **View of Arles with Irises
in the Foreground**
May 1888
Reed pen, ink and wash
over graphite on wove paper,
43.5 x 55.5 cm
Inscribed and signed lower left:
Vue d'Arles | Vincent
Museum of Art, Rhode Island
School of Design. Gift of Mrs
Murray S. Danforth, 42.212A

Selected references: Faille 1970,
no. 1461r; Heenk 1995, p. 177;
Stolwijk and Veenenbos 2002,
p. 194; Amsterdam 2005 B, cat. 46

**View of Arles with Irises
in the Foreground**

May 1888
Oil on canvas, 54 x 65 cm
Van Gogh Museum, Amsterdam
(Vincent van Gogh Foundation),
s37 V/1962

Selected references: Faille 1970,
no. 409; New York 1984, cat. 27;
Otterlo 1990, p. 219; Heenk 1995,
p. 177; Toledo 2003, cat. 9

92 Harvest in Provence

c. 12 June 1888
Reed and quill pens and
ink with watercolour,
wax crayon, and
gouache over charcoal
on wove paper laid down
on millboard, 50.5 x 61 cm
Signed lower right: *Vincent*
Inscribed lower left: *La moisson
en Provence*
Private collection, courtesy
of Heather James Fine Art

Selected references: Faille 1970,
no. 1483; Amsterdam 2005 B,
cat. 62; Van Heugten 2005,
pp. 108–13

Harvest themes were among Van Gogh's favourite means of expressing the essence of rural life. In June 1888 he concentrated fully on capturing images of traditional life in the country, just as he had done at Nuenen in 1883–85.

On 27 May Vincent asked Theo to send him some watercolours, because he wanted 'to do some pen drawings, but coloured in flat tints like Japanese prints' (614). *Harvest in Provence* was the second work that Van Gogh made in this manner, and the result was spectacular. First he made a preliminary sketch in pencil, followed by a pen-and-ink drawing, which he filled in with wax crayon and opaque watercolour. His satisfaction with the result is evident from the fact that he signed the sheet and gave it a title: 'La moisson en Provence'. He also used the motif for a large painting that is now in the Van Gogh Museum, Amsterdam (F412). This canvas formed the basis for two drawn copies: one for his friend Emile Bernard (Kupferstichkabinett, Staatliche Museen zu Berlin, F1485) and one for John Peter Russell (National Gallery of Art, Washington. Collection of Mr and Mrs Paul Mellon, F1486).

Harvest in Provence is a view over the plateau of La Crau, which 'apart from a difference in colour and the clearness of the atmosphere' reminded Van Gogh of 'the old Holland of Ruisdael's day' (639). Visible in the distance are the Abbey of Montmajour, the Mont des Cordes and Les Alpilles. RZ

**93 View of Arles
from Montmajour**
July 1888
Reed pen, quill, and pen and ink
over graphite on wove paper,
48.6 x 60 cm
Signed lower left: *Vincent*
The National Museum of Art,
Architecture and Design, Oslo,
NG.K&HB00068

Selected references: Faille 1970,
no. 1452; New York 1984, cat. 33;
Otterlo 1990, cat. 183; Stolwijk
and Veenenbos 2002, p. 195;
Amsterdam 2005B, cat. 47;
Van Heugten 2005, cat. 103

**94 Landscape near
Montmajour with a Train**
July 1888
Pen, reed pen and brown ink
over graphite on wove paper,
48.7 x 60.7 cm
Signed lower left: *Vincent*
Inscribed in a cartouche lower
right: *La campagne du côté des bords |
du Rhône vue de | Mon[t] Majour*
On loan from the
British Museum, London,
1968,0210.20

Selected references: Faille 1970,
no. 1424; Amsterdam 2005B,
cat. 86; Van Heugten 2005,
pp. 118–30; Vellekoop and
Zwikker 2007, cats 342, 343

The elaborate landscapes in large format that Van Gogh drew in July 1888 from the hill of Montmajour near Arles are among the highlights of his drawn *œuvre*. These sheets were intended to show Theo 'the epitome of a really beautiful corner of Provence' (637). On about 13 July Vincent sent Theo a roll containing five pen-and-ink drawings and told him in the accompanying letter that he already had a view belonging to this series (cat. 93): 'You have a 6th of this Montmajour series. A group of very dark pines and the town of Arles in the background' (639). As early as the end of May, Van Gogh had sent his friend Arnold Koning a description of that sheet in a letter that included an enthusiastic plea for drawing with the reed pen: 'a drawing [...] Of a group of pines on a rock, seen from a hill. Behind that foreground a vista of meadows, a road with poplars and, right in the distance, the town. The trees very dark against the sunlit meadow. Perhaps you'll get a chance to see this drawing. I did it with very thick reed pens on thin Whatman, and used a quill pen for the finer lines in the distance. I can recommend that to you, because the lines with a quill pen are more in the nature of those with a reed' (618).

In a letter to Theo, Vincent described *Landscape near Montmajour with a Train* (cat. 94) and *La Crau seen from Montmajour* (Van Gogh Museum, Amsterdam, F1420)

as 'the two views of the Crau and the countryside along the banks of the Rhône [...] the best I've done with my pen' (639).

Landscape near Montmajour with a Train shows the train to Fontvieille. While drawing, Van Gogh was looking from his vantage point on Montmajour in a northwesterly direction, towards the banks of the Rhône. The mountains of Les Alpilles appear on the horizon. In a letter to Emile Bernard, Van Gogh briefly explained why he was so satisfied with the drawing: 'It does not look Japanese, and it's *actually* the most Japanese thing that I've done. A microscopic figure of a ploughman, a little train passing through the wheat fields; that's the only life there is in it' (641). RZ

95 The Langlois Bridge with a Lady with a Parasol
Mid-July 1888
Reed pen and ink over graphite
on wove paper, 24.2 x 31.8 cm
Los Angeles County Museum
of Art. George Gard de Sylva
Collection, 1949, M.49.17.2

Selected references: Faille 1970,
no. 1471; New York 1984, cat. 24;
Davis 1995, cat. 59; Hulsker 1996,
no. 1420; Martigny 2000, pp. 212,
271, 300; Amsterdam 2005 B,
cat. 87, pp. 269–70

Before beginning his series of blossoming orchards at the end of March, Van Gogh first depicted the bridge over the Arles-Bouc canal – the 'Pont de Langlois' – making it the subject of five paintings and three works on paper; he sent a sketch of the motif to his friend Emile Bernard (587; fig. 22). Four months later, however, he made this pen-and-ink drawing after the painting *The Langlois Bridge with a Lady with a Parasol* of March (Wallraf-Richartz-Museum and Fondation Corboud, Cologne, F570). The sheet belongs to a group of fifteen pen-and-ink drawings that Van Gogh sent in mid-July to Bernard, to give him an idea of his more recent paintings. *The Langlois Bridge with a Lady with a Parasol* was, however, the only drawing made after a considerably older painting. Van Gogh's shipment had an aim, namely to tempt Bernard into carrying out a similar project, as he wrote to him on 15 July: 'let me know if you agree to make me some croquis of your Breton studies [...] I want to do at least another half a dozen subjects in pen croquis for you' (641). A week later Bernard sent him ten pen-and-ink drawings, but they were not representative enough to entice Theo to buy one of Bernard's paintings, as Vincent had hoped he would do. TM

Fig. 22 **Letter 587** from Vincent van Gogh to Emile Bernard. Arles, Sunday 18 March 1888. *The Langlois Bridge with Walking Couple* (JH1370), letter sketch. Paper, 20.3 x 13.2 cm. The Morgan Library and Museum, New York. Thaw Collection

96 Summer Evening
Mid-July 1888
Reed pen, quill and ink
over graphite on wove paper,
24 x 31.5 cm
Kunstmuseum Winterthur.
Presented by Dr Emil Hahnloser,
1928

Selected references: Faille 1970,
no. 1514; New York 1984, cat. 69;
Otterlo 1990, cat. 195; Hulsker
1996, no. 1546; Dorn 1999;
Amsterdam 2005 B, cat. 68

Summer Evening is one of fifteen drawings after paintings that Van Gogh sent in mid-July 1888 to Emile Bernard (see also cat. 95). Van Gogh had already told his friend about the painting itself (fig. 23), having sent a sketch and a short description in a letter of *c.* 19 June (fig. 24): 'Here's another landscape. Setting sun? Moonrise? Summer evening, at any rate. Town violet, star yellow, sky blue-green; the wheat fields have all the tones: old gold, copper, green gold, red gold, yellow gold, green, red and yellow bronze [...] I painted it out in the mistral. My easel was fixed in the ground with iron pegs, a method that I recommend to you' (628).

In both painting and drawing, the silhouette of Arles stands out boldly against what, after all, most closely resembles a setting sun, despite Van Gogh's view that it could just as well be seen as a rising moon. His ambivalence is not all that strange, however, for he painted the city looking in a southwesterly direction, whereas the mid-June sun sank below the horizon in the northwest. To enhance the effect of a summer evening, he deliberately placed the heavenly body directly behind the city, wedged in between one of the Roman arena's towers and the steeple of the church of the Carmelite Convent. The aureole appearing in the drawing is lacking in the painting, but ultimately emphasises the idea of a setting sun. TM

Fig. 23 **Summer Evening**, June 1888.
Oil on canvas, 74 x 92 cm. Kunstmuseum Winterthur.
Donation of Dr Emil Hahnloser, 1922 (F465)

Fig. 24 **Letter 628** from Vincent van Gogh to Emile Bernard. Arles, on or about Tuesday 19 June
1888. *Wheat Field with Setting Sun* (JH1474), *Leg of an Easel with a Ground Spike*, letter sketches. Paper,
26.8 x 20.5 cm. The Morgan Library and Museum, New York. Thaw Collection

97 Olive Trees, Montmajour

July 1888

Pencil, reed pen, brown and black
ink on wove paper, 49.1 x 61 cm
Signed lower left: *Vincent*
Musée des Beaux-Arts, Tournai

Selected references: Stolwijk and
Veenenbos 2002, pp. 18, 46, 80,
193; Amsterdam 2005 B, cat. 82;
Van Heugten 2005, no. 104;
Vellekoop and Zwikker 2007,
no. 342a, p. 139

In May 1888 Van Gogh made a series
of drawings of the surroundings of
Montmajour, a rocky outcrop about three
miles northeast of Arles. He returned in
the first half of July to make a second series
of landscapes that are an undisputed
highlight of his drawn *œuvre*.

In this period Van Gogh concentrated
on drawing, both because it was less
expensive than painting and because
it was less susceptible to disruption by
the mistral, the strong north wind typical
of the Rhône Valley and the coastal areas
of southeastern France.

In a letter written around 8 or 9 July,
Vincent told Theo that he had 'two large
new ones' (637), by which he meant *The
Rock of Montmajour with Pine Trees* (Van
Gogh Museum, Amsterdam, F1447) and
the present drawing. Although the title
of the latter has always been *Olive Trees,
Montmajour*, we see pine trees (*Pinus
halepensis*) here as well.

Both sheets are remarkable for their
free and forceful style of drawing, which
contrasts somewhat with the more
considered and harmonious compositions
of the three drawings that followed
(*Montmajour*, Rijksmuseum, Amsterdam,
F1446; *La Crau: The View from Montmajour*,
Van Gogh Museum, Amsterdam, F1420;
and cat. 94). RZ

98 **Letter 602**

from Vincent van Gogh
to Theo van Gogh
Arles, Tuesday 1 May 1888
The Yellow House (JH1413),
letter sketch
Paper, 21 x 27 cm
Van Gogh Museum, Amsterdam
(Vincent van Gogh Foundation),
b520 a-b V/1962

99 **The Yellow House**

c. 29 September 1888
Pen and ink on graph paper,
13.3 x 20.6 cm
Private collection, USA

Selected references: Faille 1970,
no. 1453; Christie's 2003, lot 52
(entry by Ronald Pickvance);
Amsterdam 2005B, cat. 97;
Vellekoop and Zwikker 2007,
no. 349d

Van Gogh dreamed of founding an artists' colony in which kindred spirits could live and work together, but the only artist who actually lived with him briefly in the Yellow House was Paul Gauguin.

On 1 May 1888 Van Gogh wrote to Theo to tell him that he had rented a house for 15 francs a month: 'The studio, the store, will remain here for the whole of the campaign here in the south, and that way I have my independence from petty squabbles over guest-houses, which are ruinous and depress me' (602; cat. 98). In that letter he made a rapid sketch of the building, which still needed to be fixed up and furnished. It was not until Theo made this possible by sending an additional 300 francs that Vincent could actually move in, in September.

That same month Vincent sent Theo this sketch (cat. 99), made from memory, of the painting he had just finished (cat. 100):

a 'croquis of a square no. 30 canvas showing the house and its surroundings under a sulphur sun, under a pure cobalt sky. That's a really difficult subject! But I want to conquer it for that very reason. Because it's tremendous, these yellow houses in the sunlight and then the incomparable freshness of the blue. All the ground's yellow, too. I'll send you another, better drawing of it than this croquis from memory; the house to the left is pink, with green shutters; the one that's shaded by a tree, that's the restaurant where I go to eat supper every day. My friend the postman lives at the bottom of the street on the left, between the two railway bridges' (691).

The piles of sand next to the pavement most probably indicate the laying of gas pipes, to which the ground floor of the Yellow House was eventually connected – to Van Gogh's satisfaction, since this enabled him to paint in the evenings as well. RZ

100 **The Yellow House
(The Street)**
September 1888
Oil on canvas, 76 x 91.5 cm
Van Gogh Museum, Amsterdam
(Vincent van Gogh Foundation),
s32 V/1962

Selected references: Faille 1970,
no. 464; Amsterdam 1990,
cat. 60; Chicago 2001, pp. 107–11,
146–47; Amsterdam 2005B,
no. 216; Vellekoop and Zwikker
2007, no. 349

Van Gogh was fond of drawing and painting parks and gardens, which for him had poetic connotations. On 5 July 1888 he informed Theo that he had found 'a new subject', and sent him a sketch to give him an impression of the painted park view (fig. 25), which he described as follows: 'A corner of a garden with round bushes and a weeping tree, and in the background, clumps of oleanders. And the lawn that has just been mown, with long wisps of hay drying in the sun. A little corner of blue green sky at the top' (636; cat. 101).

The drawing Van Gogh made that same month, after completing the work discussed above, was one of the fifteen drawings after paintings that he sent to Emile Bernard. According to Van Gogh, *The Garden: A Corner of a Garden in the Place Lamartine* (cat. 103) contained 'perhaps something like "the shaggy carpets of flowers and woven greenery" of Crivelli or Virelli' (641) – probably a reference to the late fifteenth-century painter Carlo Crivelli or his brother Vittore Crivelli, who was also a painter.

In addition to the garden view in horizontal format intended for Bernard, Van Gogh drew *A Corner of a Garden in the Place Lamartine* (cat. 102) and sent it to John Peter Russell, together with eleven other drawings after painted studies.

The park view produced for Russell makes a more finished and stylised impression than the work intended for Bernard. To Theo, too, he sent a drawn copy of the painting (Menil Collection, Houston, F1451), and told him that 'the painted studies lack clarity of touch. One more reason why I felt the need to draw them' (657).

From September 1888 Van Gogh began to associate the parks in Arles with such poets as Dante, Petrarch and Boccaccio, about whom he had read an article. He described the works painted in this context as belonging to the 'poet's garden', and later viewed *The Garden: A Corner of a Garden in the Place Lamartine*, painted in July, as the 'first idea' for this series. Thus he informed Bernard that he had two canvases of the 'poet's garden': 'among the croquis you

185

July 1888
Reed pen and ink over graphite
on wove paper surrounded by
narrow strips of marbled paper,
24.2 x 31.6 cm
Signed lower left: *Vincent*
Private collection

Selected references: Faille 1970,
no. 1450; Otterlo 1990, pp. 232–33;
Heenk 1995, p. 170; Amsterdam
2005B, cat. 88; Vellekoop and
Zwikker 2007, p. 86

→

have the first idea for it, after a smaller painted study that's already at my brother's' (696). And to Gauguin, who was shortly to come to Arles to share the Yellow House with him, he wrote that same day: 'About the room where you'll stay, I've made a decoration especially for it, the *garden of a poet* (in the croquis Bernard has there's a first idea for it, later simplified). The unremarkable public garden contains plants and bushes that make one dream of landscapes in which one may readily picture to oneself Botticelli, Giotto, Petrarch, Dante and Boccaccio. In the decoration I've tried to tease out the essence of what constitutes the changeless character of the region. And I'd have wished to paint this garden in such a way that one would think both of the old poet of this place (or rather, of Avignon), Petrarch, and of its new poet – Paul Gauguin. However clumsy this effort, you'll still see, perhaps, that while preparing your studio I've thought of you with very deep feeling' (695). RZ

Fig. 25 **Garden with Weeping Willow: Sunny Lawn in a Public Park (Arles)**, July 1888.
Oil on canvas, 60.5 x 73.5 cm. Merzbacher Collection (F428)

104 Entrance to the Public Gardens in Arles

October 1888
Oil on canvas, 72.3 x 90.8 cm
The Phillips Collection,
Washington DC, 0796

Selected references: Faille 1970, no. 566; New York 1984, cat. 108; Dorn 1990A, pp. 435–38; Passantino and Scott 1999, pp. 112–14; Houston 2002, p. 131; Stolwijk and Veenenbos 2002, p. 178

In Arles Van Gogh frequently went to paint and draw in one of the three small parks on the Place Lamartine, the square in front of the Yellow House. He painted *Entrance to the Public Gardens in Arles* in October 1888, while awaiting Paul Gauguin's arrival. The entrance to the park seen here was probably opposite Van Gogh's house. Unlike the 'poet's garden' – a series of paintings that had a symbolic meaning for Van Gogh and were intended to decorate Gauguin's room – this work is a more everyday picture of the park. In a letter dated 13 October (703) Van Gogh mentions three canvases depicting the 'poet's garden', as well as two paintings of the 'other garden', referring to his more prosaic views of gardens, including the present work.

The atmosphere and the figures – particularly the standing man wearing a straw hat – recall to some extent the caricatures of Honoré Daumier, whom Van Gogh greatly admired. This association is an obvious one, since Van Gogh wrote in a letter to Gauguin: 'you may well see nothing more beautiful than things out of Daumier, figures here are often pure Daumier' (695). And a couple of days after completing *Entrance to the Public Gardens in Arles*, he said in a letter to Theo: 'it isn't a superb and sublime country, it's all something out of Daumier come to life' (703). RZ

105 **Still-life with a Plate of Onions**
Early January 1889
Oil on canvas, 49.6 x 64.4 cm
Kröller-Müller Museum,
Otterlo, KM 111.075

Selected references: Faille 1970,
no. 604; Feilchenfeldt 1988,
p. 107; Amsterdam 1990,
cat. 79, pp. 188–90; Ten Berge,
Meedendorp, Vergeest and
Verhoogt 2003, pp. 261–64;
Feilchenfeldt 2005, pp. 302–03

'I'm going to get back to work tomorrow, I'll begin by doing one or two still-lifes to get back into the way of painting' (732), Vincent wrote to Theo on 7 January 1889, upon returning to the Yellow House after his first stay in the hospital at Arles. This canvas was one of the still-lifes mentioned in that letter. The various objects on the table represent Van Gogh's everyday surroundings: a pipe, a tobacco pouch, a letter from Theo, a book, a candle, matches, a stick of sealing wax, a coffee pot, a plate of onions and an empty bottle, possibly of absinthe.

Over the years these objects have been interpreted in various ways, but the most likely explanation for this hotchpotch is the fact that Van Gogh had to settle in after coming home, and attempted this by documenting the bits and pieces in his immediate surroundings. Still-lifes were a good way of becoming reaccustomed to canvas, brush and palette, and he did not even have to leave the house to assemble this medley of objects. The book on the table – on which *Annuaire de la Santé* and the author's name, F.-V. Raspail, are legible – is a handbook on homoeopathy, with instructions for personal use: a reference to Van Gogh's recent health problems. This book prescribes camphor, for example, as a means of combating insomnia, and Van Gogh actually used this remedy, as he told Theo in a letter written on 9 January 1889: 'The most FEARSOME thing is the insomnia [...] But I'm fighting it myself [...] with a very, very strong dose of camphor in my pillow and my mattress' (735). AV

106 Letter 756

from Vincent van Gogh
to Paul Signac
Arles, Wednesday 10 April 1889
La Crau with Peach Trees in Blossom
(JH1682), letter sketch
Paper, 20.9 x 26.9 cm
Private collection

107 Peach Trees in Blossom

April 1889
Oil on canvas, 65 x 81 cm
The Samuel Courtauld Trust,
The Courtauld Gallery, London,
P.1932.SC.176

Selected references: Faille 1970,
no. 514; London 1994, cat. 23;
Stolwijk and Veenenbos 2002,
note 33; Compton Verney 2006,
cat. 26; Vienna 2008, p. 296

In the spring of 1889 Van Gogh painted this view, one of the last works he made before having himself admitted to the asylum at Saint-Rémy. The view was probably taken from the top of a small windmill now on the eastern outskirts of Arles. The base of the windmill survives, although the upper half has been lost. (I am grateful to Martin Bailey for sharing this information with me.)

Van Gogh sent a sketch of this landscape to a friend, the artist Paul Signac, and described his painting as the depiction of 'a poor green countryside with little cottages, blue line of the Alpilles, white and blue sky. The foreground, enclosures with reed hedges where little peach trees are in blossom – everything there is *small*, the gardens, the fields, the gardens, the trees, even those mountains, as in certain Japanese landscapes, that's why this subject attracted me' (756; cat. 106).

Van Gogh saw the countryside around Arles as the Western equivalent of Japan, which was an important reason for him to leave Paris and go to the South. The light-coloured mountain top in the right background of *Peach Trees in Blossom* is reminiscent of Mount Fuji, near Tokyo, with which Van Gogh had become familiar through his great love of Japanese prints.

This work was painted in a style that differs from the Japanese manner: here we see no large areas of colour, as in *The Harvest* (Van Gogh Museum, Amsterdam, F412) – an earlier rendering of this motif – but rather brushwork that is more in keeping with Pointillism, the style in which Signac worked. RZ

CYCLES OF NATURE

The seasons of the year and their accompanying labours run like a thread through Van Gogh's *œuvre*. He spent his youth in villages and loved the countryside, as he wrote in June 1888: 'having been brought up there, snatches of memories from past times, yearnings for that infinite of which the Sower, the sheaf, are the symbols, still enchant me as before' (628). After a period of religious obsession (1876–79), his belief in the Bible had given way to a religious view of nature, 'faith in and consciousness of something higher' (333), which found expression in the eternal cycle of the seasons. At first he sought to capture in his drawings and paintings the 'sentiment' and atmosphere of the landscape, but at Nuenen, after proclaiming himself a 'peasant painter' (493), in imitation of Jean-François Millet, his main subject became the simple folk who worked the land, communing with nature – an idealised image that he never relinquished.

In the summer of 1884, therefore, when Antoon Hermans commissioned him to paint a series of designs for panels with biblical scenes to decorate his dining room, Van Gogh proposed to depict motifs from rural life that would symbolise the seasons – a sower, a ploughman, peasants lifting potatoes, the wheat harvest (cf. cat. 121), a shepherd with his flock and an ox-cart in the snow – and maintained that those subjects would whet the appetite of Hermans's dinner guests more than 'mystical personages' would (453). He might have had this idea from a similar group of works by Millet that were discussed by Alfred Sensier in his biography of the painter, Van Gogh's favourite book at Nuenen. However, Van Gogh also knew Charles-Emile Jacque's series of woodcuts after the twelve months (reproduced in *L'Illustration* in 1852) and the more everyday examples he later described as 'naïve almanac pictures – old country almanacs, where hail, snow, rain, fine weather are represented in an utterly primitive way' (628). Four of the six paintings made for Hermans have survived (see cat. 19): large horizontal compositions with figures lined up in rather static positions in landscapes that function only as backdrops. In 1882 Van Gogh had already made four small watercolours of the seasons, perhaps as ideas for larger works, but this was the only time that he portrayed them on large canvases and as part of a decorative programme.

In Provence Van Gogh was again inspired by the changing seasons and the seasonal labours to produce a series of paintings and drawings, but now with a different meaning and featuring the landscape instead of the human figure. After hectic and unhealthy Paris, the rural surroundings of Arles were literally a breath of fresh air for Van Gogh, and he began to document them in detail – with methodical thoroughness – in paintings and drawings. Although his ambitions ultimately lay in portraiture, in Provence Van Gogh achieved unprecedented mastery as a landscape painter. He had once written to Theo that to fathom the character of a region it was necessary to experience all the seasons (384), and aptly enough, he began and ended his year in Arles by painting a series of blossoming orchards.

In late March 1888 the first blossoms appeared on the trees, which for Van Gogh signalled the start of an intensive 'campaign', as he called it. 'I'm in a fury of work as the trees are in blossom and I wanted to do a Provence orchard of tremendous gaiety' (592), he told Theo. For two weeks he painted without stopping, since the trees flowered for only a short while (cats 109–11, 113–14). Because the blossoming orchards were cheerful subjects from country life, Van Gogh expected to find a market for them, and soon conceived the idea to combine these canvases into triptychs and pendants, forming decorative ensembles (cats 111, 112). Back in Paris he had already thought about series of works that could be used to decorate restaurants and country houses; the sketches that Emile Bernard sent him of the decoration of his studio probably revived that idea. In the Japanese prints he had collected in Paris, blossoming trees are ubiquitous as symbols of the burgeoning spring. Examples closer to home were Charles-François Daubigny (whose large canvas *Spring* Van Gogh knew from his visits to the Musée du Luxembourg) and César de Cock, both of whom he praised as the pre-eminent painters of 'the Norman apple tree' (RM21).

After the blossoming orchards, his next campaign – the harvest – presented itself in June. This also required constant work, for the harvest was gathered in quickly, and bad weather could bring the reaping to an abrupt halt. The result of a week of intense work in the fields in the full sun, which he revelled in 'like a cicada' (628), was an extensive series of paintings of wheat fields (cat. 115) and one of a sower (Kröller-Müller Museum, Otterlo, F422): these are studies in yellow, just as the orchards had represented white and pink, and the seascapes of Saintes-Maries blue. And he already knew what the next step would be: the vineyards in autumn. 'Perhaps now I'll have a try at doing greens. Now autumn – that gives you the whole range of tones' (631).

In the vicinity of Arles in early October, Van Gogh made the painting *The Green Vineyard* (Kröller-Müller Museum, Otterlo, F475), which was given an important place in his decorative scheme of 'poetic subjects' for the Yellow House. The four seasons formed an essential part of that decoration, because at the end of October he wrote that he still needed canvases of the other seasons before he could form some idea of the whole (715). At grape-picking time he returned to the vineyard with Gauguin, who painted *The Wine Harvest at Arles (Misères*

humaines) (1888; Ordrupgaard, Copenhagen), a canvas bursting with symbolism and largely a product of his imagination. Van Gogh's *The Red Vineyard* (1888; Pushkin State Museum of Fine Arts, Moscow, F495), on the other hand, is a faithful depiction of the countryside, showing grape pickers against a sky at sunset, a landscape that the artist himself must have considered one of the best he made in Arles, since he decided to submit it to the avant-garde exhibition of Les XX in Brussels in 1890.

In November 1888 Van Gogh made two more paintings of a sower (cat. 120), in another attempt to create his own, modern version of Millet's emblematic figure. In Van Gogh's eyes, the sower stood for the beginning of life's cycle; its pendant was the reaper, a figure he painted the following year in Saint-Rémy as a symbol of death (see cat. 138). The thought of sowing and reaping as metaphors for life itself gave him comfort: 'What else can one do, thinking of all the things whose reason one doesn't understand, but gaze upon the wheat fields. Their story is ours, for we who live on bread, are we not ourselves wheat to a considerable extent, at least ought we not to submit to growing, powerless to move, like a plant, relative to what our imagination sometimes desires, and to be reaped when we are ripe, as it is?' (785).

Until the end of his life, Van Gogh attempted to express in his landscapes how 'healthy and fortifying' (898) the countryside was. He felt best when working the whole day outdoors in the sun, as he wrote in August 1888: 'If you're well, you should be able to live on a piece of bread, while working the whole day long, and still having the strength to smoke and to drink your glass; you *need* that in these conditions. And still to feel the stars and the infinite, clearly, up there. Then life is almost magical, after all' (663).

108 **Letter 597**
from Vincent van Gogh
to Theo van Gogh
Arles, on or about
Friday 13 April 1888
Three Orchards (JH1393),
letter sketch (recto), *Small Pear
Tree in Blossom* (JH1395),
letter sketch (verso)
Paper, 21 x 27.1 cm
Van Gogh Museum, Amsterdam
(Vincent van Gogh Foundation),
b517 V/1962

'I've just done a clump of apricot trees in a little fresh green orchard' (589), Van Gogh wrote to Theo on about 25 March 1888. In all likelihood he was referring to the blossoming orchard from Edinburgh (cat. 109), because even though he continued to paint blossoming fruit trees until the last week of April, this is the only work that displays the 'fresh green' of his description. By about 30 March he had started six of the fourteen paintings of orchards he was eventually to produce in this period. 'I'm in a fury of work as the trees are in blossom' (592), he told Theo on 3 April. After all, the flowering season was not all that long. The blossoming splendour of the countryside around Arles no doubt reminded him of various Japanese prints in his collection, such as Hiroshige's *Plum Orchard at Kameido* (cat. 62), which he had previously copied in Paris (fig. 20).

For cat. 110 – which has the same format – Van Gogh moved his easel deeper into the orchard. The blue-green strips of ploughed earth between the apricot trees are also clearly recognisable in the middle distance of the first painting. The foreground includes only an oblique strip of the 'fresh green' at the front of the orchard. The trees further back are all slightly younger and smaller, apart from the tree bending to the left on the edge of the ploughed part of the orchard, which is clearly visible in the middle distance of the Edinburgh painting. A green expanse of grass stretching beyond the orchard is delimited by a line of yellow on which willows stand. A factory with a tall chimney is visible on the right in both works.

These two works are signed – one on the lower left, the other on the lower right – which concurs with Van Gogh's decision to include them in a triptych, flanking *Small Pear Tree in Blossom (Arles)* (fig. 26). He had no preconceived plan to combine his paintings of orchards, but he must have changed his mind when he saw the sketches Emile Bernard sent him around 10 April, showing decorations made for

his studio in Asnières (see letters 596 and 696). Van Gogh immediately made an arrangement of several of his earlier paintings, placing *The Pink Orchard* and *The White Orchard* on either side of *Blossoming Peach Trees* (all Van Gogh Museum, Amsterdam, F555, F403, F404 respectively). He sketched this tentative triptych in a letter to Theo of *c.* 13 April, in which he also described and sketched a more recent painting: 'I now also have a small pear tree, vertical, also flanked by two other horizontal canvases [the present works]. That will make 6 canvases of orchards in blossom [...] I dare hope for 3 more, also going together, but those are still only in the state of embryos or foetuses [see cats 111–12]. I'd really like to do this group of 9 canvases. You understand that we're free to consider the 9 canvases as the initial idea for a much larger, definitive decoration [...] which would be done after exactly the same subjects, at the same time next year' (597; cat. 108). TM

Fig. 26 **Small Pear Tree in Blossom (Arles)**, 1888.
Oil on canvas, 73 x 46 cm. Van Gogh Museum, Amsterdam
(Vincent van Gogh Foundation) (F405)

J'ai eu une lettre de Bernard
avec des sonnets qu'il a fabriqués
parmi lesquels il y en a qui sont réussis
il arrivera a faire un bon sonnet ce que
je lui souvre presque.

Aussitôt le pont de l'anglais et
la répétition de l'autre tableau le pêcher rose
secs seront envoi

---

† Mon cher Theo, merci de ta lettre
contenant les échantillons de toile
absorbante. Serai bien aise de
recevoir – mais cela ne presse aucun
3 mètres de celle à 6 fr. –
Pour ce qui est de son envoi de couleurs
il n'y avait que les gros tubes _de blanc_ tandis
que tous les autres tubes étaient
de blanc des demi gros. – S'il les a comptés
dans les mêmes proportions c'est fort bien
mais fais attention à cela –
Les tubes de blanc à 1 fr. mais le
reste ne doit être qu'à moitié prix
Je trouve son bleu de Prusse mauvais
et son cinabre. Le reste est bien
Maintenant je te dirai que je travaille
aux **2 tableaux** desquels je voulais faire
des répétitions Le pêcher rose me donne
le plus de mal

Verger rose pêchers   pêcher   Verger blanc
abricotiers   rose   pruniers
                         terrain violet à vert

Tu vois par les quatre cases de l'autre
côté que les trois vergers se tiennent plus
ou moins. J'ai maintenant aussi un
petit poirier en hauteur ~~flanqué~~
~~flanqué~~ également de deux toiles en
largeur. Cela fera 6 toiles de
vergers en fleur.
Je cherche actuellement tous les jours
à les achever un peu et à les faire tenir
ensemble.
J'ose espérer 3 autres se tenant
également mais ceux là ne sont
encore qu'à l'état d'embryons ou
de fœtus
Je voudrais bien faire cet ensemble
de 9 toiles.
Tu comprends qu'il nous est loisible
de considérer les 9 toiles de cette
année comme première pensée
d'une décoration définitive beaucoup plus
grande (celle ci se compose de toiles de
25 et de 12) qui serait exécutée
d'après les mêmes motifs absolument l'année
prochaine à la même époque.

Voici l'autre pièce de milieu
des toiles de 12
terrain violet – dans le
fond un mur avec des peupliers
droits – et un ciel très bleu
Le petit poirier a un tronc
violet et des fleurs blanches
un grand papillon jaune
Sur une des touffes
à gauche dans le coin un
petit jardin avec bordure de
roseaux jaunes et des arbustes
verts et un parterre de fleurs. – Une maisonnette
rose.
Voilà dans les détails de la décoration
de vergers en fleur que je te destinais.
Seulement les 3 dernières toiles n'existent
qu'à un état provisoire elles représentent un
très grand verger avec bordure
de cyprès et grand poiriers à
Le pont de l'anglais pour toi marche bien
et sera mieux que l'étude je pense
Suis bien pressé de retourner
travailler. Pour le Guillaumin
si cela est possible c'est sûrement
bonne affaire d'acheter. Seulement
puisqu'on parle d'un nouveau procédé
pour fixer le pastel serait peut être sage
de lui demander de fixer de cette façon en
cas d'achat. Poignée de main à toi et à Koning
                  Vincent

109 **Orchard in Blossom**
   (Apricot Trees)
March–April 1888
Oil on canvas, 54 x 65.2 cm
Signed lower left: *Vincent*
National Gallery of Scotland,
Edinburgh, NG2217

Selected references: Faille 1970,
no. 553; New York 1984, cat. 8;
Van Uitert and Hoyle 1987,
p. 214; Dorn 1990B, pp. 38–39;
Amsterdam 1990, p. 112; Hulsker
1996, no. 1387; Martigny 2000,
pp. 269, 298; New York 2007,
p. 152 (note 6)

110 **Orchard with Blossoming Apricot Trees**

March–April 1888
Oil on canvas, 54 x 65 cm
Signed lower right: *Vincent*
Private collection, Switzerland

Selected references: Faille 1970,
no. 556; New York 1984, p. 47;
Van Uitert and Hoyle 1987,
pp. 214, 339; Bührle 1990,
cat. 50; Hulsker 1996, no. 1383;
Martigny 2000, cat. 45;
Budapest 2006, cat. 53

Orchard with Peach Trees in Blossom (cat. 111) and *Orchard Bordered by Cypresses* (cat. 112) were originally intended for the third triptych Van Gogh had in mind: 'the last 3 canvases [...] are supposed to represent a very large orchard with border of cypresses and large pear trees and apple trees' (597). Both works were painted in the same orchard, from approximately the same vantage point. When painting the second work, however, Van Gogh was looking more to the right, which caused the blossoming pear trees to become the main motif. The large peach trees in *Orchard with Peach Trees in Blossom* are the same ones that Van Gogh depicted from another position in *Pink Peach Trees ('Souvenir de Mauve')* (fig. 11) and its repetition *Blossoming Peach Trees* (Van Gogh Museum, Amsterdam, F404). Thus we may conclude that all the paintings of fruit trees made by Van Gogh in this period were done in only two or three orchards just outside Arles. Their exact locations have not yet been identified.

It is not entirely clear which work was supposed to serve as the central representation in the last triptych Van Gogh was contemplating. It might have been the large painting of a cherry tree

seen against a blue sky that he was working on in mid-April but unfortunately spoiled, as he said in letters to Theo and Bernard of 19 and 20 April respectively (599 and 600). A letter written to Theo more than a month later suggests that Vincent had begun to see the two works as pendants: 'The orchard study you mention – where there's a lot of stippling [*Orchard with Peach Trees in Blossom*] – is half of the main subject of the decoration. The other half is the study of the same format, without a stretching frame [*Orchard Bordered by Cypresses*]. And those two together would give an idea of how orchards are laid out here. But I myself thought one study too feeble, the other too harsh, both of them failures' (615).

Nevertheless, these two studies hold a certain charm precisely because of their differing brushwork, which was apparently a reason for Van Gogh to consider them 'failures'. The delicately dotted *Orchard with Peach Trees in Blossom* (the one Van Gogh called 'feeble') recalls the work he made in Paris nearly a year before, whereas *Orchard Bordered by Cypresses* (the 'harsh' one) displays the wide contours and coarse brush strokes characteristic of his new approach. With regard to the latter work, or at least the comparable small study made slightly earlier (Private collection, USA, F554), of which the sketch in letter 596 (fig. 27) was made, he told Bernard that its roughness was intentional: 'At present I'm busy with the fruit trees in blossom: pink peach trees, yellow-white pear trees. I follow no system of brushwork at all; I hit the canvas with irregular strokes which I leave as they are, impastos, uncovered spots of canvas – corners here and there left inevitably unfinished – reworkings, roughnesses; well, I'm inclined to think that the result is sufficiently worrying and annoying not to please people with preconceived ideas about technique' (596). TM

Fig. 27 **Letter 596** from Vincent van Gogh to Emile Bernard. Arles, on or about Thursday 12 April 1888. *Orchard Bordered by Cypresses* (JH1390), letter sketch. Paper, 20.7 x 26.6 cm. The Morgan Library and Museum, New York. Thaw Collection

III **Orchard with Peach Trees
in Blossom**
April 1888
Oil on canvas, 65.1 x 81.3 cm
Private collection

Selected references: Faille 1970,
no. 551; New York 1984, cat. 12;
Amsterdam 1990, cat. 43;
Hulsker 1996, no. 1396;
Ten Berge, Meedendorp, Vergeest
and Verhoogt 2003, p. 215

112 Orchard Bordered by Cypresses

April 1888
Oil on canvas, 64.9 x 81.2 cm
Kröller-Müller Museum, Otterlo,
KM 108.685

Selected references: Faille 1970,
no. 513; New York 1984, cat. 11;
Amsterdam 1990, cat. 42;
Hulsker 1996, no. 1389;
Ten Berge, Meedendorp, Vergeest
and Verhoogt 2003, pp. 214–16

Flowering Orchard
April 1888 (detail of cat. 114)

The descriptions and sketches in Van Gogh's letters make it possible to identify nearly all the flowering orchards he painted in March and April 1888. The *Flowering Orchard* owned by the Metropolitan Museum of Art (cat. 114) is an exception, but in all likelihood it is one of the later depictions in the series. A letter Vincent wrote to Theo around 20 April reveals that he painted a total of fourteen orchards: 'I have 10 orchards now, not counting three small studies and a large one of a cherry tree that I worked to death' (600). Thirteen of these can be traced to extant works, which means that *Flowering Orchard* is perhaps the fourteenth. The style and execution of the painting are more in keeping with the orchards painted in 1888 than with those made a year later. It is not entirely clear what type of fruit trees Van Gogh depicted here, but they could well be plum trees that have nearly finished flowering and are already in leaf. The blossoming trees in the right background are perhaps apples, which blossom slightly later than the softer kinds of fruit, such as plums, peaches and apricots.

It is unlikely that *Flowering Orchard* was ever intended as the central panel of the last triptych Van Gogh worked on, of which cats 111 and 112 were meant to be the side panels. Not only does it differ in format – here Van Gogh used the standard no. 20 canvas and for the others no. 25 – but he had earlier written that his last triptych was 'supposed to represent a very large orchard with border of cypresses and large pear trees and apple trees' (597). *Flowering Orchard* was painted at a different location and in other respects, too, does not fit so well into that series. The unsuccessful cherry tree mentioned above, which Van Gogh said he had 'worked to death' – a larger work, as Van Gogh wrote,

that is now lost – is more likely to have belonged to this series.

The long grass in the orchard is being mown: the foremost part has already been done, and the rake and scythe leaning against the tree suggest that the mower has interrupted his work, perhaps to have lunch. In the drawing *Orchard with Arles in the Background* (cat. 113), executed in the same orchard, the bare branches suggest that it was made earlier. Indeed, it is generally assumed to have originated at the end of March, several weeks before the painting, though some doubt may be cast on this supposed discrepancy. In both drawing and painting, dandelions are recognisable and the grass is about the same height. In the drawing, moreover, the trees on the right obviously have leaves or blossoms, certainly those in the background on the horizon, where dots clearly indicate flowering. A dating to slightly later in April is therefore more plausible. Did the compelling graphic effect of the budding branches persuade Van Gogh not to finish the tree further? The theory that the tree is dead seems in any case to be contradicted by the leaves already sprouting on some of its branches.

To capture the motif of his drawing, Van Gogh took up a position slightly farther back in the orchard and more to the left with respect to the vantage point from which he made the painted version, thus bringing the towers of the Church of Saint-Trophime and the Town Hall of Arles into view. The drawing thus provides co-ordinates that enable us to establish, also for the painted version, a location to the south of the city, near the ancient Roman remains of Les Alyscamps. Visible in the right background is the roof of the Caserne Calvin, a barracks on the Boulevard des Lices. TM

113 **Orchard with Arles
in the Background**
Late March – early April 1888
Reed pen, pen, ink and graphite
on laid paper, 53.2 x 38.8 cm
The Hyde Collection, Glens Falls,
New York, 1971.81

Selected references: Faille 1970,
no. 1516; New York 1984, cat. 19;
Otterlo 1990, cat. 175; Heenk
1995, p. 176; Hulsker 1996,
no. 1376; Amsterdam 2005B,
cat. 44; Vellekoop and Zwikker
2007, p. 58

114 **Flowering Orchard**
April 1888
Oil on canvas, 72.4 x 53.3 cm
Signed lower left: *Vincent*
Lent by the Metropolitan Museum
of Art, The Mr and Mrs Henry
Ittleson Jr Purchase Fund, 1956
(56.13)

Selected references: Faille 1970,
no. 552; New York 1984, pp. 45,
48, 61, cat. 9; Arnold 1995,
pp. 408–09; Hulsker 1996,
no. 1381; New York 2007,
pp. 147, 218, cat. 108

115 Wheat Field

June 1888
Oil on canvas, 50 x 61 cm
Stichting Collectie P. en N.
De Boer, Amsterdam

Selected references: Faille 1970,
no. 564; New York 1984, cat. 45;
Hulsker 1996, no. 1475;
Martigny 2000, cat. 60;
Vienna 2008, cat. 77

In June 1888 the grain harvest around Arles largely determined Van Gogh's choice of subject, the high point being the painting *The Harvest* (fig. 10; cf. cat. 92). This work was preceded by several more modest studies, both painted and drawn, one of which was this *Wheat Field*. The farmhouse in the background of this work is the same as the one on the far right in *The Harvest*. When making the study, Van Gogh took up a lower position, having walked a bit further into the field, so that the blue cart must have been more or less behind him. While working on *The Harvest* Van Gogh commented: 'it kills the rest of what I have' (625), so powerfully did the bright areas of colour in that painting dominate the other works in his studio. More annoyingly, several of his acquaintances – the artists Dodge MacKnight and Eugène Boch – thought so too. Later in the same letter Van Gogh remarked, not without a touch of humour: 'you're really not sure what to think of yourself when you hear people say that, but I say to myself: the rest must look bloody awful, to be sure'. TM

116 Letter 714

from Vincent van Gogh
to Theo van Gogh
Arles, Saturday 27 or
Sunday 28 October 1888
Sower (JH1619), *Ploughed Field
with a Tree-trunk ('The Furrows')*
(JH1619), letter sketches
Paper, 21.1 x 26.7 cm
Van Gogh Museum, Amsterdam,
b605 V/1968

117 Sower

October 1888
Oil on canvas, 72 x 91.5 cm
Hahnloser/Jaeggli Stiftung,
Villa Flora, Winterthur

Selected references: Faille 1970,
no. 494; New York 1984, cat. 114;
Amsterdam 1988, cat. 74; Hulsker
1996, no. 1617; Chicago 2001,
cat. 69; Winterthur 2002, cat. 11

After Gauguin's arrival in Arles on Tuesday 23 October 1888 the two artists made their first excursion together to the fields of La Crau to the east of the city, where Van Gogh laid in two paintings: *Sower* (cat. 117) and *The Old Yew* (fig. 28). At the end of that week, on 27 or 28 October, he made sketches of them in a letter to Theo and added this brief announcement: 'This week I did a new study of a sower; the landscape utterly flat, the figure small and blurred. Then I did another study of ploughed field with the stump of an old yew. Like this' (714; cat. 116).

Earlier that summer Van Gogh had painted a sower (Kröller-Müller Museum, Otterlo, F422) – he sketched this in a letter to John Peter Russell (627; cat. 118) – but afterwards he was not entirely satisfied with it. In his search for an emblematic conception of this subject, this new *Sower* represents an intermediate stage, for it was the sower he made in November that most nearly approached his ideal (see cat. 120).

Of the three works, the painting from Winterthur is the closest to 'reality'. While the sowing peasants in the other two canvases perform their task against a setting sun laden with meaning, this sower appears relatively small and modest, a lone figure in a vast ploughed field that covers nearly the entire canvas. Painting with the sun at his back, Van Gogh paid close attention to the structure of the churned-up earth, which illusively recedes ever more vaguely in soft, complementary hues of purple-blue and yellow.

'I dare believe that you'll like the new *Sower*', Vincent told Theo around 29 October (715), saying that Gauguin himself immediately thought it a splendid painting. Vincent could not wait to go on working and to broaden his subject-matter, now that Gauguin was there. 'I'm writing in haste, we have heaps of work. He and I plan to go to the brothels a lot', Vincent said at the close of his letter, ending with the reassuring words: 'but only to study them.' TM

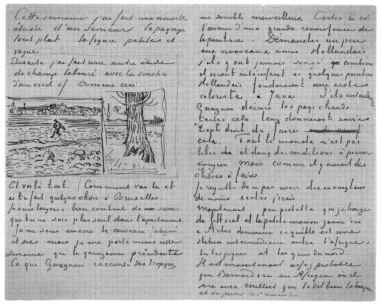

Fig. 28 **The Old Yew**, late October 1888.
Oil on canvas, 91 x 71 cm. Private collection (F573)

118 **Letter 627**

from Vincent van Gogh
to John Peter Russell
Arles, on or about
Sunday 17 June 1888
Sower with Setting Sun (JH1471),
letter sketch
Paper, 20.3 x 26.3 cm
Solomon R. Guggenheim
Museum, New York.
Thannhauser Collection,
Gift of Justin K. Thannhauser,
78.2514.19

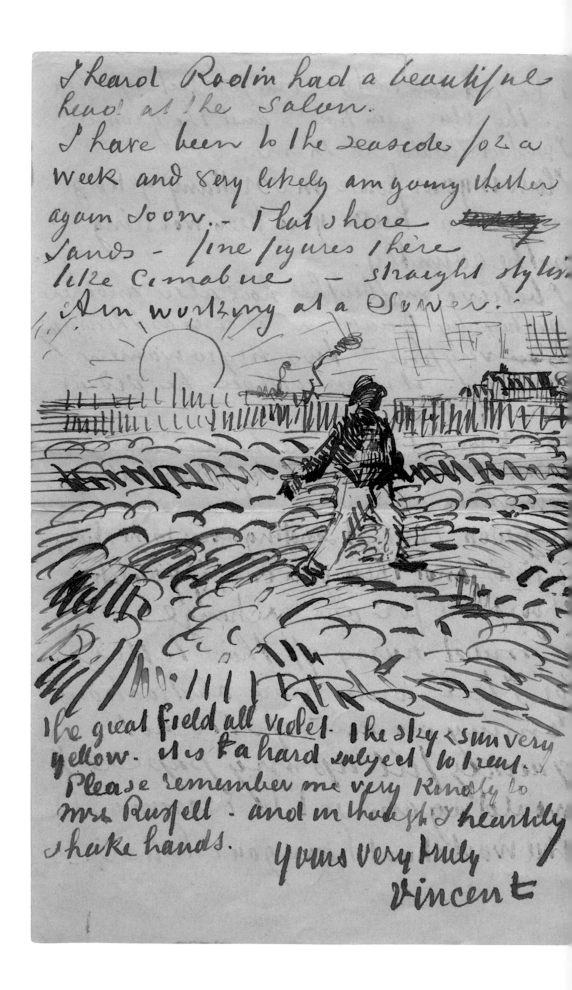

My dear ▓▓▓▓▓▓ for ever so long I have
been wanting to write to you - but then
the work has so taken me up. We have
harvest time here at present and I am
always in the fields.

And when I sit down to write I
am so abstracted by recollections of
what I have seen that I leave the
letter. For instance at the present
occasion I was writing to you and
going to say something about Arles.
as it is _ and as it was in the
old days of Boccaccio. -
Well instead of continuing the letter
I began to draw on the very paper
the head of a dirty little girl I saw
this afternoon whilst I was painting
a view of the river with a greenish yellow
sky.

This dirty "mudlark" I thought
yet had a vague florentine sort of figure
like the heads in the Monticelli
pictures. and reasoning and drawing
this wise I worked on the letter

119 **Letter 722**
from Vincent van Gogh
to Theo van Gogh
Arles, on or about Wednesday
21 November 1888
Sower with Setting Sun (JH1628),
letter sketch
Paper, 21 x 27 cm
Van Gogh Museum, Amsterdam
(Vincent van Gogh Foundation),
b604 V/1968

120 **The Sower**
November 1888
Oil on canvas, 32 x 40 cm
Van Gogh Museum, Amsterdam
(Vincent van Gogh Foundation),
s0029 V/1962

Selected references: Faille 1970,
no. 451; New York 1984, cat. 128;
Van Uitert and Hoyle 1987,
pp. 246–47; Amsterdam 1988,
pp. 184–85; Sund 1988B;
Hulsker 1996, no. 1629; Paris
1998, pp. 101–02; Amsterdam
2000, pp. 198–9; Chicago 2001,
p. 217; Amsterdam 2003, p. 190

Jean-François Millet (1814–1875), the painter of French peasant life, was an important example to Van Gogh throughout his regrettably short career as an artist. Van Gogh made several copies (the last in 1890) of Millet's *Sower* of 1850 (fig. 5), an emblematic rendering of a sower at sunset. In the summer of 1888, Van Gogh made his own variant of the subject (Kröller-Müller Museum, Otterlo, F422), but he did not find it entirely satisfactory. In November of that year he took up the theme again for a large *tableau* (Foundation E. G. Bührle, Zürich, F450), of which this smaller painting is the second version. Vincent described the first version in a letter to Theo, and added a sketch for good measure: 'Here's a croquis of the latest canvas I'm working on, another sower. Immense lemon yellow disc for the sun. Green-yellow sky with pink clouds. The field is violet, the sower and the tree Prussian Blue' (722; cat. 119). In this period Van Gogh was living at Arles and working closely with Paul Gauguin, whose *Vision of the Sermon* (National Galleries of Scotland, Edinburgh) undoubtedly inspired the diagonally placed tree trunk that is given such prominence here. Then again, Japanese prints from Van Gogh's collection could easily have served as examples too. The pollarded tree in all its autumnal glory contrasts sharply with the new life being scattered by the sower, whose labour is sanctified by the sun floating behind him like a halo. In this smaller version Van Gogh depicted the tree proportionately thicker and simplified the colours somewhat, but both works are worthy counterparts to Millet's revered example. TM

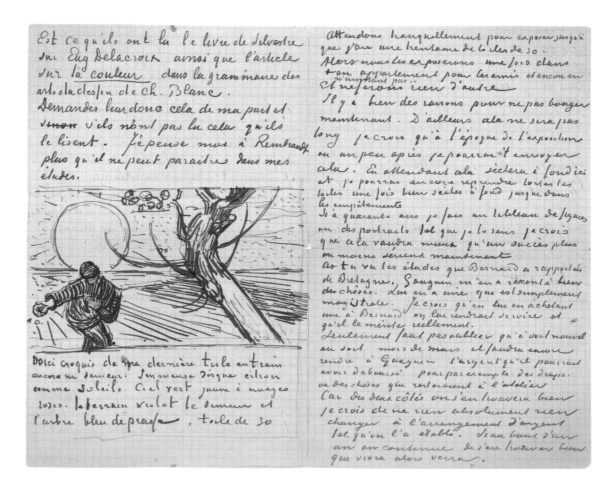

121 Wheat Fields with Reaper

July 1890
Oil on canvas, 73.6 x 93 cm
Lent by the Toledo Museum of
Art. Purchased with funds from
the Libbey Endowment, Gift of
Edward Drummond Libbey,
1935.4

Selected references: Faille 1970,
no. 559; Gerstein 1989, no. 40;
Dorn and Feilchenfeldt 1993,
p. 285; Nichols, Gerstein,
Swenson, Phillips and Berkowitz
1995, pp. 142–43; Hulsker 1996,
no. 1479; Bremen 2002, cat. 48;
Ten Berge, Meedendorp, Vergeest
and Verhoogt 2003, p. 364;
Stockholm 2004, pp. 143–46

Van Gogh's last summer, spent in Auvers,
resulted in scores of paintings featuring
wheat fields in various stages of
cultivation, but only one of them – the
present painting – shows a reaper at work.
For this reason, and owing to the fact that
it is not mentioned in the correspondence,
Wheat Fields with Reaper was, until two
decades ago, thought to be a harvest scene
painted in Arles. The village in the distance
is not Auvers-sur-Oise, but the landscape
is typical of the countryside around Auvers,
even if the exact location cannot be
pinpointed. Stylistically, this work fits in
with Van Gogh's late landscapes, although
it displays a somewhat more compact
manner than his other Auvers work. The
figure of the reaper – particularly his odd
physique, not unlike a jumping jack –
strongly recalls the peculiar 'elastic'
figures that Van Gogh began to draw
towards the end of his stay at Saint-Rémy.
Various drawings of agricultural labourers
from Van Gogh's Auvers period have
survived, including reapers wielding,
remarkably enough, scythes rather than
the sickles seen in *Wheat Fields with Reaper*.
One of those drawings, *Peasant with a Scythe*
(Van Gogh Museum, Amsterdam, F1635v),
shows a reaper in a pose similar to that
of the peasant in this painting, who holds
his scythe in a strange, horizontal way.
A second version of *Wheat Fields with Reaper*,
in the possession of the National Museum
in Stockholm since 1914 (F560), is now
generally acknowledged to be a forgery. TM

ART AND LITERATURE

Art and literature are the two subjects that dominate Van Gogh's letters. So completely are they woven into the fabric of his richly associative way of thinking that everything he saw or experienced was coloured by a literary or an artistic reference. As he wrote in a letter to Theo in February 1883: 'Books and reality and art are the same kind of thing for me' (312).

The numerous references we find in Van Gogh's letters demonstrate the stimulus, both intellectual and spiritual, that he derived from art. As he strove to become an artist himself, the works of other artists were of vital importance to him. But well before this Van Gogh had devoured paintings wherever he went, visiting museums in Holland, London and Paris, collecting prints and photographic reproductions and reading avidly about art, urging Theo to do the same. The lives and characters of the artists he admired fascinated him, and he made them his role models and, in a sense, his teachers.

Van Gogh's first real exposure to the world of art came in 1869, when, at the age of sixteen, he joined the international art dealers Goupil & Cie in The Hague. He stayed with the firm until 1876, working successively in their London and Paris branches. At Goupil, Van Gogh had exceptional opportunities to learn about art. The gallery's extensive stock of established conservative artists and its thriving business in reproductive prints and photographs of both modern and old-master paintings enabled him to build up a vast mental archive that was to be a lasting resource.

Early on, his taste for artists of The Hague and Barbizon Schools crystallised in his unbounded admiration for Jean-François Millet (1814–1875), his role model par excellence, whom he described thus in a letter to Theo: 'PÈRE Millet [...] guide in *everything*, for the younger painters' (493). Millet's ability to capture the reality of rural toil and yet invest it with grander truths was an inspiration to Van Gogh. Alfred Sensier's idealising biography of Millet (1881; cat. 160) was a revelation to him, and after reading it in 1882 he came to identify with the peasant painter on a personal level as well. The French Romantic painter Eugène Delacroix (1798–1863), whom Van Gogh admired as a revolutionary artist and for his emotive use of colour, was another hero. He enriched his knowledge by reading Théophile Silvestre's *Eugène Delacroix: documents nouveaux* (1864; cat. 168) and studied Delacroix's colour theories in Charles Blanc's *Les Artistes de mon temps* (1876).

Van Gogh discovered Dutch seventeenth-century art at an early age. Again, his view of these artists was guided by reading, especially the influential *Musées de la Hollande. Amsterdam et La Haye* (1858; cat. 167) in which Théophile Thoré (who wrote under the pseudonym W. Bürger) expressed his ideas about an art for mankind; these were in tune with Van Gogh's own. His enthusiasm was confirmed by a visit to the newly opened Rijksmuseum in Amsterdam in 1885, where he especially revered the portraits and the humanity of Rembrandt, but also admired Ruisdael, Hals and Van Goyen.

Van Gogh demonstrated his enduring reverence for Millet, Delacroix and Rembrandt in 1889 when, in the asylum at Saint-Rémy, he made his own 'translations' into colour of works by these artists (cats 125, 127, 130) from black-and-white prints that Theo had sent him. Now fully in command of the expressive technique and brilliant palette that he had mastered in Arles, he used the prints as raw material with which he could both pay homage to his artistic heroes and create free and highly personal interpretations in which, as he told Theo, 'my brush goes between my fingers as it were a bow on the violin and absolutely for my pleasure' (805).

Literature, like art, was of vital importance to Van Gogh. He had, as he said, 'a more or less irresistible passion for books' (155) and he refers to about 800 books and 150 authors in his letters. Van Gogh read in several languages: in addition to his native Dutch, he was fluent in French and English and could read and quote in German. His eloquence as a letter writer is testament to the extent to which he was steeped in literature.

Literature functioned for Van Gogh in different ways. He read to develop his mind but also to confirm his views, to feed the flame of his ideas rather than to modify his thinking. He used literary sources to support and express his own experience. Frequently he would urge correspondents – Theo, his sister Willemien or his artist friends Van Rappard, Gauguin or Bernard – to read books he had read so that they would understand more clearly his ideas about his work and his life. Reading was also a solace in periods of anguish; books were 'friends' that could alleviate his loneliness.

The pattern of Van Gogh's reading followed the phases of his life. We know little of his appetite for books early on but, as the son of a pastor in the Dutch Reformed church, he grew up in a family where literature mattered and in which the Bible played a central role. The resonant language of the Gospels echoes throughout Van Gogh's own writing. An independent literary taste emerged in 1873 with his discovery of the French historian and philosopher Jules Michelet, especially his *La Mer* (1861; cat. 161). Vincent also compiled scrapbooks of French and German Romantic poetry for Theo and for his friends.

In his intensely religious phase that began in London in 1873 and continued until 1879, Van Gogh's letters are filled with quotations from the Bible and religious literature, including Thomas à Kempis's *The Imitation of Christ* (1441) and especially John Bunyan's *A Pilgrim's Progress* (1678; cat. 172). In the 1870s Van Gogh read the Scottish philosopher Thomas Carlyle and the novels of George Eliot (cat. 169) and Charles Dickens (cat. 165), which he esteemed for their realism and socially engaged compassion, qualities that explain his fervent admiration of Harriet Beecher Stowe's best-selling anti-slavery novel *Uncle Tom's Cabin* (1852; cat. 162).

Around 1880 a distinct shift occurred in Van Gogh's reading, as religion was replaced by the fervour of his artistic vocation. In the lively cultural climate of The Hague, where he moved in 1882, he turned away from Christian writing and discovered contemporary French literature, particularly the Naturalist writers. *Still-life with Bible* from October 1885 (cat. 122) symbolises this transition: the weighty, leather-bound family Bible is juxtaposed with a recently published yellow paperback novel in French, Emile Zola's *La Joie de vivre* (1884). Van Gogh read all Zola's novels as soon as they came off the press. His vivid word pictures and unadorned portrayals of working-class life accorded with Van Gogh's belief in depicting directly what he saw.

In Paris in 1886–88 Van Gogh had ample opportunity to discover modern French writers. 'On the contrary, if one wants truth, life as it is, De Goncourt, for example, in Germinie Lacerteux, La fille Elisa, Zola in La joie de vivre and L'assommoir and so many other masterpieces paint life as we feel it ourselves and thus satisfy that need which we have, that people tell us the truth' (574), he wrote to Willemien in October 1887. *Romans Parisiens (Les Livres Jaunes)* (cat. 123), a still-life composed entirely of books, is a colourful tribute to the many French novels that Van Gogh must have read at this time.

Van Gogh's reading habits did not change radically after his move to Provence in February 1888. In his last years he used literature as a consolation but also as an entertainment. In Arles, his letters refer to Balzac, Flaubert and Maupassant among others, but a new interest is apparent in more light-hearted writing that offered a distraction from his mental turmoil. Van Gogh was much taken with the Provençal writer Alphonse Daudet's fanciful novels *Tartarin de Tarascon* (1872; cat. 164) and *Tartarin sur les Alpes* (1885) as well as Pierre Loti's exotic tales of adventure such as *Pêcheur d'Islande* (1886) and *Madame Chrysanthème* (1888; cat. 163).

In the last phase of his life at Saint-Rémy and Auvers (May 1889 to July 1890), as Van Gogh was increasingly plagued by mental illness, he found reassurance in the books he had read in his youth, such as *Uncle Tom's Cabin* and Dickens. He planned to reread all of Balzac and tackled Shakespeare's history plays, which he found 'so alive that one thinks one knows them and sees it' (784). Although literature all but disappears from the letters in the last year of Van Gogh's life, this is not necessarily an indication that he read less. Both art and literature were so deeply embedded in Van Gogh's way of thinking that it is likely that they shaped his view of the world until the end of his life.

122 Still-life with Bible

October 1885
Oil on canvas, 65.7 x 78.5 cm
Signed lower left: *Vincent*
Van Gogh Museum, Amsterdam
(Vincent van Gogh Foundation),
s8 V/1962

Selected references: Faille 1970,
no. 117; Amsterdam 1990,
cat. 10, pp. 54–55; Greer 1997;
Van Tilborgh and Vellekoop 1999,
pp. 218–25

Religion was an important theme in Van Gogh's life and work. As the son of a clergyman, he had had long discussions with his father about the meaning of faith and the role of the church. This large Bible, opened to the Book of Isaiah (ISAIE) 53, has sometimes been interpreted as Van Gogh's view of the significance of this piece of scripture for his own times. The chapter in question predicts the coming of the suffering Christ, with whom Van Gogh identified in the years of his religious mania (1876–78). In the Borinage, a region of Belgium, after all, he had tried to base his life on Christ's example: sacrificing himself and comforting others. The Bible represents the old values from which Van Gogh distanced himself when he finally resolved to pursue a career in art. Modern times are symbolised here by Emile Zola's naturalist novel *La Joie de vivre* (1884).

Even though the symbolic meaning of both books was immensely important to Van Gogh, he does not mention this at all in his letters. For him, the still-life was, above all, the prize for having slaved for months on end to master the art of modelling in various colours. As he wrote to Theo at the end of October 1885: 'I'm sending you a still-life of an open, hence an off-white Bible, bound in leather, against a black background with a yellow-brown foreground, with an additional note of lemon yellow. I painted this *in one go*, in a single day. This to show you that [...] these days it really comes quite readily to me to paint a given object, whatever the shape or colour may be, without hesitation' (537). AV

**123 Romans Parisiens
(Les Livres Jaunes)**
November–December 1887
Oil on canvas, 73.5 x 93 cm
Private collection

Selected references: Faille 1970,
no. 359; Feilchenfeldt 1988, p. 90;
Paris 1988, cat. 56; Amsterdam
1990, cat. 29; Essen 1990, cat. 17;
Hendriks and Van Tilborgh
forthcoming

Reading was extremely important to Van Gogh, as is evident from the frequent references in his letters to contemporary literature. He particularly admired the French naturalists, such as Emile Zola and the De Goncourt brothers: 'if one wants truth, life as it is, De Goncourt, for example, in Germinie Lacerteux, La fille Elisa, Zola in La joie de vivre and L'assommoir and so many other masterpieces paint life as we feel it ourselves and thus satisfy that need which we have, that people tell us the truth' (574).

Theo submitted this still-life to the exhibition of the Indépendents held in Paris in the spring of 1888. Vincent was happy about this choice, as emerges from a letter of 10 March: 'I think it's a very good idea that you put the books in the Independents' too. This study should be given the title: "*Parisian novels*"' (584). It is generally maintained that this title refers to Jean Richepin's *Braves Gens. Roman Parisien*. That is quite possible, although in those days *Roman Parisien* was a fairly common subtitle for books of this kind.

Not only the title of the painting but also the books' yellow covers make it clear that these are contemporary French novels, published in Van Gogh's time. The painting – of which a slightly smaller version, made as a preparatory study, is preserved in the Van Gogh Museum, Amsterdam (F358) – can also be seen as a homage to naturalist literature. Unlike the earlier, more spontaneous study, the present work is painted in Neo-Impressionist style. In this larger version, moreover, Van Gogh painted the covers of the books with more care and added a glass of roses.

Later on Van Gogh compared the Paris still-life with his painting *The Bedroom* (fig. 16): 'This bedroom is something like that still life of French novels with yellow, pink, green covers, you'll recall. But I believe that the execution is simpler and more virile' (707). RZ

124 Célestin François Nanteuil-
Leboeuf (1813–1873), after
Eugène Delacroix (1798–1863)
Pietà
c. 1850
Lithograph, 21.7 x 16.7 cm
Van Gogh Museum, Amsterdam
(Vincent van Gogh Foundation),
t622 V/1962

125 **Pietà (after Delacroix)**
September 1889
Oil on canvas, 42 x 34 cm
Inscribed and signed lower right:
*d'après Eug Delacroix | a apartenu à |
Diaz | Vincent*
Vatican Museums, Vatican City,
23698

Selected references: Faille 1970,
no. 757; Feilchenfeldt 1988;
Hammacher 1992, pp. 175–78;
Stolwijk and Veenenbos 2002,
p. 20

Van Gogh once wrote to his friend Bernard, 'Projects so often fall through, and the best calculations you make; while by taking advantage of chance, and working from day to day without bias, you do a whole lot of unforeseen things' (684). This small painted sketch demonstrates nicely how Van Gogh's work sometimes came about by chance. He painted it because his lithograph of Delacroix's *Pietà* (one of the prints decorating the walls of his studio; cat. 124) and some other sheets fell into oil and paint and were damaged, as he told Theo: 'I was sad about it – then in the meantime I occupied myself painting it, and you'll see it one day, on a no. 5 or 6 canvas I've made a copy of it which I think has feeling' (801).

He intended to send the sketch to his sister Willemien, to give her 'an idea of what Delacroix is', but he stressed that 'this little copy of course has no value from any point of view' (804). After the first version, he made an even larger painting that is now part of the collection of the Van Gogh Museum, Amsterdam (F630).

In a letter of 20 September Van Gogh described his working method: 'I place the black-and-white by Delacroix or Millet or after them in front of me as a subject. And then I improvise colour on it but, being me, not completely of course, but seeking memories of their paintings – but the memory, the vague consonance of colours that are in the same sentiment, if not right – that's my own interpretation' (805). RZ

Fig. 29 Eugène Delacroix (1798–1863), **Pietà**, 1850.
Oil on canvas, 35 x 27 cm. The National Museum of Art,
Architecture and Design, Oslo, NG.M.01179

126 Adrien Lavieille (1818–1862), after
Jean-François Millet (1814–1875)
The Evening
from *L'Illustration*, 61,
8 March 1873, p. 168
Wood engraving, 14.9 x 22 cm
Van Gogh Museum, Amsterdam
(Vincent van Gogh Foundation),
t138 V/1962

127 **Evening: The Watch**
October 1889
Oil on canvas, 74.5 x 93.5 cm
Van Gogh Museum, Amsterdam
(Vincent van Gogh Foundation),
s147 V/1962

Selected references: Faille 1970,
no. 647; Van Uitert and Hoyle
1987, cat. 82; Amsterdam 1988,
cat. 37; Tokyo 1993, cat. 12;
New York 2008, p. 101

After a severe attack of his illness that lasted more than a month, Van Gogh began to paint again at the beginning of September 1889. Despite the lack of models, he could devote himself to figure studies by making paintings after reproductions, such as Adrien Lavieille's wood engraving (cat. 126) after *Winter Evening* by Jean-François Millet (fig. 30). 'Good – since I'm above all ill at present, I'm trying to do something to console myself, for my own pleasure,' wrote Van Gogh on about 20 September: 'I place the black-and-white by Delacroix or Millet or after them in front of me as a subject. And then I improvise colour on it but, being me, not completely of course, but seeking memories of their paintings – but the memory, the vague consonance of colours that are in the same sentiment, if not right – that's my own interpretation' (805).

On 3 November 1889 Vincent described the finished work to Theo: 'The evening is in a range of violets and soft lilacs, with light from the lamp pale citron, then the orange glow of the fire and the man in red ochre' (816). In both this letter and a later one written in January 1890, Van Gogh emphasised that these were not just mere copies: 'It is rather translating into another language, the one of colours, the impressions of chiaroscuro and white and black' (839).

Vincent was delighted that Theo was so receptive to his translations into colour: 'You know, one of the things I like best is the Evening after Millet. Copied like that it's no longer a copy. There's a tone in it and everything is so harmonious. It's really very successful' (838). RZ

Fig. 30 Jean-François Millet (1814–1875), **Winter Evening**, 1867.
Pastel and black conté crayon on grey-brown wove paper, 43.8 x 54 cm.
Museum of Fine Arts, Boston, 17.1520. Gift of Quincy Adams Shaw
through Quincy Adams Shaw Jr, and Mrs Marian Shaw Haughton, 1917

In a letter written on 1 May 1890 Vincent thanked Theo for the reproductions of etchings that Theo had sent him during his illness: 'I read your kind letters, then the letters from home as well, and that did me an enormous amount of good in giving me back a little energy, or rather the desire to climb back up again from the dejected state I'm in. I thank you very much for the etchings – you've chosen some of the very ones that I've already liked for a long time.' One of these was *The Raising of Lazarus* after an etching by Van Gogh's great exemplar Rembrandt (cat. 128). It reminded Van Gogh of what he had read about it in 1877 in Charles Blanc's *L'Œuvre complet de Rembrandt*: 'But the Lazarus! Early this morning I looked at it and I remembered not only what Charles Blanc says of it, but indeed even that he doesn't say everything about it' (865).

It is likely that Van Gogh, now that he was on the mend after such a difficult period, felt drawn to the subject because of its parallels with his own situation.

As his starting point for the painting (cat. 130), Van Gogh took the part of the print that shows the resurrection of Lazarus. On about 2 May he sent Theo a letter with a sketch: 'Opposite this I've scribbled a croquis after a painting I've done of three figures which are in the background of the Lazarus etching. The dead man and his two sisters. The cave and the corpse are violet, yellow, white. The woman who is taking the handkerchief from the resurrected man's face has a green dress and orange hair, the other has black hair and a striped garment. Green and pink. Behind a countryside, blue hills, a yellow rising sun. The combination of colours would thus itself speak of the same thing expressed by the chiaroscuro of the etching' (866; cat. 129).

Like the colourful interpretations Van Gogh made in September–October 1889 of wood engravings after Millet, *The Raising of Lazarus* is not a literal copy, but rather a translation into colour. RZ

Mon cher Theo, encore une fois je t'ecris pour dire
que la santé continue à aller bien, pourtant
je me sens un peu éreinté par cette longue crise.
et j'ose croire que le changement projeté
me rafraichira davantage les idées
je crois que le mieux sera que j'aille
moi même voir ce médecin à la campagne
le plus tôt possible ; alors on pourra bientôt
décider si c'est chez lui ou provisoirement
à l'auberge que j'irai loger ; et ainsi on
évitera un séjour trop prolongé à Paris, chose
que je redouterais.

Arles Avril 1890

130 **The Raising of Lazarus
     (after Rembrandt)**
     May 1890
     Oil on paper on canvas,
     50 x 65 cm
     Van Gogh Museum, Amsterdam
     (Vincent van Gogh Foundation),
     s169 V/1962

     Selected references: Faille 1970,
     no. 677; Van Uitert and Hoyle
     1987, cat. 87; Amsterdam 1990,
     pp. 126–30; Hecht 2006, pp. 52–54

THE SACRIFICE FOR ART

The last fifteen months of Van Gogh's life were characterised by disappointment and despair. During his hospitalisation in the psychiatric clinic Saint-Paul-de-Mausole from May 1889 to May 1890, when he produced works that are among his best and most famous, the tenor of his letters is one of lost ideals and thwarted ambitions. Even the fact that a small circle had begun to take notice of his work – resulting in a laudatory article in the *Mercure de France* and an invitation to exhibit work at Les XX, the leading artists' circle in Brussels – did nothing to alleviate Van Gogh's feeling that so far he had failed to help art move forward and that his recurring mental and physical ailments would prevent him from doing so in the future.

Van Gogh's own view of his situation after having himself admitted to the asylum emerges from one of the first letters he wrote to Theo from Saint-Rémy: 'My hope would be that at the end of a year I'll know better than now what I can do and what I want. Then, little by little, an idea will come to me for beginning again' (776). About ten days later he wrote: 'I still have remorse, and enormously when I think of my work, so little in harmony with what I'd have wished to do. I hope that in the long run it will make me do better things, but we aren't there yet' (777). This reads like a hesitant promise: he had hit rock bottom and first needed to discover what he still had in him. Characteristic of this wariness is his abandonment of the experimentation in extreme colour combinations that had drained his spirit: 'I feel tempted to begin again with the simpler colours, the ochres for example' (779). And sure enough, we see in the work done in Saint-Rémy a more muted, more naturalistic palette, no longer the high-pitched contrasts of his Arles canvases.

In Saint-Rémy Van Gogh had to rely for the most part on one type of motif: nature and the landscape. This had much to do with his situation, since at first the doctor in attendance, Théophile Peyron, would not permit him to leave the grounds of the asylum. Time and again Van Gogh suffered relapses that resulted in temporary restrictions on his freedom of movement. Not surprisingly, the works made in the first months invariably show cropped views of the walled grounds of the asylum (cats 142, 143), or the bit of landscape that could be glimpsed from his window (cat. 134).

On the one hand, he must have found some comfort in the close-ups of the vegetation he drew and painted, and in the characteristic pine trees. Pondering and depicting nature at close quarters was calming, as he explained to his sister Wil a month after his arrival at Saint-Paul-de-Mausole. He wrote to her about the excitement that overcame him when reading 'dramatic books' such as Shakespeare's 'kings series': 'I myself, returning from this reading, am always obliged to go and gaze at a blade of grass, a pine-tree branch, an ear of wheat, to calm myself. So if you want to do as artists do, gaze upon the white and red poppies with the bluish leaves, with those buds raising themselves up on stems with gracious curves. The hours of trouble and battle will assuredly come and find us without our going to look for them' (785). Constantly having recourse to nature, even out of sheer necessity, was a counterpoise to the constant recurrence of his illness.

On the other hand, the many paintings and drawings of the walled field visible from Van Gogh's room are painful reminders of the fact that he was literally and figuratively a prisoner; it was always the same jagged wall that closed off his living space, providing a stark contrast with the hills in the distance and the expanse of sky above.

Although Van Gogh's situation and perspective had changed drastically, there was also, in an artistic sense, some measure of continuity. Stylistically, he moved ahead in the first months from the point where he had stopped in Arles. Such landscapes as *Mountains at Saint-Rémy* (cat. 137) and *The Olive Trees* (cat. 135), dating from June and July 1889, show similar areas of colour with clear outlines. Van Gogh, however, who thought that expressing the 'character' of the landscape was more important than portraying it realistically, made deliberate use of such 'exaggerations' (805).

The stylisation of forms reached a high point in *The Starry Night* (Museum of Modern Art, New York, F612), with its highly overstated enlargement of the luminous nocturnal firmament, which elicited from Theo the following cautious criticism: 'I feel that the search for style takes away the real sentiment of things. In Gauguin's last consignment there are the same preoccupations as with you, but with him there are a lot more memories of the Japanese, the Egyptians etc. As for me, I prefer to see a local Breton woman than a Breton woman with the gestures of a Japanese woman, but in art there are no limits, so it's quite permissible to do as one sees it' (813). The work of the two friends still had much in common, but here it becomes obvious that they had gone their separate ways. Their artistic estrangement certainly gave no comfort to Van Gogh. Later he was dismissive of his own experiments with abstraction, and called his depiction of stars that were 'too big' (as in *The Starry Night*) a 'new setback' (822).

Meanwhile Van Gogh had gone from the sunflower to the cypress as his favourite picturesque motif (see cats 132, 133). The way he explains his preference is typical: 'there's a lack of news to write to you, for the days are all the same, as for ideas I have no others except to think that a wheat field or a cypress are well worth the effort of looking at them from close at hand, and so on [...] The cypresses still preoccupy me, I'd like to do something with them like the canvases of the sunflowers because it astonishes me that no one has yet done them as I see them. It's beautiful as regards lines and proportions, like an Egyptian obelisk. And the green has such a distinguished quality. It's the *dark* patch in a sun-drenched landscape, but it's one of the most interesting dark notes, the most difficult to hit off exactly that I can imagine. Now they must be seen here against the blue, *in* the blue, rather. To do nature here, as everywhere, one must really be here for a long time' (783). Thus the cypress was both a painterly challenge and a motif Van Gogh could use to distinguish himself from other artists – something he had succeeded in doing with his sunflowers.

In the course of the summer of 1889 Van Gogh used not only areas of colour but also – and with increasing frequency – pronounced, individual brush strokes. Perhaps his study of cypresses had prompted him to do this, since masses of rythmical, descriptive brush strokes are necessary to suggest the twisting of the branches. In any case, it is beyond dispute that in Saint-Rémy Van Gogh the painter achieved complete mastery of brush, paint and canvas, and attained the ultimate freedom and variation in his touch.

In this period figure pieces and portraits account for little of his output. The translations into colour of black-and-white prints (sent by Theo) after the work of much-admired artists such as Millet, Delacroix, Rembrandt and Daumier are the most important of the figurative works (see cats 125, 127, 130), although of course these figures were not portrayed from life. In the spring of 1890, however, Van Gogh made quite a few sketches on paper of peasant types, partly in preparation for a new version of *The Potato Eaters* (fig. 1). The letters reveal that he was also contemplating new versions of two other important works from this period, *The Cottage* (F83) and *The Old Tower* (F84): 'if you like I'll redo the old tower at Nuenen and the cottage. I think that if you still have them I could now make something better of them from memory' (863). Homesick for the North, he thought about going back to such motifs – 'souvenirs du nord' (863), as he called them – which had been his main focus at Nuenen.

Even though he continued to suffer relapses, Van Gogh left Saint-Rémy in May 1890. He travelled north and – under the watchful eye of the homoeopathic doctor and art lover Paul Gachet, a specialist in 'melancholy' – he took up residence at an inn in Auvers-sur-Oise, some 18 miles north of Paris. Van Gogh's mood was somewhat ambivalent, as emerges from an unsent outpouring written on 24 May, four days after his arrival in the rural village: 'I feel – a failure – that's it as regards me – I feel that that's the fate I'm accepting. And which won't change any more. But one more reason, *setting aside all ambition*, we can live together for years without ruining ourselves on either side' (RM20). It is something of a paradox that a man who claimed to have given up his ambitions could keep up a level of activity that allowed him to paint an average of more than one painting a day for seventy days. It is perhaps even more paradoxical that his last landscapes in particular radiate a calm grandeur alternating with an unrest bordering on menace. Everything, however, is masterfully controlled: the seeming looseness and rich variation of the brushwork no less than the balanced and at times monumental compositions. Van Gogh's enthusiasm for his work was impressive, as were the results. Painting was life – until that also failed.

131 **Letter 783**

from Vincent van Gogh
to Theo van Gogh
Saint-Rémy-de-Provence,
Tuesday 25 June 1889
Cypresses (JH1750),
letter sketch
Paper, 21 x 27 cm
Van Gogh Museum, Amsterdam
(Vincent van Gogh Foundation),
b644 V/1962

When Van Gogh wrote to his brother on 2 July 1889 to say that he intended to send him around ten drawings of his last paintings, he described them as 'all after canvases on the go' (784). This means that the canvases in question had not yet acquired their final appearance. Recently Susan Stein (Houston 2007) even substantiated that the painting of *Cypresses* in this series (cat. 133) actually originated in interaction with the pen-and-ink drawing (cat. 132). Van Gogh began in late June to work on two canvases with cypresses in a large vertical format, the no. 30. 'I think that of the two canvases of cypresses, the one I'm making the croquis of will be the best,' he wrote to Theo on 25 June, and thanks to that sketch (cat. 131) it is clear that he had greater expectations for the canvas from the Metropolitan (the other is *Cypresses with Two Women*, Kröller-Müller Museum, Otterlo, F620). He also wrote: 'I'll send you drawings of them, with two other drawings that I've also done. That will keep me busy for the next few days' (783). By then he evidently had four drawings finished, or nearly finished, including two with cypresses (the present sheet and F1524 at the Art Institute of Chicago).

Although there were cypresses aplenty in Arles, they did not become an important subject for Van Gogh until his stay in Saint-Rémy, as he wrote in the same letter of 25 June: 'The cypresses still preoccupy me [...] It's beautiful as regards lines and proportions, like an Egyptian obelisk. And the green has such a distinguished quality. It's the *dark* patch in a sun-drenched landscape.' He conceived the plan to make a series of them, as he had done earlier with sunflowers, 'because it astonishes me that no one has yet done them as I see them'. Together with the olive groves that he likewise discovered in Saint-Rémy, the cypresses became an important new Provençal subject for Van Gogh.

In the pen-and-ink drawing, Van Gogh used a wide reed pen to gather together the fitful cypress branches into elegant 'quotation marks' that lend the trees a decorative rhythm and capture the feel of a windy day. The less dense character of the drawing technique makes these cypresses seem airier than those in the painting. Using thinner pens Van Gogh drew the undulating clouds, which have lost some of their contrast owing to the faded ink. In proportion the crescent moon is considerably larger than in the painting and placed more in the corner. X-radiographs reveal that Van Gogh later changed the position of the sickle on the canvas, probably after he had sent the drawing to his brother.

Theo was decidedly unenthusiastic about the series of pen-and-ink drawings, and told Vincent so on 16 July: 'The latest drawings look like they've been done in a fury and are a little more distanced from nature. When I see one of these subjects in a painting I'll understand them more' (792). Disappointment followed, for when Vincent finally sent him the paintings, he found some passages too stylised. This was one of the reasons why Van Gogh used less paint for a time and tempered his undulating lines to some extent. *Cypresses* and *Cypresses with Two Women* are among his most heavily impasted works. Mindful of Adolphe Monticelli, he had used a specific technique that was not entirely without risk: 'I've worked their foregrounds with thick impastos of white lead which gives firmness to the ground. I believe that Monticellis were very often prepared in this way. One then places other colours on top. But I don't know if the canvases are strong enough for this work' (783). TM

Enfin il en convient qu'il trouve ~~une certaine~~ des consolations dans la compagnie de sa femme ce que est très bien vu mais enfin pour mon propre usage il ne m'apprend absolument rien sur le sens de la vie dans n'importe quel sens. De mon côté je pourrais le trouver un peu blasé et m'étonner de ce qu'il ait fait imprimer de ces jours ci un livre comme cela et qu'il vende cela à raison de fl 3.50.

Enfin je préfère alphonse Karr sauterelle Droz parceque c'est un peu plus vivant encore que ceci. Il est vrai que je suis peut être ingrat n'appréciant même pas l'abbé constantin et autres productions littéraires qui illuminent le doux règne du naïf Carnot.

Il paraît que ce livre a fait grande impression sur nos bonnes soeurs et Wil m'en avait du moins parlé mais les bonnes femmes et les livres cela fait deux.

J'ai relu avec bien du plaisir Zadig ou la destinée de Voltaire C'est comme Candide Là au moins le puissant auteur fait entrevoir qu'il y reste une possibilité que la vie ait un sens quoique on convient dans la conversation que les choses de ce monde n'allaient pas toujours au gré des plus sages.

Pour moi je ne sais que désirer travailler ici ou ailleurs me paraît d'abord à peu près la même chose et étant ici y rester le plus simple

Seulement des nouvelles à l'écrire cela manque car les jours sont tous les mêmes des idées je n'en ai pas d'autres que de penser qu'un champ de blé ou un cyprès valent bien la peine de les regarder de près et ainsi de suite

J'ai un champ de blé très jaune et très clair peutêtre la toile la plus claire que j'aie faite

Les cyprès me préoccupent toujours je voudrais en faire une chose comme les toiles des tournesols parceque cela m'étonne qu'on ne les ait pas encore fait comme je les vois

C'est beau comme lignes et comme proportions comme une obelisque egyptienne.

Et le vert est d'une qualité si distinguée

c'est la tâche noire dans un paysage ensoleillé mais elle est une des notes noires les plus intéressantes les plus difficiles à taper juste que je puisse imaginer

Or il faut les voir ici contre le bleu dans le bleu pour mieux dire

Pour faire la nature ici comme partout il faut bien y être longtemps.

Aussi un montchenard ne me donne pas la note vraie et intime car la lumière est mystérieuse et monticelli et Delacroix sentaient cela. Alors Pissarro en parlait très bien dans le temps et je suis encore bien loin de pouvoir faire comme il disait qu'il le faudrait

Tu me feras naturellement plaisir en m'envoyant les couleurs si c'est possible bientôt mais fais surtout là dedans comme tu peux dans que cela t'éreinte trop.

Ainsi si tu préfères me l'envoyer en deux fois cela est bon aussi

Je crois que des deux toiles de cyprès celle dont je fais le croquis sera la meilleure. Les arbres y sont très grands et massifs. L'avant plan très bas des ronces et broussailles. Derrière des collines violettes un ciel vert et rose avec un croissant de lune. L'avant plan surtout est très empâté des touffes de ronces ~~jaunes~~ à reflets jaunes violets verts. Je t'en enverrai des dessins avec deux autres dessins que j'ai encore fait.

132 **Cypresses**
June 1889
Reed pen, graphite, quill and
brown and black ink on wove
paper, 62.3 x 41.7 cm
Brooklyn Museum, New York.
Frank L. Babbott Fund and the
A. Augustus Healy Fund, 38.123

Selected references: Faille 1970,
no. 1525; New York 1986, cat. 18;
Otterlo 1990, cat. 231; Heenk
1995, p. 186; Hulsker 1996,
no. 1747; Amsterdam 2005 B,
cat. 108

133 **Cypresses**
June 1889
Oil on canvas, 93.3 x 74 cm
Lent by the Metropolitan Museum
of Art, New York. Rogers Fund,
1949 (49.30)

Selected references: Faille 1970,
no. 613; New York 1986, cat. 15;
Amsterdam 1990, cat. 90; Jirat-
Wasiutynski 1993; Hulsker 1996,
no. 1746; Chicago 2001, cat. 107;
Ten Berge, Meedendorp, Vergeest
and Verhoogt 2003, pp. 298–99;
Amsterdam 2005 B, cat. 109;
Houston 2007, cat. 158

134 Wheat Field with White Cloud (Landscape from Saint-Rémy)

June 1889
Oil on canvas, 70.5 x 88.5 cm
Ny Carlsberg Glyptotek,
Copenhagen, SMK 1840

Selected references: Faille 1970, no. 611; Amsterdam 1990, cat. 85; Hulsker 1996, no. 1723; Paris 1996, cat. 42; Bremen 2002, cat. 17; Ten Berge, Meedendorp, Vergeest and Verhoogt 2003, pp. 289, 290

From his room in the asylum at Saint-Rémy, Van Gogh looked out over an enclosed wheat field, which he glowingly described as 'a perspective in the manner of Van Goyen, above which in the morning I see the sun rise in its glory' (776, 23 May 1889). Van Gogh depicted this rewarding subject in several paintings and drawings, of which *Wheat Field with White Cloud (Landscape from Saint-Rémy)* was one of the first (see also cat. 138). He described it to Theo in a letter of 9 June: 'In the foreground a field of wheat, ravaged and knocked to the ground after a storm. A boundary wall and beyond, grey foliage of a few olive trees, huts and hills. Finally, at the top of the painting a large white and grey cloud swamped by the azure. It's a landscape of extreme simplicity – in terms of coloration as well. It would be suitable as a pendant to that study of the bedroom that's damaged' (779). By this he meant *The Bedroom* (fig. 16), a painting in which he had likewise sought to express simplicity and, above all, peace and quiet. As in nearly all the other views of the enclosed field, Les Alpilles are clearly visible on the right. Van Gogh's vision of the scene forced him to pull these mountains closer into the picture, since in reality they are more to the side of the asylum. Only in the drawing *Enclosed Wheat Field with Sun and Cloud* (Kröller-Müller Museum, Otterlo, F1728), made slightly earlier, and to some extent also in *Enclosed Field with Rising Sun* (cat. 140), is the focus on a much vaster horizon, which does more justice to the Van Goyenesque perspective so admired by the artist. TM

135 The Olive Trees

June–July 1889
Oil on canvas, 72.6 x 91.4 cm
The Museum of Modern Art,
New York. Mrs John Hay
Whitney Bequest, 1998, 581.1998

Selected references: Graetz 1963,
pp. 184–85; Faille 1970, no. 712;
Rewald 1978, pp. 312, 321–22;
Washington 1983, cat. 24;
New York 1986, cat. 13;
Amsterdam 1990, cat. 92;
Hulsker 1996, no. 1740; Ten
Berge, Meedendorp, Vergeest
and Verhoogt 2003, pp. 398–99;
Elderfield 2004, pp. 67, 83

Early in June 1889, when Van Gogh received a new shipment of paint, brushes and canvas from Theo and was given permission by the doctor in Saint-Rémy to work outside the walls of the 'maison de santé' Saint-Paul-de-Mausole, he set out at once to explore his immediate surroundings, focusing on two typically Provençal subjects that he had never before considered as independent themes: cypresses and olive trees. *The Olive Trees*, one of his earliest depictions of an olive grove, is most probably the work he mentioned in a letter to Theo of c. 18 June: 'At last I have a landscape with olive trees, and also a new study of a starry sky' (782). The latter is a reference to *The Starry Night* (Museum of Modern Art, New York, F612). In both works the stylisation of line has been carried to great lengths, creating an undulating graphic pattern with clear contours. Van Gogh felt that this manner of working – which he later compared to the curling lines of wood engravings – was a way of maintaining his ties with the artistic ideas of Gauguin and Bernard. In the same letter he thus went on to say: 'Although I haven't seen the latest canvases either by Gauguin or Bernard, I'm fairly sure that these two studies I speak of are comparable in sentiment. When you've seen these two studies for a while [...] I'll perhaps be able to give you, better than in words, an idea of the things Gauguin, Bernard and I sometimes chatted about and that preoccupied us.' TM

136 Olive Trees with Les Alpilles in the Background

Late June – early July 1889
Pencil, reed pen, quill and ink
on wove paper, 47.1 x 62.4 cm
Private collection

Selected references: Faille 1970, no. 1544; New York 1986, p. 109; Otterlo 1990, cat. 235; Hulsker 1996, no. 1741; Vellekoop and Zwikker 2007, pp. 241, 242

'So that you may have an idea of what I have on the go I'm sending you ten or so drawings today, all after canvases on the go,' Vincent wrote on 2 July 1889 to Theo (784). Among them was this drawing, in which he used both pen and reed pen to translate the swirling brush strokes of *The Olive Trees* (cat. 135) into equally dashing lines and stripes of ink. Every one of these sheets testifies to the virtuosity he had meanwhile acquired in drawing with the pen (see also cat. 132), even though the 'legibility' of these drawings has been impaired by the fading of the ink: originally the sheet would have appeared more elaborate, particularly the sky and middle passages.

Remarkably, Van Gogh was not entirely happy with the series, as emerges from the same letter: 'The drawings appear to me to have little colour this time, and this is very probably due to the over-smooth paper.' Van Gogh, who preferred to work on laid paper, used a smooth wove paper for these sheets. By 'little colour' he did not, in fact, mean actual colour in the drawings. Since as early as his Hague period, he had aimed to suggest colour in his drawings by means of black and white contrasts. TM

137 Mountains at Saint-Rémy

July 1889

Oil on canvas, 71.8 x 90.8 cm

Solomon R. Guggenheim
Museum, New York.
Thannhauser Collection,
Gift of Justin K. Thannhauser,
1978, 78.2514.24

Selected references: Faille 1970,
no. 622; New York 1986, cat. 20;
Krens 1992, pp. 22, 184–85;
Hulsker 1996, no. 1766; Martigny
2000, pp. 91, 97, 116; Van der
Veen 2009, pp. 221–23

Of the more stylised and sometimes very heavily impasted works that Van Gogh produced in June and July 1889, this view of Les Alpilles, the chain of mountains near the asylum, remained one of his favourites. 'People will tell me that mountains aren't like that,' he wrote to Theo on *c.* 20 September, 'and that there are black contours as wide as a finger. But anyway it seemed to me that it expressed the passage in Rod's book – one of the very rare passages of his in which I find something good – on a lost land of dark mountains in which one noticed the darkish huts of goatherds, where sunflowers bloomed' (805). The novel in question by Edouard Rod, *Le Sens de la vie*, was a fairly recent publication, which Van Gogh had read at the request of his sister Willemien. That he associated his painting so closely with a passage from a novel he did not actually like shows his sensitivity to evocative descriptions of things that had always moved him, such as simple peasant cottages. In *Mountains at Saint-Rémy*, the cottage seems to play a rather minor role, despite Van Gogh's best intentions, and the sunflowers, although admittedly present, are difficult to recognise as such and look rather odd against the backdrop of olive trees. In any case, the viewer's eye is caught by the impressive mountains, rendered with supple brush strokes, featuring in the middle the crest of 'Les deux trous', also recognisable in the left background of *The Olive Trees* (cat. 135). TM

Wheat Field with Reaper at Sunrise

September 1889
Oil on canvas, 74 x 92 cm
Van Gogh Museum, Amsterdam
(Vincent van Gogh Foundation),
s49 V/1962

Selected references: Faille 1970,
no. 618; Van Uitert and Hoyle
1987, pp. 252–53; Amsterdam
1988, cat. 26; Sund 1988b, p. 674;
Amsterdam 1990, cat. 97; Essen
1990, pp. 148–50; Hulsker 1996,
no. 1773; Bremen 2002, cat. 22;
Ten Berge, Meedendorp, Vergeest
and Verhoogt 2003, pp. 304–5;
Dallas 2007, cat. 28

In the summer of 1885 Van Gogh drew reapers galore at Nuenen and toyed with the idea of making a large painting of the wheat harvest, with a reaper and a woman binding wheatsheaves. Later on, in Arles, we encounter the subject as staffage in several harvest scenes, but it was in Saint-Rémy that Van Gogh first gave the figure of the reaper a clear symbolic meaning, as he had done earlier with the sower (see cats 117, 120). He wrote to Theo: 'A reaper, the study is all yellow, terribly thickly impasted, but the subject was beautiful and simple. I then saw in this reaper – a vague figure struggling like a devil in the full heat of the day to reach the end of his toil – I then saw the image of death in it, in this sense that humanity would be the wheat being reaped [...] But in this death nothing sad, it takes place in broad daylight with a sun that floods everything with a light of fine gold' (800). Van Gogh was referring here to the first version of a reaper in a field, *Wheat Field with Reaper* (Kröller-Müller Museum, Otterlo, F617), of which this painting is a repetition. In this neater, more resolved variant, he painted the sky green instead of yellow and worked with a thinner impasto, although afterwards he preferred the first, more spontaneous version (see letter 822). In both paintings the sun is depicted rather low for a scene unfolding 'in the full heat of the day', as the artist wrote. TM

139 Enclosed Field with Peasant

October 1889
Oil on canvas, 73.6 x 92.9 cm
Indianapolis Museum of Art.
Gift of Mrs James W. Fesler in
memory of Daniel W. and
Elizabeth C. Marmon, 44.74

Selected references: Faille 1970,
no. 641; New York 1986, cat. 28;
Amsterdam 1990, cat. 96;
Hulsker 1996, no. 1795;
Toledo 2003, cat. 18

After painting the second version of *Wheat Field with Reaper at Sunrise* (cat. 138), Van Gogh placed his easel in late September or early October in what was by now the completely mown and ploughed wheat field behind the asylum, in order to paint *Enclosed Field with Peasant*. Of the many views of the enclosed wheat field, this is one of the most impressive, with its keen observation of the rugged Alpilles, here depicted with more fidelity to nature than in any of his other works. Also the field in the foreground shows more clearly than other paintings the differences in level of this terrain.

Van Gogh immediately viewed *Enclosed Field with Peasant* as a sequel to *Wheat Field with Reaper at Sunrise*, by which he meant the first version, started back in late June (Kröller-Müller Museum, Otterlo, F617), because on 8 October he wrote to Theo: 'It's another harsh study, and instead of being almost entirely yellow it makes an almost completely violet canvas. Broken and neutral violets [...] I think that this will complement the reaper and will make it easier to see what it is. For the reaper appears done at random, and this with it will balance it [...] I seriously ask you to show them *together*, if someone or other comes to see the studies, because of the opposition of the complementaries' (810). Over the years, however, the intended complementary colour contrast has weakened, owing to the fading of the purple hues in *Enclosed Field with Peasant*, for which Van Gogh most likely used geranium lake, an unstable organic red pigment, which, when mixed with other pigments, tends to fade away completely on prolonged exposure to light. TM

**140 Enclosed Field
with Rising Sun**
Mid-November –
mid-December 1889
Black chalk, reed pen,
pen and ink on pink laid paper,
47.4 x 62 cm
Staatliche Graphische
Sammlung Munich

Selected references: Faille 1970,
no. 1552; New York 1986, cat. 38;
Otterlo 1990, cat. 237; Hulsker
1996, no. 1863; Bremen 2002,
cat. 25; Amsterdam 2005B, cat. 116

It is not clear whether Van Gogh made this
large drawing after the painting *Enclosed
Field with Rising Sun* (Private collection, F737)
or the other way around, or whether he
worked on them both at the same time. The
framing of the image and detailing in both
drawing and painting are nearly identical
(only the sun is depicted proportionately
larger in the drawing), and the two works
also display technical similarities: Van Gogh
drew and painted mainly with short, distinct
lines. He began working on the painting
around mid-November and carried on
until some time in December, at which
point he sent it to Theo in Paris. It was
intended for the exhibition of Les XX in
January/February 1890 in Brussels, where
he was to be represented by a total of six
paintings. Whether Vincent sent Theo the
drawing along with the painting, as is
sometimes assumed, cannot be determined
from their correspondence.

Van Gogh began the drawing *Enclosed
Field with Rising Sun* with black chalk,
afterwards working it up in pen and ink.
Unlike the drawings made that summer
and many others, this sheet displays roughly
equal proportions of chalk and ink.
Although he had previously used pen and
ink to draw in detail over a cursory sketch
in pencil or chalk, here he also did the
opposite, using chalk to draw over the ink.
Rather a lot of paper remained blank, lending
the depiction a sunny character. This
'open' method of working with short lines
recalls the new, less heavily impasted
manner of painting that Van Gogh employed
in this period, which he described to Theo
in a letter of 7 December as follows: 'I
prepare the thing [the canvas] with sorts of
washes with spirits, and then proceed with
touches or hatchings of colour with spaces
between them. This imparts atmosphere
and uses less paint' (824). TM

257

141 **The Poplars at Saint-Rémy**
October 1889
Oil on canvas, 61.6 x 45.7 cm
The Cleveland Museum of Art.
Bequest of Leonard C.
Hanna Jr, 1958.32

Selected references: Faille 1970,
no. 638; New York 1986, pp. 301,
303; Hulsker 1996, no. 1797;
Argencourt, Diederen
et al. 1999, no. 108

The olive trees, cypresses and pines so
characteristic of Provence were a real
discovery for Van Gogh, whereas in
portraying these poplars at Saint-Rémy he
ventured to paint a species of tree found
throughout Europe. This had to do with
the season, since the artist was mainly
interested in the autumnal effect, which is
less striking in the species mentioned
above. 'We're having some superb autumn
days, and [...] I'm taking advantage of
them,' he wrote on 5 October to Theo,
'I have a study of two yellowed poplars on
a background of mountains' (808). At the
same time he was working on a mulberry
tree in autumn colours (*Mulberry Tree*,
Norton Simon Museum of Art, Pasadena,
F637), in a similar palette of powerful
yellow-browns and deep shades of blue.
He found the poplars close to the asylum
at the foot of Les Alpilles, where there
were various quarries. Old sawn and
hewn blocks of stone, visible here in the
foreground, are still scattered around
the area. TM

142 Hospital at Saint-Rémy

Autumn 1889
Oil on canvas, 92.2 x 73.4 cm
The Armand Hammer Collection.
Gift of the Armand Hammer
Foundation. Hammer Museum,
Los Angeles, AH.90.81

Selected references: Faille 1970,
no. 643; Paris n.d., cat. 34;
Los Angeles 1971, cat. 37;
New York 1986, cat. 32, pp. 143–
45; Amsterdam 1990, cat. 102,
pp. 231–35

From May 1889 to May 1890, Van Gogh stayed at a home for the mentally ill, the asylum of Saint-Paul-de-Mausole, housed in a former Romanesque monastery at Saint-Rémy in the south of France. During the first month of his stay, when he was not yet allowed to leave the grounds, he worked outdoors in the neglected walled garden. He depicted this garden many times in the course of his year-long residence. For Van Gogh, working was a welcome distraction and the best remedy against his recurring mental crises.

After suffering a serious attack of his illness in the autumn of 1889, Van Gogh spent much time in the garden, painting the large pine trees. He wrote to Theo on c. 8 October 1889: 'I also have two views of the park and the asylum in which this place appears most agreeable' (810). This canvas, one of the two works mentioned here, does indeed make an agreeable impression, owing to the tall trees reaching high into the blue sky and to Van Gogh's swirling, forceful and colourful brush strokes. 'I tried to reconstruct the thing as it may have been by simplifying and accentuating the proud, unchanging nature of the pines and the cedar bushes against the blue' (810). The low viewpoint heightens the impression of spaciousness radiated by this setting, with its shimmering southern skies. AV

143 **Pine Trees near the Wall of the Asylum**

May/early June or
October/November 1889
Reed pen, pen, brush and ink,
graphite on pink laid paper,
63.5 x 48 cm
Tate, 4716. Bequeathed
by C. Frank Stoop, 1933

Selected references: Faille 1970,
no. 1497; New York 1986, cat. 4;
Otterlo 1990, cat. 212; Heenk
1995, pp. 184–85; Hulsker 1996,
no. 1852; Bremen 2002, cat. 5;
Amsterdam 2005B, cat. 101;
Vellekoop and Zwikker 2007,
pp. 210–11

'Since I've been here, the neglected garden planted with tall pines under which grows tall and badly tended grass intermingled with various weeds has provided me with enough work' (776), Vincent wrote to Theo around 23 May 1889, several weeks after arriving at the asylum at Saint-Rémy. This drawing is generally dated to the period when he was not yet allowed to work outside the grounds. The blooming irises in the left foreground seem to confirm this, but there are also arguments for dating the drawing to the autumn. The picture is in keeping with paintings (and pencil sketches) of the garden made in October/November, which also display closely observed tree branches standing out against the sky. Moreover, Van Gogh drew on pink laid paper, which he used for a number of drawings made in the autumn (see, among others, cat. 140), and which he had probably not used before this time. Even though another drawing datable to May/June – *Trees in the Garden of the Asylum* (Van Gogh Museum, Amsterdam, F1501) – was also drawn on pink laid paper and is similar in style, that sheet does not show – as its title suggests – a view from inside the walls of the asylum, but from outside (given the receding view in the background, which is not visible as such from any place within the garden). That drawing, too, is perhaps datable to the autumn. Since Van Gogh did not write much about his drawing activities in Saint-Rémy and neither sheet can be pinpointed in the correspondence, it is difficult to give them a more precise place in his *œuvre*. TM

144 The White Mas among the Olive Trees

December 1889
Oil on canvas, 73.5 x 60.5 cm
Signed lower right: *Vincent*
Private collection

Selected references: Faille 1970, no. 664; New York 1986, pp. 58, 318; Amsterdam 1988, p. 189; Hulsker 1996, no. 1865; Vellekoop and Zwikker 2007, p. 299, note 5

Van Gogh's manner of painting gradually changed after the summer of 1889, as is evident in the series of olive groves that he produced in November and December, to which *The White Mas among the Olive Trees* belongs. The rounded, flamboyant brush strokes of a work such as *The Olive Trees* (cat. 135) of June made way for short varied strokes that provided more rhythmic punctuation to the increasingly staccato structure. Moreover, Van Gogh's more sparing use of paint resulted in thinner layers. The later olive groves stand out because of their autumnal colour scheme, which naturally features earthier tones. Whereas Van Gogh had previously sought the full sunlight to show to best advantage the silver-green of the foliage, he now focused on early evening skies that required a saturated palette. This work differs somewhat from the other olive groves in the series owing to its inclusion of a mas, a Provençal farmhouse, and to its vertical format.

In Saint-Rémy Van Gogh remained in touch with a few good friends from Arles. He sent *The Cottage among the Olive Trees and Fields with a Tree* (Private collection, F663) to the postman Joseph Roulin, who had meanwhile been transferred. 'Yesterday I sent 2 canvases to Marseilles,' Vincent wrote to Theo on 3 January 1890. 'I made a present of them to my friend Roulin, a white farmhouse among the olive trees and a wheat field with a background of lilac mountains and a dark tree' (836). In late December 1889 Van Gogh had suffered a relapse that lasted about a week. It is not inconceivable that he wanted to give Roulin a present, since it had been exactly one year since his friend had been so helpful in the painful days after the ear incident. TM

145 Landscape with a Bridge over the Oise

Late May – early June 1890
Brush, opaque watercolour and oils, pen and ink, pencil on pink laid paper, 47.8 x 62.8 cm
Tate, 4714. Bequeathed by C. Frank Stoop, 1933

Selected references: Faille 1970, no. 1639; New York 1986, cat. 74; Otterlo 1990, cat. 245; Hulsker 1996, no. 2023; Martigny 2000, cat. 86; Toledo 2003, cat. 19; Amsterdam 2005B, cat. 119; Madrid 2007, cat. 11; Vienna 2008, cat. 128

On 20 May Van Gogh arrived in Auvers-sur-Oise after an overnight stay in Paris, but it immediately became apparent that he had taken few painting and drawing materials with him, for the next day he wrote to Theo: 'I'd also ask you for 10 metres of canvas if that wouldn't inconvenience you, but if it would inconvenience you, since it's near the end of the month, you could send 20 sheets of Ingres paper [...] There's a lot to draw here' (874). Theo probably sent both, for not only did Vincent begin to paint rather soon, but this sketchy study in pencil – which Van Gogh, with real feeling for rhythm and simplicity, worked up in watercolour, oil paint (in the sky and other places) and pen and ink (in such details as the cows and the figures with the wheelbarrow) – most probably originated in the first weeks after his arrival. From a high vantage point near the railway on the north bank of the River Oise, Van Gogh looked towards the newly built iron bridge that linked Auvers and Méry-sur-Oise. Factories are visible behind the trees and on the left. By no means did Van Gogh avoid signs of the modern world in his work. Indeed, his awareness of living in an era of change is voiced in a letter written to Theo a week later: 'Here [in Auvers] we're far enough from Paris for it to be the real countryside, but nevertheless, how changed since Daubigny. But not changed in an unpleasant way [...] the development of a new society in the old one has nothing disagreeable about it; there's a lot of well-being in the air' (875). TM

146 Vineyards with a View of Auvers

June 1890
Oil on canvas, 65.1 x 80.3 cm
Saint Louis Art Museum, 8:1953.
Funds given by Mrs Mark C.
Steinberg

Selected references: Faille 1970,
no. 762; New York 1986, pp. 135,
136; Berlin 1996, p. 136; Martigny
2000, p. 114; Stolwijk and
Veenenbos 2002, p. 49;
Compton Verney 2006, p. 112

In a letter written immediately after his arrival in Auvers, Vincent told Theo that he found the village 'really beautiful': 'it's the heart of the countryside, distinctive and picturesque' (873). He hoped to do 'a few canvases of that really seriously' (873), and in any case his doctor, Paul Gachet, had told him to 'work a great deal, boldly' (873).

On 13 June Vincent wrote to his sister Willemien to tell her that he had 'been working a lot and quickly; by doing so I'm trying to express the desperately swift passage of things in modern life' (886). The following day, in a letter to Theo, he described his recent works, one of which was *Vineyards with a View of Auvers*: 'I have a vineyard study, which Mr Gachet liked very much the last time he came to see' (887). This painting, so much admired by Dr Gachet, gives an impression of the magnificent colours of the countryside, where Van Gogh found life so 'healthy and fortifying' (898). The landscape is rendered in various shades of green, yellow and blue, which are enlivened by the red of roofs and poppies.

To give Theo some idea of his paintings, Vincent included in this letter a detailed description of the colours of another work, 'a large landscape' that he had painted the day before: *Landscape with a Carriage and Train* (State Pushkin Museum, Moscow, F760). Like that painting, *Vineyards with a View of Auvers* is characterised by the high vantage point from which Van Gogh captured the view. RZ

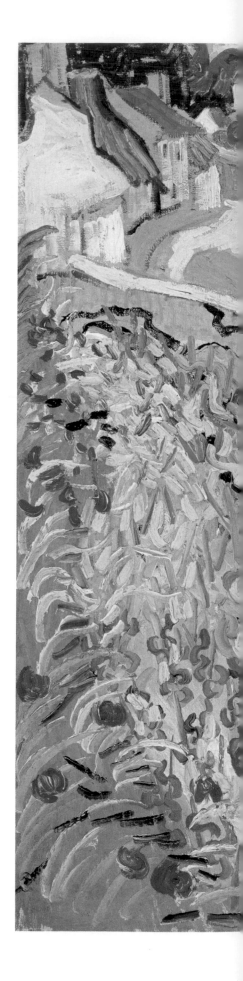

147 Letter RM23
from Vincent van Gogh
to Paul Gauguin
Auvers-sur-Oise, on or about
Tuesday 17 June 1890
Road with a Cypress and Star
(JH1983), *Ears of Wheat, Ears
of Wheat*, letter sketches
Paper, 21.8 x 33.8 cm
Van Gogh Museum, Amsterdam
(Vincent van Gogh Foundation),
b691 V/1962

148 Ears of Wheat
June 1890
Oil on canvas, 64 x 48 cm
Van Gogh Museum, Amsterdam
(Vincent van Gogh Foundation),
s88 V/1962

Selected references: Faille 1970,
no. 767; New York 1986, p. 243;
Hulsker 1996, no. 767; Seoul
2007, pp. 163, 253

This painted study made in Auvers presents a picture plane completely filled with ears of wheat, comparable to the decorative studies that Van Gogh had previously made in Saint-Rémy of picture-filling profusions of roses and arums (Van Gogh Museum, Amsterdam, F749, F610). He had, however, conceived a special plan for his studies of ears of wheat, as emerges from a draft of a letter to Paul Gauguin, dated c. 17 June 1890 and supplied with a little sketch after *Ears of Wheat*: 'Look, an idea which will perhaps suit you. I'm trying to do studies of wheat like this, however I can't draw it – nothing but ears, blue-green stems, long leaves like ribbons, green and pink by reflection, yellowing ears lightly bordered with pale pink due to the dusty flowering. A pink bindweed at the bottom wound around a stem. On it,

on a very alive and yet tranquil background, I would like to paint portraits' (RM23; cat. 147). If we compare the background with those of two paintings of slightly later vintage, in which he actually painted his model against ears of wheat – *Girl against a Background of Wheat* (Private collection, F774) and *Girl against a Background of Wheat* (National Gallery of Art, Washington, F788) – it is striking that he abandoned the study's closely observed, natural setting in favour of more stylised backdrops, thereby more pointedly creating 'a very alive and yet tranquil background'. The realistically conceived details in the study were thought to detract too much from the sitter, who in both paintings is realised by means of forceful contours and bright areas of colour. TM

149 **Vase with Field Flowers and Thistles**
June 1890
Oil on linen mounted on canvas,
66 x 45 cm
Private collection

Selected references: Faille 1970,
no. 763; New York 1986, cat. 67;
Mothe 1987, p. 82; Gachet
and Mothe 1994, pp. 139–40;
Kostenevich 1995, p. 250;
Hulsker 1996, no. 2030; Paris
1999, pp. 167–68, 219; Chavannes
and Van Tilborgh 2007, p. 550

This powerfully painted and angular-looking bunch of summer wildflowers is the only one of the six or seven flower still-lifes known from the Auvers period to be described in the artist's correspondence. In a letter written on 17 June Van Gogh told Theo: 'At the moment I have two studies on the go – one a bouquet of wild plants, thistles, ears of wheat, leaves of different types of greenery. One almost red, the other very green, the other yellowing' (889). The round table occurs in three other flower still-lifes painted in Auvers. It was probably a deeper pink originally, so that it contrasted with the greens incorporated elsewhere in the canvas. Unfortunately, the tabletop has faded over the years, owing to Van Gogh's use of an unstable organic red pigment.

In the same letter Van Gogh thanks his brother for sending him more canvas. He had run out some time earlier, and, as he sometimes did in this situation, had turned to household textiles as an alternative. This still-life, for example, is painted on a piece of thin, red-striped cloth of the kind typically used for tea towels. The fabric, called *torchon*, is still manufactured in France. Van Gogh used similar supports for *Vase with Cornflowers and Poppies* (Private collection, F280) and *Daubigny's Garden* (Van Gogh Museum, Amsterdam, F765). The latter work was already finished when he wrote to Theo on 17 June about *Vase with Field Flowers and Thistles*. The second study Van Gogh mentioned in that letter – 'a white house amid greenery with a star in the night sky and an orange light at the window and dark greenery and a sombre pink note' (State Hermitage Museum, St Petersburg, F766) – is also painted on a kind of *torchon*, although it is not known if it is also red-striped. TM

150 Roses

May 1890
Oil on canvas, 71 x 90 cm
National Gallery of Art,
Washington. Gift of Pamela
Harriman in memory of
W. Avrell Harriman 1991.67.1

Selected references: Faille 1970,
no. 681; New York 1986, cat. 53;
Ottawa 1999, p. 16; Washington
2001, p. 174

During the last weeks of his stay in the asylum at Saint-Rémy, Van Gogh painted four flower still-lifes, sending a report of these activities to Theo on 11 May 1890: 'At the moment the improvement is continuing, the whole horrible crisis has disappeared like a thunderstorm, and I'm working here with calm, unremitting ardour to give a last stroke of the brush. I'm working on a canvas of roses on bright green background [the present work] and two canvases of large bouquets of violet Irises, one lot against a pink background in which the effect is harmonious and soft through the combination of greens, pinks, violets. On the contrary, the other violet bouquet (ranging up to pure carmine and Prussian blue) standing out against a striking lemon yellow background with other yellow tones in the vase and the base on which it rests is an effect of terribly disparate complementaries that reinforce each other by their opposition' (870). Two days later he informed Theo: 'I've also just finished a canvas of pink roses against yellow-green background in a green vase' (872). For both pairs of flower paintings Van Gogh used one canvas horizontally and another vertically.

The above-mentioned 'canvas of roses', the current painting, has changed in appearance since Van Gogh painted it: the originally pink flowers are now almost completely white, and this discoloration has effaced the original contrast with the green. The vase recurs in the vertical still-life with irises in the collection of the Van Gogh Museum, Amsterdam (F678), and the angle from which it was painted also corresponds to the viewpoint in that work.

When Van Gogh left Saint-Rémy, these still-lifes were not yet dry, so he left them with an employee at the asylum who sent them on to Auvers at the end of June. In a letter written earlier that month to his sister Willemien, Van Gogh looked back on the previous period: 'in the last few days at St-Rémy I worked like a man in a frenzy, especially on bouquets of flowers. Roses and violet Irises' (879). RZ

151.1 **Letter 902**
from Vincent van Gogh
to Theo van Gogh
Auvers-sur-Oise,
Wednesday 23 July 1890
Daubigny's Garden (JH2106),
letter sketch (recto)
Paper, 17 x 21.8 cm
Van Gogh Museum, Amsterdam
(Vincent van Gogh Foundation),
b699 a-c V/1962

152 **Daubigny's Garden**
June/July 1890
Oil on canvas, 56 x 101.5 cm
Inscribed lower right: *le jardin
de Daubigny*
Collection Rudolf Staechelin.
On extended loan to the
Kunstmuseum Basel

Selected references: Faille 1970,
no. 777; New York 1986, cat. 84;
Amsterdam 1990, cat. 127;
Hulsker 1996, no. 2105;
Basel 2009, cat. 68

The landscape painter Charles-François Daubigny, who was much admired by Van Gogh, died in 1878 in Auvers. Shortly before his death he had this house built, and his widow was still living there when Van Gogh depicted it from the adjacent garden. 'I have an idea for doing a more important canvas of Daubigny's house and garden, of which I already have a small study' (889), he told Theo in a letter of 17 June. He painted that small study (Van Gogh Museum, Amsterdam, F765) in a square format (50 x 50 cm). For the present painting (overleaf), the 'more important canvas', Van Gogh chose a so-called 'double square' (50 x 100 cm), a format much used by Daubigny himself and seemingly chosen by Van Gogh as a tribute to him. He used this format in Auvers for thirteen canvases, most of which display landscape motifs.

Van Gogh was presumably still working on *Daubigny's Garden* around 10 July, at which time he wrote to Theo: 'Now the third canvas is *Daubigny's garden*, a painting I'd been thinking about ever since I've been here' (898). That Van Gogh was working on this painting and not on the other version in the same format (Hiroshima Museum of Art, F776) is apparent from, among other things, the small sketch enclosed two weeks later in the last letter he was ever to send to Theo (902; cat. 151.1) – on 23 July – which more closely resembles the second, more stylised version. The painting discussed here is more keenly observed, although Van Gogh intentionally pulled the church into the composition, since from his position it would not have been visible.

Van Gogh also painted flowering gardens at Arles and Saint-Rémy. Although no gardener himself, he recognised the healthy aspect of gardening. So did his mother, to whom he wrote in July from Auvers, while working on *Daubigny's Garden*: 'precisely for one's health, as you say – it's very necessary to work in the garden and to see the flowers growing' (899). TM

Le jardin de Daubigny

avant plan d'herbe verte à rose

à gauche un buisson vert à lilas et une souche de plante
à feuillages blanchâtre. Au milieu un parterre
de roses. à droite une claie un mur et au dessus
du mur un noisetier à feuillage violet.

Puis une haie de lilas une rangée de tilleuls arrondis
jaunes. La maison elle même dans le fond rose
à toit de tuiles bleuâtres. Un banc et 3 chaises une figure
noire à chapeau jaune et sur l'avant plan un chat noir
Ciel vert pâle.

Anvers 23 Juillet 90

651 B   2

le jardin de Daubigny

151.2 Letter 902
from Vincent van Gogh
to Theo van Gogh
Auvers-sur-Oise,
Wednesday 23 July 1890
Wheat Fields (JH2103),
letter sketch (verso)
Paper, 17 x 21.8 cm
Van Gogh Museum, Amsterdam
(Vincent van Gogh Foundation),
b699 a-c V/1962

**153 Wheat Fields after the Rain
(The Plain of Auvers)**
July 1890
Oil on canvas, 73.5 x 92.1 cm
Carnegie Museum of Art,
Pittsburgh. Acquired through the
generosity of the Sarah Mellon
Scaife Family, 68.18

Selected references: Faille 1970,
no. 781; Lane 1985, pp. 102–03;
New York 1986, cat. 73; Gerstein
1989, no. 39; Hulsker 1996, no.
2102; Bremen 2002, cat. 47

In his very last letter to Theo – dated Wednesday 23 July 1890, four days before he shot himself in the chest – Van Gogh sent sketches of 'two no. 30 canvases depicting immense stretches of wheat after the rain' (902). One of these (cat. 151.2) is a drawn copy of *Wheat Fields after the Rain (The Plain of Auvers)* (cat. 153). The alternating areas of colour, indicating that some fields have already been mown or cultivated with other crops, zigzag in stripes towards the horizon, above which drift clouds, broadly painted with comma-like curls. As he did more often in his later landscapes, Van Gogh here combined two viewing angles, creating a powerful effect of depth: the foreground – which is observed from very close up, as though looking down on it – was worked out with short, multi-coloured strokes of paint. The eye is then drawn across the 'bump' in the foreground to the more linearly conceived fields in the distance. Using simple but selectively applied brush strokes – red dots for poppies, a vertical line with a transverse line for an ear of wheat, and so on – Van Gogh showed himself to be a consummate artist who understood very well how to make a motif succinct and yet clearly decipherable. With regard to a number of large landscapes painted slightly before this, he had written to Theo earlier in July: '[I] almost believe that these canvases will tell you what I can't say in words, what I consider healthy and fortifying about the countryside' (898). *Wheat Fields after the Rain (The Plain of Auvers)* makes a similar impression, but neither it nor those earlier landscapes, despite their 'healthy and fortifying' effect, were to be able to prevent the artist from taking his own life. TM

154 **Letter** RM25
from Vincent van Gogh
to Theo van Gogh
Auvers-sur-Oise,
Wednesday 23 July 1890
Paper, 21.8 x 34 cm
Van Gogh Museum, Amsterdam
(Vincent van Gogh Foundation),
b700 V/1962

This unfinished letter to Theo, a draft of the one that Vincent actually sent on 23 July, was found on Vincent's person after he shot himself in the fields on 27 July 1890. Theo noted in pencil on the sheet: 'lettre qu'il portait sur lui le 27 Juillet jour du sinistre' (the letter he had on him on 27 July, that horrible day).

The draft and the sent letter begin in much the same way, although the sent letter is slightly softer in tone. Vincent thanks Theo for a 50-franc note (the final payment in ten years of unbroken financial support), refers to a certain domestic tension in Theo's household, to Theo's negotiations with his employers the art dealers Boussod, Valadon et Cie for a pay rise, and to the difficulties of the art market. In the sent letter he then asserts: 'I'm applying myself to my canvases with all my attention' (902; cats 151.1–2). He continues on a practical and positive note, including sketches of four recent paintings (cats 152, 153) and asking for a supply of paints for himself and Anton Hirschig, a Dutch artist who was also lodging at the Auberge Ravoux. This letter ends warmly, promising 'More soon.'

In the draft, Van Gogh seeks to reassure Theo 'in a moment of relative crisis', assuring him 'I'll always consider that you're something other than a simple dealer in Corots, that through my intermediacy you have your part in the very production of certain canvases, which even in calamity retain their calm' (RM25). But then this unfinished letter tails off on a despairing note: 'Ah well, I risk my life for my own work and my reason has half foundered in it – very well – but you're not one of the dealers in men; as far as I know and can judge I think you really act with humanity, but what can you do'. The last sentence is unfinished.

We will never know why Van Gogh took his own life, but these last letters hint that a combination of factors – a sense of being a burden, the difficulties of the art market, fear of recurring illness, loneliness and despair – may have led him to it. AD

Les autres peintres quoi qu'ils en
pensent instinctivement se tiennent à distance
des discussions sur le commerce actuel.
Eh bien vraiment nous ne pouvons
faire parler que nos tableaux
mais pourtant mon cher frère il y a
ceci que toujours je l'ai dit et je te
le redis encore une fois avec toute
la gravité que puisse donner
les efforts de pensée assidument faits
pour chercher à faire aussi bien
qu'on peut — je te le redis encore
que je considèrerai toujours que
tu es autre chose qu'un simple marchand
de Corots que par mon intermédiaire
tu as ta part à la production même
de certaines toiles que même dans
la débacle gardent leur calme.
Car là nous en sommes et c'est
là tout ou au moins le principal
que je puisse avoir à te dire dans
un moment de crise relative
Dans un moment où les choses
sont fort tendues entre marchands
de tableaux — d'artistes morts — et artistes vivants
Eh bien mon travail à moi j'y
risque ma vie et ma raison y
fondrée à moitié — bon —

mais tu n'es pas dans les marchands
d'hommes pour autant que je sache
et puisse prendre parti je te trouve
agissant réellement avec humanité
mais que veux tu

CHRONOLOGY

1853–76: EARLY YEARS

30 March 1853: Vincent Willem van Gogh was born in Groot-Zundert, the eldest child of the Reverend Theodorus van Gogh and Anna Cornelia van Gogh-Carbentus.

1 May 1857: his brother Theodorus (Theo) (1857–1891) was born. Vincent had four other siblings: Anna Cornelia (1855–1930), Elisabeth (Lies) Huberta (1859–1936), Willemien (Wil) Jacoba (1862–1941) and Cornelis (Cor) Vincent (1867–1900).

1861–69: Van Gogh attended several schools, where he learnt English, French and German.

30 July 1869: Van Gogh was appointed a junior apprentice at the art dealer Goupil & Cie in The Hague, where his uncle was a partner. Van Gogh began to collect engravings and prints, eventually assembling a large collection over his lifetime.

29 September 1872: Van Gogh's surviving correspondence with his brother Theo began shortly after Theo visited him in The Hague.

December 1872: Theo accepted a job with the Brussels branch of Goupil, and on 13 December Vincent congratulated him: 'I'm so glad that both of us are now in the same line of business, and in the same firm; we must correspond often' (2).

May 1873 – May 1875: Vincent van Gogh was transferred to Goupil's London branch. He visited the British Museum, the National Gallery, the Wallace Collection, the South Kensington Museum (now the Victoria and Albert Museum), the Dulwich Picture Gallery and the Royal Academy of Arts. On 16 June 1874, he wrote to Theo: 'There are beautiful things at the Royal Academy this year' (23). The two brothers corresponded regularly, exchanging opinions on art and literature; they met at the family home each Christmas. During this period Van Gogh became fixated by religion; his letters grew increasingly pious, and contained excerpts from the Bible and sermons. He showed indifference towards commercial art dealing and became convinced that he should instead fulfil a social duty.

May 1875: Van Gogh was transferred to Paris.

Christmas 1875: After taking leave without permission to visit his family, now living at Etten, he learnt that he was to be dismissed on 1 April 1876.

April 1876: he returned to England, working as a teacher in Ramsgate and Isleworth.

29 October 1876: he delivered a sermon at the Wesleyan Methodist Church, Richmond. On 3 November 1876, he wrote: 'Theo, your brother spoke for the first time in God's house last Sunday' (96). In November he was appointed a volunteer worker at a church in Turnham Green, where he preached and taught Sunday school.

1

2

3

4

1877–80: DORDRECHT, AMSTERDAM AND BELGIUM (THE BORINAGE AND BRUSSELS)

January 1877: Van Gogh decided not to return to England after Christmas 1876. His parents found him a position in a bookshop in Dordrecht, but he was not satisfied with this, wanting to be an evangelist.

May 1877 – May 1878: he pursued theological studies in Amsterdam but became frustrated, feeling divorced from 'practical work' (145).

August 1878 – July 1879: his father helped him gain temporary appointments as an evangelist in the Borinage, Belgium, but each time his fanatical behaviour led to these being terminated.

August 1879: he moved to Cuesmes where he worked as a preacher without pay. Depressed, living in poverty and disillusioned with formal religion, he increasingly spent his time drawing.

10 August 1879: Theo visited, but after an argument about his brother's future the two did not communicate until June 1880.

c. **1 November 1879**: Theo was given a permanent position with Goupil in Paris, and by June 1880 he was managing the Boulevard Montmartre branch, dealing mainly in Barbizon and Hague School paintings. In 1884 Goupil became Boussod, Valadon & Cie, and a few years later Theo, who was interested in the avant-garde, began to buy and sell Impressionist works.

During 1880 Van Gogh's family began to give up hope of a normal middle-class life for him, and his inability to conform to social conventions left him lonely and dejected. Between about 22 and 24 June 1880, in the first letter after a silence of almost a year, he wrote to Theo: 'my torment is none other than this, what could I be good for, couldn't I serve and be useful in some way?' (155).

August 1880: encouraged by Theo, Van Gogh decided to become an artist, at the age of twenty-seven.

October 1880: he moved to Brussels in search of galleries, a better studio and contact with other artists. 'For a long time now I haven't seen enough paintings or drawings &c., and the mere sight of a few good things here in Brussels has raised my morale' (159).

5

Page 284
Vincent van Gogh aged nineteen, January 1873. Van Gogh Museum, Amsterdam (Vincent van Gogh Foundation)

Page 285
Theo van Gogh, Vincent van Gogh's brother, 1882. Van Gogh Museum, Amsterdam (Vincent van Gogh Foundation)

1   **The Revd Theodorus van Gogh, Vincent van Gogh's father**, undated. Van Gogh Museum, Amsterdam (Vincent van Gogh Foundation)

2   **Anna Cornelia van Gogh-Carbentus, Vincent van Gogh's mother**, 1880/90. Van Gogh Museum, Amsterdam (Vincent van Gogh Foundation)

3   **Vincent van Gogh aged thirteen**, 1866. Van Gogh Museum, Amsterdam (Vincent van Gogh Foundation)

4   **Willemien van Gogh, Vincent van Gogh's sister**, undated. Van Gogh Museum, Amsterdam (Vincent van Gogh Foundation)

5   **The Goupil Gallery, The Hague**, late nineteenth century. Van Gogh Museum, Amsterdam (Vincent van Gogh Foundation)

1881–83: BRUSSELS, ETTEN AND THE HAGUE

Now committed to being an artist, Van Gogh worked tenaciously, trying to produce competent landscape and figure drawings. With no formal training, he relied heavily on teaching manuals and was often preoccupied with the technique of perspective.

February 1881: Theo assumed direct responsibility for his elder brother's living expenses, and was to support him financially for the rest of his life.

Late March – late April 1881: Van Gogh worked in the studio of the painter Anthon van Rappard, who remained a close friend and source of advice throughout most of his Dutch period. The pair corresponded regularly until April 1885, when an unfortunate difference of opinion put an end to their acquaintance.

End of April 1881: Van Gogh returned to the family home in Etten, where he continued to work. By mid-September 1881 Van Gogh wrote to Theo of his hard-earned improvement: 'I've learned to measure and to see [...] I must now draw constantly. Examine and draw everything that's part of a peasant's life [...] I'm no longer so powerless in the face of nature as I used to be' (172).

25 December 1881: Van Gogh moved to The Hague after an argument with his father.

January 1882: he received lessons in drawing, watercolour and oils from the Hague School painter Anthon Mauve, his cousin by marriage.

March 1882: Van Gogh received his first commission, for twelve views of The Hague, from his uncle Cornelis Marinus van Gogh (Uncle Cor). His relationship with his model Sien Hoornik, a former prostitute, caused further tension with his family. Mauve broke off relations with him when he took the unmarried, pregnant Sien and her daughter into his house.

1882–83: despite the disapproval of his family and friends regarding his living situation, Van Gogh continued to progress as an artist. On 11 March 1883, he wrote to Theo: 'I've found my work [...] something which I live for heart and soul [...] I have a certain faith in art, a certain trust that it's a powerful current that drives a person' (327).

1883–86: DRENTHE, NUENEN AND ANTWERP

September 1883: Van Gogh decided to break up with Sien and to move to rural Drenthe. After three months in extreme isolation there, he returned to the home of his parents, who had moved to Nuenen. There he continued to live and work for almost two years. As ever, Van Gogh taught himself. Guided largely by the work and ideas of his greatest exemplar Jean-François Millet, described in the biography by Alfred Sensier, he concentrated on subjects that eulogised simple country life, such as still-lifes, cottages and agricultural labourers.

26 March 1885: Van Gogh's father died suddenly of a stroke.

April 1885: Van Gogh completed the important painting *The Potato Eaters* (fig. 1) and sent it to Theo in Paris. Although discouraged by the unfavourable response to this work, Van Gogh persevered in improving his painting. Inspired by the colour theories he read during August in Théophile Silvestre's *Eugène Delacroix. Documents nouveaux*, he experimented further with colour, for example in a series of autumn landscapes. On 28 October 1885 he wrote to Theo: 'Presently my palette is thawing, and the bleakness of the earliest beginnings has gone' (537).

24 November 1885: struggling to find models and unable to work outside in the cold weather, Van Gogh moved to Antwerp where he was able to visit museums and the academy, and hoped for more opportunities to sell work: 'it feels to me like a return from exile [...] And in the meantime my powers have matured somewhat' (543). It was in Antwerp that Van Gogh discovered Japanese woodblock prints.

6

7

6 **Anthon van Rappard,** undated. Van Gogh Museum, Amsterdam (Vincent van Gogh Foundation)

7 **Emile Bernard,** c. 1887. Van Gogh Museum, Amsterdam (Vincent van Gogh Foundation)

8 **Vincent van Gogh (seen from behind) and Emile Bernard on the banks of the Seine at Asnières,** c. 1886. Van Gogh Museum, Amsterdam (Vincent van Gogh Foundation)

9 **The Yellow House, Arles,** undated. Postcard. Van Gogh Museum, Amsterdam (Vincent van Gogh Foundation)

1886–88: PARIS

February 1886: after discussing a move to Paris, and agreeing to wait until Theo could rent a larger apartment, Van Gogh arrived unexpectedly, writing on 28 February: 'Don't be cross with me that I've come all of a sudden. I've thought about it so much [...] Will be at the Louvre from midday, or earlier if you like' (567).

Then the art capital of the Western world, Paris was a revelation to Van Gogh. In **March–April 1886** he worked briefly in the studio of Fernand Cormon. Through Theo, Van Gogh came into contact with the work of the Impressionists. In a letter of September or October 1886 to the English artist Horace Mann Livens Van Gogh reflected: 'In Antwerp I did not even know what the Impressionists were, now I have seen them and though not being one of the club yet I have much admired certain Impressionist pictures' (569).

Van Gogh was also inspired by the heavy impasto and bright palette of the recently deceased Adolphe Monticelli. While visiting exhibitions and studios he met many artists of the younger generation, some of whom he was later to correspond with, such as Emile Bernard, the Australian John Peter Russell, Paul Signac and Paul Gauguin.

Throughout his two years in Paris, Van Gogh experimented with the Impressionist brush stroke to cultivate an individual style, producing self-portraits, portraits of acquaintances, including the dealer Alexander Reid (cat. 67) and the colour merchant Julien ('Père') Tanguy (fig. 19), views of Paris and many still-lifes, particularly of flowers, which he conceived as 'gymnastics' in colour. He described this in the same letter to Livens:

'seeking oppositions of blue with orange, red and green, yellow and violet, seeking the broken and neutral tones to harmonise brutal extremes. Trying to render intense colour and not a grey harmony' (569).

Van Gogh continued to collect Japanese woodblock prints in Paris. Admiring their simplicity, linearity, flat colour and spatial organisation, he developed a strong affinity with Japan, which later became in his mind a metaphor for 'the painters' paradise' (691).

19 February 1888: Van Gogh was showing signs of mental and physical stress induced by the strain of urban life, and after a visit to the studio of the pointillist painter Georges Seurat with Theo, he left Paris for the south of France.

1888–89: ARLES

During his fourteen months in Arles, Van Gogh made around 200 paintings and over 100 works on paper, beginning with winter landscapes and launching into a spectacular series of orchards. His letters from this period reflect a newfound confidence.

20 February 1888: Van Gogh took a room at the Hôtel Carrel.

On or about **16 March 1888**, he wrote to Theo: 'I feel I'm in Japan' (585), an articulation of his idealised conception of Provence. In a letter to John Peter Russell dated 19 April 1888, he described 'the rich coulour [sic] and rich sun of the glorious south' (598) that was to have such a dramatic impact on his palette. He explored his surroundings on foot, often working outside 'laden like a porcupine with sticks, easel, canvas' (626).

22 March – c. 3 May: Van Gogh showed three paintings at the Salon des Artistes Indépendants in Paris.

1 May 1888: Van Gogh rented the east wing of the Yellow House (2 Place Lamartine) as his studio 'for the whole of the campaign here in the south' (602). He later described it in a letter to his

8

9

sister Wil: 'a little yellow house with green door and shutters, whitewashed inside – on the white walls – very brightly coloured Japanese drawings – red tiles on the floor – the house in full sun – and a bright blue sky above it' (626).

7 May 1888: Van Gogh took a room in the Café de la Gare, 30 Place Lamartine, run by Joseph and Marie Ginoux.

Early June 1888: Van Gogh visited Saintes-Maries-de-la-Mer, drawing the boats and village with a hand-cut reed pen and ink. The technique he developed, in part derived from the graphic qualities of Japanese woodblock prints, allowed him great spontaneity and also informed his paintings. On or about 5 June 1888, he wrote to Theo: 'tell me, in Paris would I have drawn in an hour the drawing of the boats? [...] this was done without measuring, letting the pen go' (620).

In this period Van Gogh was at the height of his powers, using line and colour autonomously, but always in the service of expressing the true essence and character of the subject he had observed; it was then that he produced some of his greatest still-lifes, landscapes and portraits. He expressed his pantheistic view of nature in paintings and drawings of sowers and the rotating seasons in the wheat fields.

17 September 1888: Van Gogh moved into the Yellow House to live as well as work.

23 October 1888: his long-cherished dream of an artist's colony seemed within reach when, after protracted negotiations, Paul Gauguin finally arrived in Arles. Van Gogh and Gauguin lived and worked together for just over nine weeks but tensions arose between the two men, whose temperaments were ill suited to collaboration.

23 December 1888: Van Gogh suffered his first mental breakdown and cut off part of his ear. He was admitted to hospital the next day.

24 December 1888: Theo travelled to Arles, visited Vincent in hospital, and returned to Paris the next day with Gauguin.

7 January 1889: Van Gogh left hospital.

9 January 1889: Theo and Jo Bonger, the sister of his friend Andries Bonger, were engaged; they married on 18 April in Amsterdam and moved to 8 Cité Pigalle, Paris.

Mid-January – May 1889: Van Gogh suffered several breakdowns and went in and out of hospital. Despite periods of recovery, he became fearful of the unpredictable nature of his condition, and agreed to be admitted to an asylum.

10

11

12

8 May 1889: Van Gogh was admitted to the Saint-Paul-de-Mausole asylum at Saint-Rémy. He suffered attacks episodically; his doctor considered his illness to be a form of epilepsy.

May 1889 – May 1890: Van Gogh continued to work in his lucid periods. Within the asylum, he painted the interior and garden; when confined to his room he painted the view from the window and made interpretations of works by artists he admired, including Millet (cat. 127), Delacroix (cat. 125) and Rembrandt (cat. 130) from lithographs sent by Theo. When well enough, he was allowed to work outside, producing landscapes in which he employed an exaggerated stylisation, often focusing on motifs such as pine and cypress trees, and olive groves. On 20 September 1889, he wrote to Theo: 'These are exaggerations from the point of view of the arrangement, their lines are contorted like those of the ancient woodcuts' (805).

September–October 1889: he showed two paintings at the 'Ve Exposition de la Société des Artistes Indépendants' in Paris.

28 January – 23 February 1890: Van Gogh showed six paintings at the exhibition of Les XX in Brussels. The Belgian artist Anna Boch bought *The Red Vineyard* (1888; Pushkin State Museum of Fine Arts, Moscow, F495).

31 January 1890: birth of Vincent-Willem, son of Theo and Jo.

1 February 1890: the critic Albert Aurier praised Van Gogh's work in an article in the avant-garde magazine *Mercure de France*, 'Les Isolés: Vincent van Gogh'.

20 March – 27 April 1890: Van Gogh showed ten paintings at the Salon des Indépendants in Paris.

16 May 1890: Van Gogh left the asylum. He stayed briefly in Paris with Theo, who arranged for him to lodge at the Auberge Ravoux in Auvers-sur-Oise. Dr Paul Gachet, an amateur painter, collector and homeopathic doctor, cared for Van Gogh, who painted portraits of Gachet (fig. 6) and his family, and produced a series of 'double-square' format landscapes (cat. 152, fig. 2).

27 July 1890: Van Gogh shot himself in the chest while out in the fields surrounding Auvers. An unfinished draft of a letter to Theo written on 23 July was found in his pocket: 'Ah well, I risk my life for my own work and my reason has half foundered in it' (RM25).

29 July 1890: Van Gogh died of his wounds with Theo at his side.

30 July 1890: Van Gogh was buried at Auvers. His funeral was attended by many artists and friends, including Bernard and Père Tanguy.

September 1890: Theo's health deteriorated rapidly as a result of syphilis.

9 October 1890: Theo suffered a mental and physical collapse and went into hospital three days later.

25 January 1891: Theo died and was buried at Utrecht.

1911: Ambroise Vollard published *Lettres de Vincent van Gogh à Emile Bernard*, edited by Emile Bernard.

1914: Jo had Theo's remains transferred to the cemetery at Auvers so that he could lie beside his brother. She published the first major edition of Van Gogh's letters to Theo: *Vincent van Gogh. Brieven aan zijn broeder*.

13

14

10 **Paul Gauguin aged 43**, 1891. Musée de Pont-Aven

11 **Aerial view of the asylum of Saint-Paul-de-Mausole, Saint-Rémy, with Les Alpilles in the background**, c. 1940. Van Gogh Museum, Amsterdam (Vincent van Gogh Foundation)

12 **Jo van Gogh-Bonger, Theo's wife, with their son Vincent-Willem van Gogh**, April 1890. Van Gogh Museum, Amsterdam (Vincent van Gogh Foundation)

13 **The Auberge Ravoux, Auvers-sur-Oise**, 1890. Van Gogh Museum, Amsterdam (Vincent van Gogh Foundation)

14 **The graves of Vincent and Theo van Gogh, Auvers-sur-Oise**, 1952. Van Gogh Museum, Amsterdam (Vincent van Gogh Foundation)

BIBLIOGRAPHIC SOURCES

Alexandria 1998
Saskia de Bodt and Manfred Sellink, *Nineteenth-century Dutch Watercolors and Drawings from the Museum Boijmans Van Beuningen, Rotterdam*, exh. cat., Art Services International, Alexandria, Virginia, 1998

Amsterdam 1980
Vincent van Gogh in zijn Hollandse jaren: Kijk op stad en land door Van Gogh en zijn tijdgenoten 1870–1890, exh. cat., Van Gogh Museum, Amsterdam, 1980–81

Amsterdam 1988
Philip Conisbee, Sjraar van Heugten and Louis van Tilborgh, *Van Gogh and Millet*, exh. cat., Van Gogh Museum, Amsterdam, 1988–89

Amsterdam 1990
Evert van Uitert, Louis van Tilborgh and Sjraar van Heugten, *Vincent van Gogh Paintings*, exh. cat., Van Gogh Museum, Amsterdam, 1990

Amsterdam 2000
Andreas Blühm and Louise Lippincott, *Light! The Industrial Age, 1750–1900. Art and Science, Technology and Society*, exh. cat., Van Gogh Museum, Amsterdam, and Carnegie Museum of Art, Pittsburgh, 2000–01

Amsterdam 2003
Chris Stolwijk, Sjraar van Heugten, Leo Jansen and Andreas Blühm (eds), *Vincent's Choice: Van Gogh's 'Musée Imaginaire'*, exh. cat., Van Gogh Museum, Amsterdam, 2003

Amsterdam 2005A
Een park met twee gezichten. Van Goghs parkgezicht en andere werken uit de Noro Foundation, exh. cat., Van Gogh Museum, Amsterdam, 2005–06

Amsterdam 2005B
Colta Ives, Susan A. Stein, Sjraar van Heugten and Marije Vellekoop, *Vincent van Gogh: The Drawings*, exh. cat., Van Gogh Museum, Amsterdam, and Metropolitan Museum of Art, New York, 2005

Argencourt, Diederen et al. 1999
Louise d'Argencourt, Roger Diederen et al., *European Paintings of the Nineteenth Century, Vol. I: Aligny – Gro*, catalogue of the collection of the Cleveland Museum of Art, 1999

Arles 1989
Ronald Pickvance, *Van Gogh et Arles, Exposition du Centenaire*, exh. cat., Ancien Hôpital Van Gogh, Arles, 1989

Arnold 1995
Matthias Arnold, *Vincent van Gogh: Werk und Wirkung*, Munich, 1995

Bakker 2003
Nienke Bakker, 'On Rustics and Labourers: Van Gogh and "the People"', in Amsterdam 2003, pp. 87–98

Basel 2009
Bernhard Mendes Bürgi, Gottfried Boehm, Walter Feilchenfeldt, Carel Blotkamp, Laura Coyle and Nina Zimmer, *Vincent van Gogh – Between Heaven and Earth: The Landscapes*, exh. cat., Kunstmuseum Basel, 2009

Belluno 2003
Da Van Gogh a Picasso dal Los Angeles Contemporary Museum of Art, exh. cat., Palazzo Crepadona, Belluno, 2003–04

Ten Berge, Meedendorp, Vergeest and Verhoogt 2003
Jos ten Berge, Teio Meedendorp, Aukje Vergeest and Robert Verhoogt, *The Paintings of Vincent van Gogh in the Collection of the Kröller-Müller Museum*, Otterlo, 2003

Berlin 1996
Johann Georg Prinz von Hohenzollern and Peter-Klaus Schuster, *Manet bis Van Gogh. Hugo von Tschudi und der Kampf um die Moderne*, exh. cat., Nationalgalerie, Berlin, and Neue Pinakothek, Munich, 1996–97

Birmingham 1991
French Impressionism: Treasures from the Midlands, exh. cat., Birmingham Museum and Art Gallery, 1991

Bowness 1969
Alan Bowness, 'A Van Gogh Discovery', *Burlington Magazine*, May 1969, pp. 299–300

Bremen 2002
Dorothee Hansen and Wulf Herzogenrath, *Van Gogh: Fields. 'The Field with Poppies' and the Artists' Dispute*, exh. cat., Kunsthalle Bremen, 2002 (Toledo 2003 is a modified version of this catalogue)

Brescia 2005
Gauguin/Van Gogh, exh. cat., Museo di Santa Giulia, Brescia, 2005–06

Bristol 2005
The Stuff of Life, exh. cat., City Museum and Art Gallery, Bristol, Laing Art Gallery, Newcastle-upon-Tyne, and National Gallery, London, 2005

Budapest 2006
Judit Geskó (ed.), *Van Gogh in Budapest*, exh. cat., Museum of Fine Arts, Budapest, 2006–07

Bührle 1990
H. Anda-Bührle, Christian Bührle and Margaret Hahnloser-Ingold, *The Passionate Eye: Impressionism and Other Master Paintings from the Collection of Emile G. Bührle, Zürich*, Zürich, 1990

Chavannes and Van Tilborgh 2007
Meta Chavannes and Louis van Tilborgh, 'A Missing Van Gogh Unveiled', *Burlington Magazine*, 149, August 2007, pp. 546–50

Chicago 2001
Douglas W. Druick, Peter Kort Zegers et al., *Van Gogh and Gauguin: The Studio of the South*, exh. cat., The Art Institute of Chicago, and Van Gogh Museum, Amsterdam, 2001–02

Christie's 2003
Impressionist and Modern Art, auction catalogue, Christie's, London, 24 June 2003

Christie's 2006
Impressionist and Modern Art, auction catalogue, Christie's, New York, 6 February 2006

Christie's 2007
Impressionist and Modern Art, auction catalogue, Christie's, New York, 9 May 2007

Clark 1996
Selections from the Sterling and Francine Clark Art Institute, Williamstown, 1996

Compton Verney 2006
Martin Bailey, *Van Gogh and Britain: Pioneer Collectors*, exh. cat., Compton Verney, Warwickshire, and Dean Gallery, Edinburgh, 2006

Dallas 2007
Dorothy Kosinski (ed.), *Van Gogh's Sheaves of Wheat*, exh. cat., Dallas Museum of Art, 2007

Davis 1995
Bruce Davis, *Master Drawings in the Los Angeles County Museum of Art*, Los Angeles, 1995

Dorn 1990A
Roland Dorn, *Décoration. Vincent van Goghs Werkreihe für das Gelbe Haus in Arles*, Hildesheim, Zürich and New York, 1990

Dorn 1990B
Roland Dorn, 'Emile Bernard and Vincent van Gogh', in MaryAnne Stevens et al., *Emile Bernard 1868–1941. A Pioneer of Modern Art*, exh. cat., Städtische Kunsthalle, Mannheim, and Van Gogh Museum, Amsterdam, 1990, pp. 30–47

Dorn 1999
Roland Dorn, 'Vincent van Gogh Soir d'été, 1888', in Dieter Schwarz (ed.), *Van Gogh, Van Doesburg, de Chirico, Picasso, Guston, Weiner, Mangold, Richter: Texte zu Werken im Kunstmuseum Winterthur*, Düsseldorf and Winterthur, 1999, pp. 11–41

Dorn 2000
Roland Dorn, 'The Arles Period: Symbolic Means, Decorative Ends', in *Van Gogh Face to Face: The Portraits*, exh. cat., The Detroit Institute of Arts, Museum of Fine Arts, Boston, and Philadelphia Museum of Art, 2000–01, pp. 135–71

Dorn and Feilchenfeldt 1993
Roland Dorn and Walter Feilchenfeldt, 'Genuine or Fake? On the History and Problems of Van Gogh Connoisseurship', in Tsukasa Kodera and Yvette Rosenberg (eds), *The Mythology of Vincent van Gogh*, Tokyo, 1993, pp. 263–307

Dumas and Van der Mast 1990
Charles Dumas and Michiel van der Mast (eds), *Van Gogh en Den Haag*, Zwolle, 1990

Elderfield 2004
John Elderfield, *MoMA. Modern Painting and Sculpture*, catalogue of the collection, New York, 2004

Essen 1990
Roland Dorn, Fred Leeman et al., *Vincent van Gogh and the Modern Movement, 1890–1914*, exh. cat., Museum Folkwang, Essen, and Van Gogh Museum, Amsterdam, 1990–91

Faille 1928
J.-B. de la Faille, *L'œuvre de Vincent van Gogh: Catalogue raisonné*, 4 vols, Paris and Brussels, 1928

Faille 1970
J.-B. de la Faille, *The Works of Vincent van Gogh: His Paintings and Drawings*, revised edition, Amsterdam, 1970

Faille 1992
J.-B. de la Faille, *Vincent van Gogh: The Complete Works on Paper. Catalogue Raisonné*, San Francisco, 1992 (a reprint of the third volume of Faille 1928 with a revised version of the part of Faille 1970 that concerns works on paper)

Feilchenfeldt 1988
Walter Feilchenfeldt, *Vincent van Gogh and Paul Cassirer, Berlin: The Reception of Van Gogh in Germany from 1901 to 1914*, Zwolle, 1988

Feilchenfeldt 2005
Walter Feilchenfeldt, *By Appointment Only. Cézanne, Van Gogh and Some Secrets of Art Dealing*, Wädenswill, 2005

Fowle 1991
Frances Fowle, 'The Hague School and the Scots. A Taste for Dutch Pictures', *Apollo*, 134, August 1991, pp. 108–11

Gachet and Mothe 1994
Paul Gachet and Alain Mothe, *Les 70 jours de van Gogh à Auvers*, Paris, 1994

Gerstein 1989
Marc S. Gerstein, *Impressionism: Selections from Five American Museums*, New York, 1989

Glasgow 1990
Richard Bionda and Carel Blotkamp (eds), *The Age of Van Gogh: Dutch Painting, 1880–1895*, exh. cat., Burrell Collection, Glasgow, and Van Gogh Museum, Amsterdam, 1990–91

Graetz 1963
H. E. Graetz, *The Symbolic Language of Vincent van Gogh*, New York, Toronto and London, 1963

Greer 1997
Joan Greer, '"Een man van smerten ende versocht in krankheyt." Het christologische beeld van de kunstenaar in Van Goghs Stilleven met open bijbel', *Jong Holland*, 3, 1997, pp. 30–42

Van Haarlem 2004
P. van Haarlem, 'Middelmatige schilderijen bij Christie's en Sotheby's gaan zeer wisselend', *Kunst & Antiek Revue*, 19, 2004, 9, April–May, pp. 29–42

The Hague 2005
Fred Leeman and John Sillevis, *De Haagse School en de jonge Van Gogh*, exh. cat., Gemeentemuseum, The Hague, 2005

Hammacher 1992
A. M. Hammacher, 'Les Deux Versions de la "Pietà" de Van Gogh d'après Delacroix: une histoire documentaire', *Monumenti Musei e Gallerie Pontificie, Bolletino*, 12, 1992

Hecht 2006
Peter Hecht, *Van Gogh en Rembrandt*, Amsterdam, 2006

Heenk 1995
Elizabeth Nicoline Heenk, *Vincent van Gogh's Drawings: An Analysis of Their Production and Uses*, unpublished dissertation, Courtauld Institute of Art, University of London, 1995

Hendriks and Van Tilborgh 2006
Ella Hendriks and Louis van Tilborgh, *New Views on Van Gogh's Development in Antwerp and Paris: An Integrated Art-historical and Technical Study of His Paintings in the Van Gogh Museum*, dissertation, University of Amsterdam, 2006

Hendriks and Van Tilborgh forthcoming
Ella Hendriks and Louis van Tilborgh, *Vincent van Gogh Paintings 2, Antwerp, Paris and Amsterdam*, to be published in 2010

's-Hertogenbosch 1987
Evert van Uitert, Carol Zemel et al., *Van Gogh in Brabant: Paintings and Drawings from Etten and Nuenen*, exh. cat., Noordbrabants Museum, 's-Hertogenbosch, 1987–88

Van Heugten 1996
Sjraar van Heugten, *Vincent van Gogh, Drawings, vol. 1. The Early Years, 1880–83*, Amsterdam, 1996

Van Heugten 1997
Sjraar van Heugten, *Vincent van Gogh, Drawings, vol. 2. Nuenen 1883–85*, Amsterdam, 1997

Van Heugten 2005
Sjraar van Heugten, *Van Gogh: Master Draughtsman*, Amsterdam, 2005

Van Heugten and Pabst 1995
Sjraar van Heugten and Fieke Pabst, *The Graphic Work of Vincent van Gogh*, Zwolle, 1995

Van Heugten and Stolwijk 2003
Sjraar van Heugten and Chris Stolwijk, 'A Passion for Art: Vincent van Gogh's Taste', in Amsterdam 2003, pp. 9–24

Homburg 1996
Cornelia Homburg, *The Copy Turns Original: Vincent van Gogh and a New Approach to Traditional Practice*, Amsterdam and Philadelphia, 1996

Houston 2002
Art Beyond-isms: Masterworks from El Greco to Picasso in the Phillips Collection, organised by the Phillips Collection, Washington DC, exh. cat., Museum of Fine Arts, Houston, Phoenix Art Museum, Albright-Knox Art Gallery, Buffalo, Denver Art Museum, Frist Center for the Visual Arts, Nashville, 2002–04

Houston 2007
Susan A. Stein et al., *Masterpieces of European Painting, 1800–1920, from The Metropolitan Museum of Art*, exh. cat., Museum of Fine Arts, Houston, 2007

Hulsker 1996
Jan Hulsker, *The New Complete Van Gogh: Paintings, Drawings, Sketches*, revised and enlarged edition, Amsterdam and Philadelphia, 1996

Jansen 2003
Leo Jansen, 'Vincent van Gogh's Belief in Art as Consolation', in Amsterdam 2003, pp. 13–24

Jansen, Luijten and Bakker 2009
Leo Jansen, Hans Luijten and Nienke Bakker (eds), *Vincent van Gogh: The Letters. The Complete Illustrated and Annotated Edition*, 6 vols, London and New York, 2009

Jansen, Luijten and Bakker online
Leo Jansen, Hans Luijten and Nienke Bakker (eds), *Vincent van Gogh: The Letters*, electronic edition, www.vangoghletters.org

Jirat-Wasiutynski 1993
Vojtech Jirat-Wasiutynski, 'Vincent van Gogh's Paintings of Olive Trees and Cypresses from St-Rémy', *Art Bulletin*, 75, December 1993, pp. 656–58, 667

Journal 2001
Rachel Esner, Sjraar van Heugten, John Leighton and Chris Stolwijk (eds), *Van Gogh Museum Journal*, Van Gogh Museum, Amsterdam, 2001

Journal 2002
Rachel Esner, Sjraar van Heugten, Leo Jansen, John Leighton and Chris Stolwijk (eds), *Van Gogh Museum Journal*, Van Gogh Museum, Amsterdam, 2002

Kostenevich 1995
Albert Kostenevich, *Hidden Treasures Revealed: Impressionist Masterpieces and Other Important French Paintings Preserved by the State Hermitage Museum, St Petersburg*, St Petersburg, 1995

Krens 1992
Thomas Krens (ed.), *Guggenheim Museum: Thannhauser Collection*, catalogue of the collection, New York, 1992

Lane 1985
John R. Lane (ed.), *Museum of Art, Carnegie Institute Collection Handbook*, catalogue of the collection, Pittsburgh, 1985

Las Vegas 1999
European and American Masters, exh. cat., Bellagio Gallery of Fine Art, Las Vegas, 1999

Van Lindert and Van Uitert 1990
Juleke van Lindert and Evert van Uitert, *Een eigen expressie. Vincent van Gogh en zijn portretten*, Amsterdam, 1990

London 1974
Drawings from the Kröller-Müller National Museum, Otterlo, exh. cat., Courtauld Institute Galleries, London, and Hatton Gallery, University of Newcastle-upon-Tyne, 1974

London 1992
Martin Bailey and Debora Silverman, *Van Gogh in England: Portrait of the Artist as a Young Man*, exh. cat., Barbican Art Gallery, London, 1992

London 1994
John House et al., *Impressionism for England: Samuel Courtauld as Patron and Collector*, exh. cat., Courtauld Institute Galleries, London, 1994

Los Angeles 1971
The Armand Hammer Collection, exh. cat., Los Angeles County Museum of Art, Royal Academy of Arts, London, and National Gallery of Ireland, Dublin, 1971–72

Louisville 2002
Vivien Hamilton (ed.), *Millet to Matisse: Nineteenth- and Twentieth-century French Painting from Kelvingrove Art Gallery, Glasgow*, exh. cat., The Speed Art Museum, Louisville, Kentucky, 2002

Luijten 2003
Hans Luijten, 'Rummaging Among My Woodcuts: Van Gogh and the Graphic Arts', in Amsterdam 2003, pp. 99–112

Van Maanen 2006
Oda van Maanen, 'Onderzoek en restauratieverslag van het schilderij *Tuin met vlinders* van Vincent van Gogh' ('Report of the Examination and Conservation of the Painting *Grass and Butterflies* by Vincent van Gogh'), 2006–07

Madrid 2007
Guillermo Solana (ed.), *Van Gogh: los últimos paisajes (Auvers-sur-Oise, 20 de mayo – 29 de julio 1890)*, exh. cat., Museo Thyssen-Bornemisza, Madrid, 2007

Martigny 2000
Ronald Pickvance, *Van Gogh*, exh. cat., Fondation Pierre Gianadda, Martigny, 2000

Meedendorp 2007
Teio Meedendorp, *Drawings and Prints of Vincent van Gogh in the Collection of the Kröller-Müller Museum*, Otterlo, 2007

Millard 1974
Charles W. Millard, 'A Chronology for Van Gogh's Drawings of 1888', *Master Drawings*, 12, 1974, no. 2, pp. 156–65

Minnesota 1962
The Nineteenth Century: One Hundred and Twenty-five Master Drawings, exh. cat., University Gallery, Minnesota, and Solomon R. Guggenheim Museum, New York, 1962

Montebello 1994
Philippe de Montebello, *The Metropolitan Museum of Art Guide*, New York, 1994

Mothe 1987
Alain Mothe, *Vincent van Gogh à Auvers-sur-Oise*, Paris, 1987

New York 1973
Drawings from the Kröller-Müller National Museum, Otterlo, exh. cat., Museum of Modern Art, New York, Art Institute of Chicago, National Gallery of Canada, Ottawa, Marion Koogler McNay Art Institute, San Antonio, and Museum of Modern Art, Mexico City, 1973–74

New York 1984
Ronald Pickvance, *Van Gogh in Arles*, exh. cat., Metropolitan Museum of Art, New York, 1984

New York 1986
Ronald Pickvance, *Van Gogh in Saint-Rémy and Auvers*, exh. cat., Metropolitan Museum of Art, New York, 1986–87

New York 1990
From Van Gogh to Picasso, from Kandinsky to Pollock: Masterpieces of Modern Art, exh. cat., Solomon R. Guggenheim Museum, New York, 1990

New York 2006
Cézanne to Picasso: Ambroise Vollard, Patron of the Avant-Garde, exh. cat., Metropolitan Museum of Art, New York, Art Institute of Chicago, Musée d'Orsay, Paris, 2006–07

New York 2007
Leo Jansen, Hans Luijten and Nienke Bakker, *Vincent van Gogh: Painted with Words. The Letters to Emile Bernard*, exh. cat., The Morgan Library, New York, 2007–08

New York 2008
Sjraar van Heugten, Joachim Pissarro and Chris Stolwijk (eds), *Van Gogh and the Colors of the Night / Van Gogh en de kleuren van de nacht*, exh. cat., Museum of Modern Art, New York, and Van Gogh Museum, Amsterdam, 2008

Nichols, Gerstein, Swenson, Phillips and Berkowitz 1995
Lawrence W. Nichols, Marc S. Gerstein, Christine Swenson, Robert F. Phillips and Roger M. Berkowitz, *Toledo Treasures: Selections from the Toledo Museum of Art*, New York, 1995

Ottawa 1999
Colin B. Bailey and John Collins, *Van Gogh's 'Irises': Masterpiece in Focus*, exh. cat., National Gallery of Canada, Ottawa, 1999

Otterlo 1990
Johannes van der Wolk, Ronald Pickvance and E. B. F. Pey, *Vincent van Gogh: Drawings*, exh. cat., Kröller-Muller Museum, Otterlo, 1990

Paris 1960
Marc Edo Tralbant, *Vincent van Gogh, 1853–1890*, exh. cat., Musée Jacquemart-André, Paris, 1960

Paris 1988
Françoise Cachin, Bogomila Welsh-Ovcharov and Monique Nonne, *Van Gogh à Paris*, exh. cat., Musée d'Orsay, Paris, 1988

Paris 1996
Anne-Birgitte Fonsmark (ed.), *Manet, Gauguin, Rodin... Chefs-d'œuvre de la Ny Carlsberg Glyptotek de Copenhague*, exh. cat., Musée d'Orsay, Paris, 1996

Paris 1998
Louis van Tilborgh and Marie-Pierre Salée, *Millet–Van Gogh*, exh. cat., Musée d'Orsay, Paris, 1998–99

Paris 1999
Ann Distel and Susan A. Stein, *Cézanne to Van Gogh: The Collection of Doctor Gachet*, exh. cat., Grand Palais, Paris, Metropolitan Museum of Art, New York, and Van Gogh Museum, Amsterdam, 1999

Paris n.d.
The Armand Hammer Collection, exh. cat., Musee du Louvre (Cabinet des Dessins), and Musée Jacquemart André, Paris, year unknown

Passantino and Scott 1999
Erika D. Passantino and David W. Scott (eds), *The Eye of Duncan Phillips: A Collection in the Making*, New Haven and London, 1999

Pickvance 2006
Ronald Pickvance, 'Van Gogh', *Burlington Magazine*, 148, July 2006, pp. 500–02

Rewald 1978
John Rewald, *Post-Impressionism: From Van Gogh to Gauguin*, London, 1978

Roskill 1971
Mark W. Roskill, 'Van Gogh's Exchanges of Work with Emile Bernard in 1888', *Oud Holland*, 86, 2–3, 1971, pp. 142–79

Seattle 2004
Van Gogh to Mondrian: Modern Art from the Kröller-Müller Museum, Otterlo, exh. cat., Seattle Art Museum, and Hogh Museum of Art, Atlanta, 2004–05

Seoul 2007
Sounjou Seo, Chris Stolwijk and Sjraar van Heugten (eds), *Van Gogh: Voyage into the Myth*, exh. cat., Seoul Museum of Art, 2007–08

Seznec 1950
Jean J. Seznec, 'Literary Inspiration in Van Gogh', *The Magazine of Art*, 43, 8, December 1950, pp. 126–33

Soth 1994
Lauren Soth, 'Van Gogh's Images of Women Sewing', *Zeitschrift für Kunstgeschichte*, 57, 1, 1994, pp. 105–10

Sotheby's 1990
Impressionist and Modern Art from the Collection of the late Mrs A. A. Bremmer-Hollmann, The Hague, auction catalogue, Sotheby's, Amsterdam, 12 December 1990

Sotheby's 2005
Impressionist and Modern Works on Paper, auction catalogue, Sotheby's, London, 21 June 2005

Sotheby's 2006
Impressionist and Modern Art, auction catalogue, Sotheby's, New York, 3 May 2006

Spencer-Longhurst 1993
Paul Spencer-Longhurst, *The Barber Institute of Fine Arts, University of Birmingham: Handbook*, Birmingham, 1993

Stockholm 2004
Görel Cavalli-Björkman et al., *Falskt & Äkta*, exh. cat., Nationalmuseum, Stockholm, 2004

Stolwijk 2003
Chris Stolwijk, 'Van Gogh's Nature', in Amsterdam 2003, pp. 25–36

Stolwijk and Veenenbos 2002
Chris Stolwijk and Han Veenenbos, *The Account Book of Theo van Gogh and Jo van Gogh-Bonger*, Amsterdam and Leiden, 2002

Sund 1988A
Judy Sund, 'Favoured Fictions: Women and Books in the Art of Van Gogh', *Art History*, 2, 1988, 2, June, pp. 255–67

Sund 1988B
Judy Sund, 'The Sower and the Sheaf: Biblical Metaphor in the Art of Vincent van Gogh', *Art Bulletin*, 70, 1988, 4, pp. 660–76

Sund 1992
Judy Sund, *True to Temperament: Van Gogh and French Naturalist Literature*, Cambridge, 1992

Sutton 1990
Peter C. Sutton, *Northern European Paintings in the Philadelphia Museum of Art, from the Sixteenth through the Nineteenth Century*, Philadelphia, 1990

Van Tilborgh 2006
Louis van Tilborgh, *Van Gogh and Japan*, Amsterdam, 2006

Van Tilborgh 2008
Louis van Tilborgh, *Van Gogh and the Sunflowers*, Amsterdam, 2008

Van Tilborgh and Vellekoop 1999
Louis van Tilborgh and Marije Vellekoop, *Vincent van Gogh, Paintings, vol. 1. The Dutch Period, 1881–85*, Amsterdam, 1999

Tokyo 1993
Vincent van Gogh and His Time: Van Gogh and Millet from the Vincent van Gogh Museum and the H. W. Mesdag Museum, exh. cat., Seiji Togo Memorial Yasuda Kasai Museum of Art, Tokyo, 1993–94

Toledo 2003
Dorothee Hansen, Lawrence W. Nichols and Judy Sund, *Van Gogh: Fields*, exh. cat., Toledo Museum of Art, 2003 (a modified version of Bremen 2002)

Van Uitert and Hoyle 1987
Evert van Uitert and Michael Hoyle (eds), *The Rijksmuseum Vincent van Gogh*, Amsterdam, 1987

Van der Veen 2003
Wouter van der Veen, 'An Avid Reader: Van Gogh and Literature', in Amsterdam 2003, pp. 49–60

Van der Veen 2009
Wouter van der Veen, *Van Gogh: A Literary Mind*, Zwolle and Amsterdam, 2009

Vellekoop and Van Heugten 2001
Marije Vellekoop and Sjraar van Heugten, *Vincent van Gogh, Drawings, vol. 3: Antwerp and Paris, 1885–88*, Amsterdam, 2001

Vellekoop and Zwikker 2007
Marije Vellekoop and Roelie Zwikker, *Vincent van Gogh, Drawings, vol. 4: Arles, Saint-Rémy and Auvers-sur-Oise, 1888–90*, Amsterdam, 2007

Vienna 1996
Roland Dorn, Klaus Albrecht Schröder and John Sillevis, *Van Gogh und die Haager Schule*, exh. cat., Bank Austria Forum, Vienna, 1996

Vienna 2005
Goya bis Picasso. Meisterwerke der Sammlung Jan Krugier und Marie-Anne Krugier-Poniatowski, exh. cat., Albertina, Vienna, 2005

Vienna 2008
Van Gogh: Heartfelt Lines, exh. cat., Albertina, Vienna, 2008

Washington 1983
John Rewald, *The John Hay Whitney Collection*, exh. cat., National Gallery of Art, Washington DC, 1983

Washington 2001
Jeannene M. Przyblyski, John McCoubrey and Richard Shiff, *Impressionist Still-life*, exh. cat., The Phillips Collection, Washington DC, and the Museum of Fine Arts, Boston, 2001–02

Welsh-Ovcharov 1998
Bogomila Welsh-Ovcharov, 'The Ownership of Vincent van Gogh's "Sunflowers"', *Burlington Magazine*, March 1998, pp. 184–92

Winterthur 2002
Fred Leeman, *Der Sämann – Vincent van Gogh. Werke aus der Sammlung Arthur und Hedy Hahnloser-Bühler und aus Schweizer und internationalem Museumsbesitz*, exh. cat., Villa Flora, Winterthur, 2002–03

Yokohama 1995
Vincent van Gogh Collection from the Kröller-Müller Museum, Otterlo, The Netherlands, exh. cat., Yokohama Museum of Art and Nagoya City Art Museum, 1995–96

Zemel 1985
Carol Zemel, 'The "Spook" in the Machine: Van Gogh's Pictures of Weavers in Brabant', *Art Bulletin*, 67, 1, 1985, pp. 123–37

Zwikker 2003
Roelie Zwikker, 'Van Gogh's Teachers', in Amsterdam 2003, pp. 37–48

LENDERS TO THE EXHIBITION

Joe L. Allbritton

Amsterdam
Rijksmuseum
Van Gogh Museum (Vincent van Gogh
Foundation)

Antwerp
Koninklijk Museum voor Schone Kunsten

Bern
Kunstmuseum

Birmingham
The Barber Institute of Fine Arts,
University of Birmingham

Boston
Museum of Fine Arts

Brussels
Royal Museums of Fine Arts
of Belgium

Cambridge
The Fitzwilliam Museum

Cleveland
Cleveland Museum of Art

The Steven and Alexandra Cohen Collection

Copenhagen
Ny Carlsberg Glyptotek

Stichting Collectie P. en N. De Boer

Edinburgh
National Gallery of Scotland

Frankfurt am Main
Städel Museum

Glasgow
Culture Sport Glasgow on behalf
of Glasgow City Council

Groningen
Groninger Museum

The Hague
Gemeentemuseum Den Haag

Indianapolis
Indianapolis Museum of Art

Collection Jan Krugier and Marie-Anne
Krugier-Poniatowski

London
The British Library
The British Museum
The National Gallery
The Samuel Courtauld Trust,
The Courtauld Gallery
Tate

Los Angeles
The J. Paul Getty Museum
The Hammer Museum
Los Angeles County Museum of Art

Manchester
The Whitworth Art Gallery,
University of Manchester

Moscow
Pushkin State Museum of Fine Arts

Munich
Staatliche Graphische Sammlung

Nahmad Collection, Switzerland

New York
Brooklyn Museum
The Hyde Collection, Glens Falls
The Metropolitan Museum of Art
The Museum of Modern Art
Solomon R. Guggenheim Museum

Oslo
The National Museum of Art,
Architecture and Design

Ottawa
National Gallery of Canada

Otterlo
Kröller-Müller Museum

The Henry and Rose Pearlman Foundation

Philadelphia
Philadelphia Museum of Art

Pittsburgh
Carnegie Museum of Art

Rhode Island
Museum of Art, Rhode Island School
of Design

Rotterdam
Museum Boijmans Van Beuningen

Saint Louis
Saint Louis Art Museum

Collection Rudolf Staechelin

Toledo
Toledo Museum of Art

Tournai
Musée des Beaux-Arts

The Triton Foundation, The Netherlands

Vatican City
Vatican Museums

Washington DC
National Gallery of Art
The Phillips Collection

Williamstown
Sterling and Francine Clark Art Institute

Winterthur
Hahnloser/Jaeggli Stiftung, Villa Flora
Kunstmuseum Winterthur

Zurich
Kunsthaus

and others who wish to remain anonymous

LIST OF UNILLUSTRATED WORKS

160 Alfred Sensier (1815–1877)
La Vie et l'œuvre de Jean-François Millet, 1881
Book, 23.3 x 16.3 x 3.8 cm
The British Library, London,
7856.f.6

161 Jules Michelet (1798–1894)
La Mer, 1861
Book, 18.3 x 12 x 2.3 cm
The British Library, London,
7298.a.19

162 Harriet Beecher Stowe (1811–1896)
Uncle Tom's Cabin, 1867
Book, 17.5 x 10 x 3 cm
The British Library, London,
12704.gg.44

163 Pierre Loti (1850–1923)
Madame Chrysanthème, 1888
Book, 23.3 x 16.3 x 3.8 cm
The British Library, London,
12515.l.24

164 Alphonse Daudet (1840–1897)
Tartarin de Tarascon, 1887
Book, 18.5 x 12.4 x 2.3 cm
The British Library, London,
12548.pp.35

165 Charles Dickens (1812–1870)
Contes de Noel, 1843
Book, 21.7 x 13.5 x 1.4 cm
The British Library, London,
12623.ee.5

166 Victor Hugo (1802–1885)
Les Misérables, 1862
Book, 17.6 x 11.9 x 4 cm
The British Library, London,
012548.a.10

167 W. Bürger (Théophile Thoré) (1807–1869)
Musées de la Hollande. Amsterdam et La Haye: Etudes sur l'école hollandaise, 1862
Book, 18.4 x 12.3 x 2.4 cm
The British Library, London,
7854.d.19

168 Théophile Silvestre (1823–1876)
Eugène Delacroix: documents nouveaux, 1864
Book, 19.3 x 13 x 1.8 cm
The British Library, London,
10663.aa.22

169 George Eliot (Mary Anne Evans) (1819–1880)
Felix Holt, the Radical, 1856
Book, 20.3 x 14.2 x 4.3 cm
The British Library, London,
12624.b.8

170 Honoré de Balzac (1799–1850)
Le Père Goriot, 1883
Book, 23 x 16 x 3.5 cm
The British Library, London,
012547.g.37

171 Voltaire (1694–1778)
Candide, ou L'Optimisme, 1867
Book, 24.4 x 16.5 x 2.7 cm
The British Library, London,
12512.i.17

172 John Bunyan (1628–1688)
The Pilgrim's Progress, 1875
Book, 18.5 x 13.2 x 2.8 cm
The British Library, London,
YA1993a20116

173 Guy de Maupassant (1850–1893)
Pierre et Jean, 1888
Book, 19.8 x 13.1 x 2.3 cm
The British Library, London,
CUP 410.e.14

174 Emile Zola (1840–1902)
L'Assommoir, 1877
Book, 18.4 x 12 x 5.4 cm
The British Library, London,
12517.e.26

PHOTOGRAPHIC ACKNOWLEDGEMENTS

Amsterdam, courtesy Van Gogh Museum (Documentation): figs 6, 14, 18

Brussels, © Royal Museums of Fine Arts of Belgium/Guy Cussac: cat. 55

Martin P. Bühler: cat. 152

Florence, © Scala: fig. 13; Digital Image/Los Angeles County Museum of Art/Art Resource: cats 69, 95; Digital Image/The Metropolitan Museum of Art, New York/Art Resource: cats 8, 10, 72, 75, 114, 133; Digital Image/The Museum of Modern Art, New York/Art Resource: cat. 135

Roy Fox: cat. 86

Bob Goedewaagen: cat. 45

Erik Gould: cat. 90

Ole Haupt: cat. 134

Jacques Lathion: cats 42, 46, 93

London, © The Trustees of the British Museum: cats 61–63, 94, 128

London, © The National Gallery: cat. 80

London, © Tate, 2009: cats 21, 143, 145

Joseph Mikuliak: cat. 76

Eric Mitchell: cat. 77

Moscow, © The State Pushkin Museum of Fine Arts: cat. 53

New York, © Christie's Images Limited (2007): cat. 17

Eamonn O'Mahony: cat. 3

Pittsburgh, © 2009 Carnegie Museum of Art: cat. 153

John Stoel: cat. 23

Toledo, Image Source: cat. 121

Vatican City, Vatican Museums: cat. 125

Washington, courtesy of the Board of Trustees, National Gallery of Art: cats 39, 150

Bruce M. White: cat. 59

Zürich, © 2009 Kunsthaus: cat. 88

INDEX

All references are to page numbers;
bold numbers refer to illustrations.

BENEFACTORS OF THE ROYAL ACADEMY OF ARTS

ROYAL ACADEMY TRUST

MAJOR BENEFACTORS

The Trustees of the Royal Academy Trust are grateful to all its donors for their continued loyalty and generosity. They would like to extend their thanks to all those who have made a significant commitment, past and present, to the galleries, the exhibitions, the conservation of the Permanent Collection, the Library collections, the Royal Academy Schools, the education programme and other specific appeals.

HM The Queen
Her Majesty's Government
The 29th May 1961 Charitable Trust
Barclays Bank
BAT Industries plc
The late Tom Bendhem
The late Brenda M Benwell-Lejeune
British Telecom
John and Susan Burns
Mr Raymond M Burton CBE
Sir Trevor and Lady Chinn
The John S Cohen Foundation
Sir Harry and Lady Djanogly
The Dulverton Trust
Alfred Dunhill Limited
The John Ellerman Foundation
The Eranda Foundation
Ernst & Young
Esso UK plc
Mr and Mrs Eugene V Fife
The Foundation for Sports and the Arts
Friends of the Royal Academy
John Frye Bourne
Jacqueline and Michael Gee
Glaxo Holdings plc
Diane and Guilford Glazer
Mr and Mrs Jack Goldhill
Maurice and Laurence Goldman
Mr and Mrs Jocelin Harris
The Philip and Pauline Harris
    Charitable Trust
The Charles Hayward Foundation
Robin Heller Moss
Heritage Lottery Fund
The Malcolm Hewitt Wiener Foundation
IBM United Kingdom Limited
The Idlewild Trust
Lord and Lady Jacobs
The JP Jacobs Charitable Trust
The Japan Foundation
Gabrielle Jungels-Winkler
Mr and Mrs Donald Kahn
Lillian Jean Kaplan Foundation
The Kresge Foundation
The Samuel H Kress Foundation
The Kirby Laing Foundation
The late Mr John S Latsis
The Leverhulme Trust
Lex Service plc
The Linbury Trust
Sir Sydney Lipworth QC and Lady Lipworth
John Lyons Charity
Ronald and Rita McAulay
McKinsey and Company Inc
John Madejski OBE DL
The Manifold Trust
Mr and Mrs John L Marion
Marks and Spencer
The Mercers' Company
The Monument Trust
The Henry Moore Foundation
The Moorgate Trust Fund
Mr and Mrs Minoru Mori
The Museums, Libraries and Archives Council
National Westminster Bank
Stavros S Niarchos
The Peacock Charitable Trust
The Pennycress Trust
PF Charitable Trust
The Pidem Fund
The Pilgrim Trust
The Edith and Ferdinand Porjes Trust
The Porter Foundation
John Porter Charitable Trust
Rio Tinto
John A Roberts FRIBA
Simon and Virginia Robertson
The Ronson Foundation
The Rose Foundation
Rothmans International plc
Dame Jillian Sackler DBE
Jillian and Arthur M Sackler

Mrs Jean Sainsbury
The Saison Foundation
The Basil Samuel Charitable Trust
Mrs Coral Samuel CBE
Sea Containers Ltd
Shell UK Limited
Miss Dasha Shenkman
William and Maureen Shenkman
The Archie Sherman Charitable Trust
Sir Hugh Sykes DL
Sir Anthony and Lady Tennant
Ware and Edythe Travelstead
The Trusthouse Charitable Foundation
The Douglas Turner Trust
Unilever plc
The Weldon UK Charitable Trust
The Welton Foundation
The Garfield Weston Foundation
The Maurice Wohl Charitable Foundation
The Wolfson Foundation
and others who wish
to remain anonymous

PATRONS

The Royal Academy is delighted to thank all its Patrons for generously supporting the following areas over the past year: exhibitions, education, the Royal Academy Schools, the Permanent Collection and Library, and Anglo-American initiatives; and for assisting in the general upkeep of the Academy.

Platinum
Mr and Mrs John Coombe
Mr and Mrs Patrick Doherty
Mrs Helena Frost
Mr and Mrs David Shalit

Gold
His Excellency the American Ambassador
Sir Ronald and Lady Cohen
The Cowley Foundation
Lady Getty
Anya Hindmarch
Mr and Mrs Ronald Lubner
Prof and Mrs Anthony Mellows
Lady Jane Rayne
Mrs Inna Vainshtock
Mr and Dr Winkler
W Randall Work and Mandy Gray

Silver
Mrs Cynthia Arno
Mrs Leslie Bacon
Mrs Gary Brass
Mrs Elie Brihi
Lady Brown
Sir Charles and Lady Chadwyck-Healey
Sir Trevor and Lady Chinn
Mrs Jennifer Cooke
The de Laszlo Foundation
Benita and Gerald Fogel
Mrs George Fokschaner
Mr and Mrs Eric Franck
Jaqueline and Jonathan Gestetner
Michael and Morven Heller
Mr and Mrs Alan Hobart
Mr and Mrs Jon Hunt
S Isern-Feliu
Mr and Mrs S Kahan
Mr Nand Khemka and Princess Jeet Nabha Khemka
Mr D H Killick
Mrs Aboudi Kosta
Lady Lever of Manchester
Mark and Liza Loveday
Mr Nicholas Maclean
Mr and Mrs Richard Martin
The Mulberry Trust
Mr and Mrs D J Peacock
The Lady Henrietta St George
Mr and Mrs Schneer
Mr and Mrs Kevin Senior
The Countess of Shaftesbury
Mrs Stella Shawzin
Richard and Veronica Simmons
Jane Spack
Sir James and Lady Spooner
Mrs Elyane Stilling
Sir Hugh Sykes DL

Bronze
Mrs Marina Atwater
Jane Barker
Stephen J Barry Charitable Trust
James M Bartos
The Duke of Beaufort

Mrs J K M Bentley
Mr Michael Bradfield
Mr Charles Brett
Miss Deborah Brett
Mr Edward Brett
Mr Ernest Brett
Mr Paul Brett
Mrs Marcia Brocklebank
Mr and Mrs Charles H Brown
Jeremy Brown
Lord Browne of Madingley
Mr Raymond M Burton CBE
Mr F A A Carnwath CBE
Jean and Eric Cass
Mrs Vivien Chappell
Mr and Mrs George Coelho
Denise Cohen Charitable Trust
Mrs Cathy Corbett
Mr and Mrs Sidney Corob
Julian Darley and Helga Sands
The Countess of Dartmouth
Peter and Andrea de Haan
Mrs Norah de Vigier
Dr Anne Dornhorst
Lord Douro
Ms Noreen Doyle
Mr and Mrs Maurice Dwek
Mrs Sheila Earles
Lord and Lady Egremont
Miss Caroline Ellison
Mary Fedden RA
Mr and Mrs David Fenton
Bryan Ferry
Lord and Lady Foley
Mrs Pamela Foster-Brown
Mrs Jocelyn Fox
Mr Monty Freedman
Arnold Fulton
Patricia and John Glasswell
Mark Glatman
Lady Gosling
Piers and Rosie Gough
Mr Mark Hendriksen
Mr and Mrs Christoph Henkel
Ms Alexandra Hess
Ms Joanna Hewitt
Mrs Pauline Hyde
Mrs Sabine Israel
Sir Martin and Lady Jacomb
Mrs Raymonde Jay
Fiona Johnstone
Mrs Joseph
Dr Elisabeth Kehoe
Mr Gerald Kidd
Mr and Mrs James Kirkman
Mr Leon Krayer
Norman A Kurland and Deborah A David
Mr Peter Lloyd
Miss R Lomax-Simpson
The Marquess of Lothian
Gillian McIntosh
Andrew and Judith McKinna
Sally and Donald Main
Mr Michael Manser RA and Mrs Jose Manser
Mr Marcus Margulies
Zvi and Ofra Meitar Family Fund
Dean Menegas
Ms Carole Meyers
Mrs Diana Mocatta
Mrs Alan Morgan
Mrs Joy Moss
Marion and Guy Naggar
Dr Ann Naylor
Elaine and David Nordby
Ann Norman-Butler
North Street Trust
Mr Michael Palin
John H Pattisson
Mr and Mrs A Perloff
Mr Philip Perry
Mrs Eve Pilkington
Mr and Mrs Anthony Pitt-Rivers
Mr Harry Plotnick
Mrs Jasmin Prokop
Mr Mike Pullen
John and Anne Raisman
Lord Rothschild
H M Sassoon Charitable Trust
Carol Sellars
Dr Lewis Sevitt
Mr James B Sherwood
Mr David Shovel
Mrs Victor Silverton
Alan and Marianna Simpson
Mr and Mrs Mark Franklin Slaughter
Mr Smith

Brian D Smith
Mr and Mrs David T Smith
Mr Malcolm Smith
Mrs D Susman
Lord and Lady Taylor
Mr Ian Taylor
Miss M L Ulfane
John and Carol Wates
Edna and Willard Weiss
Anthony and Rachel Williams
and others who wish
to remain anonymous

BENEFACTOR PATRONS

Mr and Mrs William Brake
Mrs Sue Hammerson
Joan H Lavender
The Lord Marks of Broughton
Sir Anthony and Lady Tennant

BENJAMIN WEST GROUP PATRONS

Chairman
Lady Judge

Gold
Lady J Lloyd Adamson

Silver
Mrs Adrian Bowden
Mr and Mrs Paul Collins
Charles and Kaaren Hale
Lady Judge
Scott and Christine Morrissey
Mr and Mrs John R Olsen
Mr Leigh Seippel
Frank and Anne Sixt

Bronze
Ms Ruth Anderson
Ms Michal Berkner
Wendy Brooks and Tim Medland
Mrs Kathie Child-Villiers
Ms Maryn Coker
Mr Jeffrey E Eldredge
Ms Clare Flanagan
Cyril and Christine Freedman
Mr Andrew Hawkins
Suzanne and Michael Johnson
Mr and Mrs Kenneth Lieberman
Charles G Lubar
Neil Osborn and Holly Smith
Lady Purves
Mr and Mrs K M Rubie
Sylvia Scheuer
Carl Stewart
Carole Turner Record
Frederick and Kathryn Uhde
Mrs Yoon Ullmo
Prof Peter Whiteman QC
John and Amelia Winter
Mary Wolridge
and others who wish
to remain anonymous

SCHOOLS PATRONS GROUP

Chairman
John Entwistle OBE

Platinum
Campbell Rigg
Matthew and Sian Westerman

Silver
Lord and Lady Aldington
John Entwistle OBE

Bronze
Mrs Inge Borg Scott
Ian and Tessa Ferguson
Prof Ken Howard RA and Mrs Howard
Philip Marsden
Peter Rice
Anthony and Sally Salz
Mr Ray Treen
and others who wish
to remain anonymous

CONTEMPORARY PATRONS GROUP

Chairman
Susie Allen

Patrons
Viscountess Bridgeman
Alla Broeksmit
Dr Elaine C Buck
Jenny Christensson
Loraine da Costa
Helen and Colin David
Belinda de Gaudemar
Chris and Angie Drake
Caroline Hansberry
Mrs Susan Hayden
Penelope Mather
Jean-Jacques Murray
Barbara Pansadoro
Mr Andres Recoder and
    Mrs Isabelle Schiavi
Richard and Susan Shoylekov
John Tackaberry
Inna Vainshtock
Dr Yvonne von Egidy-Winkler
Cathy Wills
Mary Wolridge
and others who wish
to remain anonymous

TRUSTS AND FOUNDATIONS

The Atlas Fund
The Ove Arup Foundation
Aurelius Charitable Trust
The Peter Boizot Foundation
The Bomonty Charitable Trust
The Charlotte Bonham-Carter
    Charitable Trust
William Brake Charitable Trust
The Britten-Pears Foundation
R M Burton 1998 Charitable Trust
C H K Charities Limited
P H G Cadbury Charitable Trust
The Carew Pole Charitable Trust
The Carlton House
    Charitable Trust
The Clore Duffield Foundation
John S Cohen Foundation
The Ernest Cook Trust
The Sidney and Elizabeth Corob
    Charitable Trust
The Coutts Charitable Trust
Alan Cristea Gallery
The de Laszlo Foundation
The D'Oyly Carte Charitable Trust
The Dovehouse Trust
The Gilbert and Eileen Edgar
    Foundation
The Eranda Foundation
Lucy Mary Ewing Charitable Trust
The Fenton Arts Trust
The Margery Fish Charity
The Flow Foundation
Gatsby Charitable Foundation
Goethe Institut London
The Golden Bottle Trust
The Great Britain Sasakawa
    Foundation
Sue Hammerson Charitable Trust
The Charles Hayward Foundation
The Hellenic Foundation
Heritage Lottery Fund
A D Hill 1985 Discretionary
    Settlement
The Harold Hyam Wingate
    Foundation
Institut fuer
    Auslandsbeziehungen e.V.
The Ironmongers' Company
The Japan Foundation
Stanley Thomas Johnson Foundation
The Emmanuel Kaye Foundation
The Kindersley Foundation
The Kobler Trust
The Lankelly Chase Foundation
Lapada Association of Art & Antique Dealers
Lark Trust
The David Lean Foundation
The Leche Trust
A G Leventis Foundation
The Leverhulme Trust
The Lynn Foundation
The Maccabaeans

The McCorquodale Charitable Trust
Mactaggart Third Fund
The Simon Marks Charitable Trust
The Paul Mellon Centre for Studies in British Art
The Paul Mellon Estate
The Mercers' Company
Margaret and Richard Merrell Foundation
The Millichope Foundation
The Henry Moore Foundation
The Mulberry Trust
The J Y Nelson Charitable Trust
Newby Trust Limited
OAK Foundation Denmark
The Old Broad Street Charity Trust
The Peacock Charitable Trust
The Pennycress Trust
PF Charitable Trust
The Stanley Picker Charitable Trust
The Pidem Fund
The Edith and Ferdinand Porjes Charitable Trust
The Fletcher Priest Trust
The Privy Purse Charitable Trust
Pro Helvetia
Mr and Mrs J A Pye's Charitable Settlement
The Radcliffe Trust
Rayne Foundation
T Rippon & Sons (Holdings) Ltd
The Rootstein Hopkins Foundation
The Rose Foundation
The Rothschild Foundation
Schroder Charity Trust
The Sellars Charitable Trust
The Archie Sherman Charitable Trust
The South Square Trust
Spencer Charitable Trust
Stanley Foundation Limited
Oliver Stanley Charitable Trust
The Steel Charitable Trust
Peter Storrs Trust
Strand Parishes Trust
The Joseph Strong Frazer Trust
The Swan Trust
Swiss Cultural Fund in Britain
Thaw Charitable Trust
Sir Jules Thorn Charitable Trust
Tiffany & Co
Tillotson Bradbery Charitable Trust
The Albert Van den Bergh Charitable Trust
The Bruce Wake Charity
Celia Walker Art Foundation
Warburg Pincus International LLC
The Wax Chandlers' Company
Weinstock Fund
The Garfield Weston Foundation
Wilkinson Eyre Architects
The Spencer Wills Trust
The Maurice Wohl Charitable Foundation
The Wolfson Foundation
The Hazel M Wood Charitable Trust
The Worshipful Company of Painter-Stainers
The Xander Foundation

AMERICAN ASSOCIATES OF THE ROYAL ACADEMY TRUST

Burlington House Trust
Mr and Mrs James C Slaughter

Benjamin West Society
Mr Francis Finlay
Mrs Deborah Loeb Brice
Mrs Nancy B Negley

Benefactors
Mrs Edmond J Safra
The Hon John C Whitehead
Mr and Mrs Frederick B Whittemore

Sponsors
Mrs Drue Heinz HON DBE
David Hockney CH RA
Mr Arthur L Loeb
Mrs Lucy F McGrath
Mr and Mrs Hamish Maxwell
Diane A Nixon
Mr Arthur O Sulzberger and Ms Allison S Cowles

Patrons
Mr and Mrs Steven Ausnit
Mr Donald A Best
Mrs Mildred C Brinn
Mrs Benjamin Coates
Anne S Davidson
Ms Zita Davisson
Mr and Mrs Stanley De Forest Scott
Mrs June Dyson
Mr and Mrs Lawrence S Friedland
Mr and Mrs Leslie Garfield
Ms Helen Harting Abell
Dr Bruce C Horten
The Hon W Eugene Johnston and Mrs Johnston
Mr William W Karatz
Mr and Mrs Wilson Nolen
Lady Renwick
Congressman Frederick W Richmond
Mr and Mrs Peter M Sacerdote
Mrs Mary Sharp Cronson
Mrs Frederick M Stafford

Ms Louisa Stude Sarofim
Ms Joan Stern
Martin J Sullivan OBE
Ms Britt Tidelius
Dr and Mrs Robert D Wickham
Mr Robert W Wilson

Donors
Mr James C Armstrong
Mr Constantin R Boden
Dr and Mrs Robert Bookchin
Mrs Edgar H Brenner
Mr and Mrs Philip Carroll
Laura Christman and William Rothacker
Mr Richard C Colyear
Mrs Beverley C Duer
Mr Robert H Enslow
Mr Ralph A Fields
Mrs Katherine D Findlay
Mr and Mrs Christopher Forbes
Mr and Mrs Gordon P Getty
Mr O D Harrison Jr
Mr and Mrs Gustave M Hauser
Mrs Judith Heath
Ms Elaine Kend
Mr and Mrs Nicholas L S Kirkbride
Mr and Mrs Gary Kraut
The Hon Samuel K Lessey Jr
Annette Lester
Mr Henry S Lynn Jr
Ms Clare E McKeon
Ms Christine Mainwaring-Samwell
Ms Barbara T Missett
The Hon William Nitze and Mrs Nitze
Mrs Charles W Olson III
Cynthia Hazen Polsky and Leon B Polsky
Mrs Patsy Preston
Mrs Nanette Ross
Mrs Martin Slifka
Mrs Judith Villard
Mr and Mrs William B Warren

Corporate and Foundation Support
Annenberg Foundation
Bechtel Foundation
The Blackstone
　Charitable Foundation
The Brown Foundation
Fortnum & Mason
Gibson, Dunn & Crutcher
The Horace W Goldsmith
　Foundation
Hauser Foundation
Leon Levy Foundation
Loeb Foundation
Henry Luce Foundation
Lynberg & Watkins
Sony Corporation of America
Starr Foundation
Thaw Charitable Trust

CORPORATE MEMBERS OF THE ROYAL ACADEMY

Launched in 1988, the Royal Academy's Corporate Membership Scheme has proved highly successful. Corporate membership offers benefits for staff, clients and community partners and access to the Academy's facilities and resources. The outstanding support we receive from companies via the scheme is vital to the continuing success of the Academy and we thank all members for their valuable support and continued enthusiasm.

Premier Level Members
A T Kearney Limited
The Arts Club
Barclays plc
BNY Mellon
CB Richard Ellis
Deutsche Bank AG
FTI Consulting
GlaxoSmithKline plc
Goldman Sachs International
Hay Group
HSBC plc
JTI
King Sturge LLP
KPMG
LECG Ltd
Lombard Odier Darier Hentsch
Schroders plc
Smith and Williamson
Standard Chartered

Corporate Members
All Nippon Airways
Aon
Apax Partners LLP
AXA Insurance
BNP Paribas
The Boston Consulting Group
Bovis Lend Lease Limited
British American Business Inc.
British American Tobacco
Calyon
Canon Europe
Capital International Limited
Christie's

Citi
Clifford Chance LLP
Concateno Plc
Ernst & Young LLP
Exxon Mobil
F & C Asset Management plc
GAM
Heidrick & Struggles
Insight Investment
John Lewis Partnership
JP Morgan
Lazard
Louis Vuitton
Man Group plc
Mizuho International plc
Momart Limited
Morgan Stanley
Nedrailways
Novo Nordisk
Pentland Group plc
Rio Tinto
The Royal Bank of Scotland
The Royal Society of Chemistry
Slaughter and May
Société Générale
Timothy Sammons Fine Art Agents
Trowers & Hamlins
Veredus Executive Resourcing
Vision Capital
Weil, Gotshal & Manges

SPONSORS OF PAST EXHIBITIONS

The President and Council of the Royal Academy would like to thank the following sponsors and benefactors for their generous support of major exhibitions in the last ten years:

2009
GSK Contemporary
　GlaxoSmithKline
Wild Thing: Epstein, Gaudier-Brzeska, Gill
　2009–2013 Season supported by JTI
　BNP Paribas
　The Henry Moore Foundation
Anish Kapoor
　JTI
　Richard Chang
　Richard and Victoria Sharp
　Louis Vuitton
　The Henry Moore Foundation
J. W. Waterhouse:
The Modern Pre-Raphaelite
　2009–2013 Season supported by JTI
　Champagne Perrier-Jouët
　GasTerra
　Gasunie
241st Summer Exhibition
　Insight Investment
Kuniyoshi. From the
Arthur R. Miller Collection
　2009–2013 Season supported
　by JTI Canon
　Travel partner: Cox & Kings
Premiums and RA Schools Show
　Mizuho International plc
RA Outreach Programme
　Deutsche Bank AG

2008
GSK Contemporary
　GlaxoSmithKline
Byzantium 330–1453
　J. F. Costopoulos Foundation
　A. G. Leventis Foundation
　Stavros Niarchos Foundation
　Travel Partner: Cox & Kings
Miró, Calder, Giacometti, Braque:
Aimé Maeght and His Artists
　BNP Paribas
Vilhelm Hammershøi:
The Poetry of Silence
　OAK Foundation Denmark
　Novo Nordisk
240th Summer Exhibition
　Insight Investment
Premiums and RA Schools Show
　Mizuho International plc
RA Outreach Programme
　Deutsche Bank AG
From Russia: French and Russian Master Paintings
1870–1925 from Moscow and St Petersburg
　E.ON
　2008 Season supported by Sotheby's

2007
Paul Mellon's Legacy:
A Passion for British Art
　The Bank of New York Mellon
Georg Baselitz
　Eurohypo AG
239th Summer Exhibition
　Insight Investment
Impressionists by the Sea
　Farrow & Ball
Premiums and RA Schools Show
　Mizuho International plc

RA Outreach Programme
　Deutsche Bank AG
The Unknown Monet
　Bank of America

2006
238th Summer Exhibition
　Insight Investment
Chola: Sacred Bronzes of Southern India
　Travel Partner: Cox & Kings
Premiums and RA Schools Show
　Mizuho International plc
RA Outreach Programme
　Deutsche Bank AG
Rodin
　Ernst & Young

2005
China: The Three Emperors, 1662–1795
　Goldman Sachs International
Impressionism Abroad: Boston and French Painting
　Fidelity Foundation
Matisse, His Art and His Textiles:
The Fabric of Dreams
　Farrow & Ball
Premiums and RA Schools Show
　Mizuho International plc
Turks: A Journey of a Thousand Years, 600–1600
　Akkök Group of Companies
　Aygaz
　Corus
　Garanti Bank
　Lassa Tyres

2004
236th Summer Exhibition
　A T Kearney
Ancient Art to Post-Impressionism: Masterpieces
from the Ny Carlsberg Glyptotek, Copenhagen
　Carlsberg UK Ltd
　Danske Bank
　Novo Nordisk
The Art of Philip Guston (1913–1980)
　American Associates of the
　Royal Academy Trust
The Art of William Nicholson
　RA Exhibition Patrons Group
Vuillard: From Post-Impressionist
to Modern Master
　RA Exhibition Patrons Group

2003
235th Summer Exhibition
　A T Kearney
Ernst Ludwig Kirchner:
The Dresden and Berlin Years
　RA Exhibition Patrons Group
Giorgio Armani: A Retrospective
　American Express
　Mercedes-Benz
Illuminating the Renaissance:
The Triumph of Flemish Manuscript Painting in Europe
　American Associates of the
　Royal Academy Trust
　Virginia and Simon Robertson
Masterpieces from Dresden
　ABN AMRO
　Classic FM
Premiums and RA Schools Show
　Walker Morris
Pre-Raphaelite and Other Masters:
The Andrew Lloyd Webber Collection
　Christie's
　Classic FM
　UBS Wealth Management

2002
234th Summer Exhibition
　A T Kearney
Aztecs
　British American Tobacco
　Mexico Tourism Board
　Pemex
　Virginia and Simon Robertson
Masters of Colour:
Derain to Kandinsky. Masterpieces
from The Merzbacher Collection
　Classic FM
Premiums and RA Schools Show
　Debenhams Retail plc
*RA Outreach Programme**
　Yakult UK Ltd
Return of the Buddha:
The Qingzhou Discoveries
　RA Exhibition Patrons Group

2001
233rd Summer Exhibition
　A T Kearney
Botticelli's Dante: The Drawings
for Dante's Divine Comedy
　RA Exhibition Patrons Group
The Dawn of the Floating World (1650–1765). Early
Ukiyo-e Treasures from the Museum of Fine Arts, Boston
　Fidelity Foundation
Forty Years in Print: The Curwen Studio and
Royal Academicians
　Game International Limited

Frank Auerbach, Paintings and Drawings 1954–2001
　International Asset Management
Ingres to Matisse:
Masterpieces of French Painting
　Barclays
Paris: Capital of the Arts 1900–1968
　BBC Radio 3
　Merrill Lynch
Premiums and RA Schools Show
　Debenhams Retail plc
*RA Outreach Programme**
　Yakult UK Ltd
Rembrandt's Women
　Reed Elsevier plc

2000
1900: Art at the Crossroads
　Cantor Fitzgerald
　The Daily Telegraph
232nd Summer Exhibition
　A T Kearney
Apocalypse: Beauty and Horror
in Contemporary Art
　Eyestorm
　The Independent
　Time Out
Chardin 1699–1779
　RA Exhibition Patrons Group
The Genius of Rome 1592–1623
　Credit Suisse First Boston
Premiums and RA Schools Show
　Debenhams Retail plc
*RA Outreach Programme**
　Yakult UK Ltd
The Scottish Colourists 1900–1930
　Chase Fleming Asset
　Management

* Recipients of a Pairing Scheme Award, managed by Arts + Business. Arts + Business is funded by the Arts Council of England and the Department for Culture, Media and Sport

OTHER SPONSORS

Sponsors of events, publications and other items in the past five years:

Carlisle Group plc
Castello di Reschio
Cecilia Chan
Country Life
Guy Dawson
Derwent Valley Holdings plc
Dresdner Kleinwort Wasserstein
Lucy Flemming McGrath
Fosters and Partners
Goldman Sachs International
Gome International
Gucci Group
Hines
IBJ International plc
John Doyle Construction
Harvey and Allison McGrath
Martin Krajewski
Marks & Spencer
Michael Hopkins & Partners
Morgan Stanley Dean Witter
The National Trust
Prada
Radisson Edwardian Hotels
Richard and Ruth Rogers
Rob van Helden
Warburg Pincus
The Wine Studio